I0796283

ATLAS OF THE BIBLICAL WORLD

Atlas of the Biblical World

by Robert A. Mullins and Mark Vitalis Hoffman

Cartographer Nick Rowland FRGS

Fortress Press
Minneapolis

ATLAS OF THE BIBLICAL WORLD

Cover design: Alisha Lofgren
Cover images: (*clockwise starting with upper left corner*) *Augusteum at Sebaste (Samaria); *view from Qumran looking west, Cave 4 in foreground; *Mount of Olives from Temple Mount showing traditional Palm Sunday Route; replica horned altar at Beer-sheba; * Synagogue at Capernaum, first century CE homes in foreground; stele of Seti I at Beth-shan ; *Synagogue at Capernaum; St. Stephen's Gate in Jerusalem. [*Copyright © Mark G. V. Hoffman. Used by permission]

Typesetting and interior design: Tim Dowley Associates

Print ISBN: 978-1-5064-0126-3
eBook ISBN: 978-1-5064-0127-0

The paper used in the publication meets the minimum requirements of American National Standard for Information Sciences — Permanence of Paper for Printed Library Materials, ANSI Z329.48-1984.

Manufactured in U.S.A.

19 20 21 22 23 9 8 7 6 5 4 3 2

Photograph Acknowledgments

The Dead Sea 18–19
Copyright © Mark G. V. Hoffman

Excavated site of Jericho 20
Berthold Werner Wiki Commons

Judean Hills 40–41
Dreamstime

Sarcophagus of Ahiram 52
Copyright © Robert A. Mullins

Panorama from Beth-shan 56
Copyright © Mark G. V. Hoffman

The Valley of Elah 58
Copyright © Mark G. V. Hoffman

Assyrian relief of siege: Capillon 74–75
Wiki Commons

Altar and excavated steps, Dan 79
Copyright © Mark G. V. Hoffman

Broken Tel Dan Stele with "House of David" inscription 84
Copyright © Mark G. V. Hoffman

Hezekiah's tunnel, Jerusalem 98
Tamar Hayardeni Wiki Commons

The Code of Hammurabi Stele 102
Luestling Wikimedia Commons

Persian Relief
Dreamstime 104–105

Coin of Antiochus Epiphanes IV 118
Zev Radovan/Bible Land Pictures

Sea of Galilee 124–125
Copyright © Mark G. V. Hoffman

Shepherds' Fields, Bethlehem 132
Wiki Commons

Aerial view, excavations at Capernaum 138
© Jacek Sopotnick Dreamstime

Theater at Caesarea Maritima 148
Copyright © Mark G. V. Hoffman

Greaco-Roman remains at Perga 152
Paul VanDerWErf Wiki Commons

The Forum, Rome 158
© scaliger Dreamstime

The foundations of [the Bible] are laid in human history and geography. However high toward the heavens it may reach in doctrine and promise, its foundations lay hold of the earth.

J. H. VINCENT

Contents

Part 3: A People Divided

Part 4: Invasion and Occupation

Part 5: Jesus and the Emergence of Christianity

List of maps

Timelines

Photographs

Illustrations

Preface

This atlas is intended to serve both as a collection of maps useful for biblical study and as a survey of biblical history. With a subject so vast and with space limited, the authors had to make choices about what to include. It is hoped that what remains is a helpful introduction to the Bible's people, places, and events. The volume is organized chronologically rather than by the order of biblical books, but it does parallel the biblical narrative and is thoroughly cross-referenced. It should be easy to consult this atlas as one reads the Bible and place the biblical events within the larger history and context of the biblical lands. A Gazetteer is included for convenience in locating sites.

This atlas provides more than just maps with historical commentary. Geography is important, because it accounts for why things happened where they did. History—based on archaeology and extra-biblical artifacts in addition to the Bible—is important because it clarifies what happened. With better clarity about where and what events in the Bible occurred, we are better able to interpret the biblical story and understand why things happened from the perspective of what God has been doing since the beginning.

Dr. Robert Mullins, professor of biblical studies at Azusa Pacific University and co-director of the archaeological excavations at Abel Beth Maacah, has written chapters 1–45. Mark Vitalis Hoffman, professor of New Testament at United Lutheran Seminary, and frequent traveler to and photographer of archaeological sites in Israel, has written chapters 46–69. The cartography is the work of Cambridge-based Nick Rowland. Page layout and design has been carried out by Bounford.com, Great Gransden, Cambridgeshire, while the index and gazetteer have been compiled by Christopher Pipe of Watermark, Cromer.

Chronology

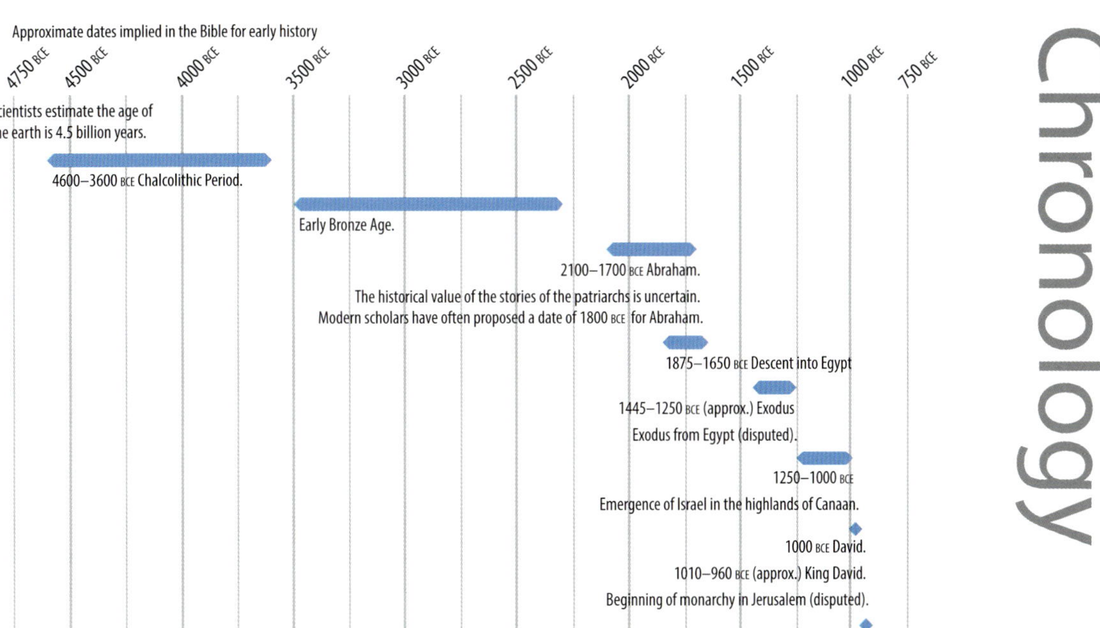

(From 922 BCE on, the implied biblical dates are generally compatible with those of modern scholarship.)

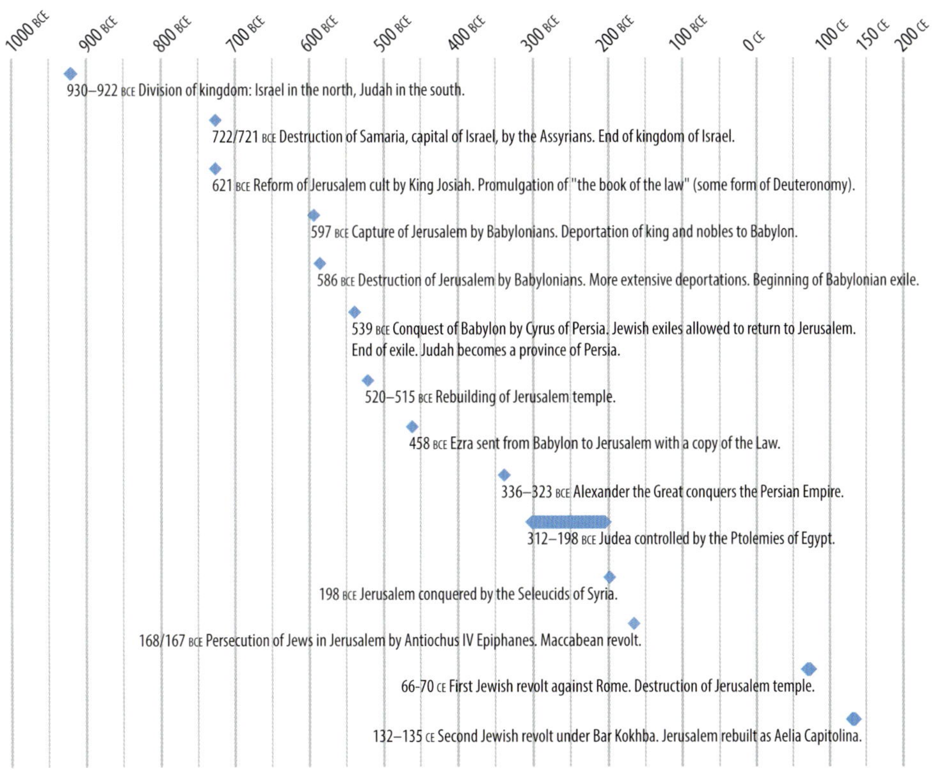

Introduction

The history of any land is largely determined by its geographical setting. This is especially true for the Levant, a term commonly used in scholarly circles to denote territories represented today by the countries of Lebanon, Syria, Israel, the Palestinian territories, and Jordan. The strategic location of the Levant at the meeting point of three continents (Europe, Asia, and Africa) made it an important land bridge in antiquity and helps explain its diverse population.

The Biblical World

Throughout its long and varied history, the Levant was successively dominated by a multitude of nations—Egyptians, Assyrians, Babylonians, Persians, Greeks, and Romans. A tripartite division of the world centering on the Levant is reflected in the Table of Nations (Genesis 10), according to which Noah's three sons begat the populations of three continents: Shem (Asia), Ham (Africa), and Japheth (Europe and Asia Minor).

Movement between Egypt and Mesopotamia took place along the Fertile Crescent. This arc of arable land, framed by the Mediterranean Sea in the west, mountains in the north and east, and arid deserts to the south, began in southern Mesopotamia, where the Tigris and Euphrates Rivers emptied into the Persian Gulf. It then curved westward across northern Syria and dropped down into Lebanon and Israel before turning westward once more, into Egypt. What made this crescent "fertile" was the natural availability of water for agriculture. Mesopotamia and Egypt possessed abundant rivers, while the Levant depended primarily on rainfall. Unsurprisingly, the most used trade routes and the majority of ancient cities lay within this curved swath of land.

Mesopotamia (Greek for "between rivers") takes its name from the Tigris and Euphrates Rivers. For much of its history, Mesopotamia fell into two parts: Babylonia in the south and Assyria in the north. Egypt also comprised two halves: Upper Egypt in the south and Lower Egypt in the north. The Nile River originates in the higher elevations of central East Africa and flows northward to the Mediterranean Sea. Anatolia (the Greek name for Turkey) was the homeland of the Hurrians and Hittites. The New Testament designation for this region is Asia Minor. Powerful city-states such as Tyre and Sidon on the coast of Lebanon (called "Phoenicia" by the Greeks) fueled an extensive network of sea trade throughout the Mediterranean basin. Syria (the Greek name for Aram) was composed of several smaller Aramean kingdoms in the time of the Israelite kings. The most prominent among them to emerge was Aram-Damascus, which became a powerful enemy of the northern kingdom of Israel in the ninth century BCE.

The Levant is called by a variety of names, each denoting a slightly different and not always well-defined territory. Canaan included southern Lebanon, present-day Israel, the Palestinian territories, and western Jordan. Palestine took its name from "Philistia" (the land of the Philistines) on the southern coast of Israel. After the Bar Kokhba Revolt (132–135 CE), the Romans applied this term to the much larger area of *Provincia Syria Palaestina*, later shortened to *Palaestina*. In 1207 BCE, the Merenptah Stele mentions an ethnic group called Israel located somewhere in the western highlands of Canaan. David later adopted it as the official name of his kingdom. The name remains in use today for the modern Jewish state.

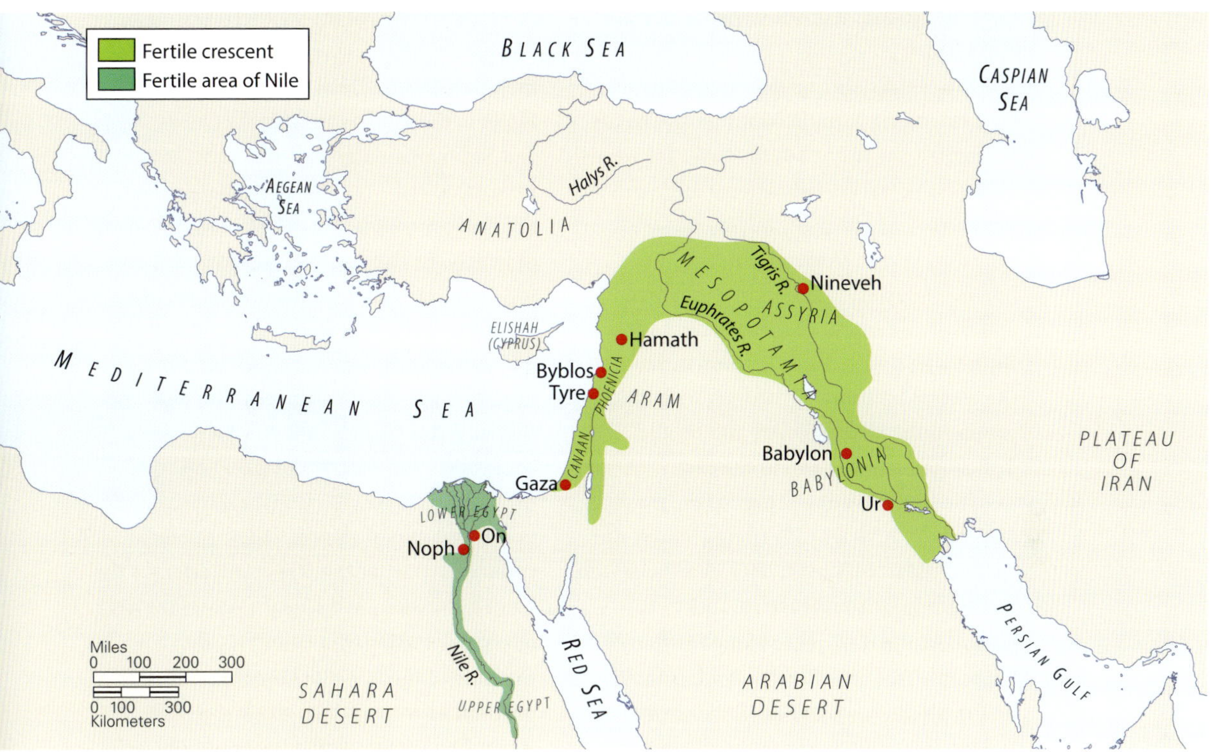

The Land of the Bible

Most events of the Hebrew Bible and the New Testament are set within the boundaries of ancient Israel. This tiny historical stage, no larger than the state of New Jersey or the nation of Belgium, remains one of the most beautiful and topographically diverse regions on earth. The heartland of biblical Israel stretched "from Dan to Beersheba" (e.g., Judg 20:1; 1 Sam 3:20; 1 Kgs 4:25)—only 150 miles (250 km) from north to south as the crow flies. Over this distance, one witnesses a dramatic shift from the lush and well-watered north to the dry and arid south. This coincides with a drop in rainfall from about 25 inches per year at Dan to around 8 inches per year in Beersheba. Israel's natural boundary was the Mediterranean Sea in the west (Num 34:6) and the Jordan River in the east (Num 34:12), some 55 miles (90 km) by air.

Though its complicated geological history produced a highly fragmented landscape, the topography of Israel and western Jordan can be simplified into six geographic zones—four north-south (Coastal Plain, Hill Country, Jordan Valley, Transjordanian Plateau) and two east-west (Jezreel Valley and Negev of Judah).

The Coastal Plain begins wide in the south and narrows to the north. It is interrupted at one point where the headland of Mt. Carmel juts into the Mediterranean Sea. This mountain marked the southern boundary of Phoenicia in the days of the northern kingdom of Israel—the same mountain on which Elijah challenged the syncretistic worship of Baal (1 Kings 18).

The southern part of the coastal plain formed the heartland of Philistia with its five key cities (Gaza, Ashkelon, Ashdod, Gath, and Ekron).

The Hill Country comprises a line of hills extending from Lebanon in the north to the Red Sea in the south. Two east-west valleys (the Jezreel/Esdraelon Valley and the Negev of Judah) cut this mountainous range into three blocks: Galilee in the north, Samaria and Judah in the center, and the Wilderness Highlands in the south. Both valleys served as corridors linking the coastal highway in the west with trade routes in the Jordan Valley and on the Transjordanian Plateau in the east.

The Jordan Valley is part of the much larger Syro-African Rift, a huge tear in the earth crust stretching 4,000 miles (6,400 km) in length from southeastern Turkey to central East Africa. The deepest point of the rift is the Dead Sea some 1,300 ft (400 m) below sea level. Two well-known bodies of water in the Jordan Valley are the Sea of Galilee (the lowest freshwater lake in the world) and the Dead Sea (the lowest point on earth). Two rivers from Lebanon and two springs at the foot of Mt. Hermon jointly form the Upper Jordan River to fill the Sea of Galilee, which then exits to fill the Dead Sea by way of the Lower Jordan River.

Transjordan ("across the Jordan") is largely a plateau on the western edge of modern Jordan. Several deep east-west gorges cut through this area. Four ravines (Yarmuk, Jabbok, Arnon, Zered), called wadi in Arabic, divided the plateau into five major regions from north to south: Bashan, Gilead, Ammon, Moab, and Edom. Only Gilead was an integral part of ancient Israel. In New Testament times, northern Transjordan belonged to the Decapolis, while the southern part of the plateau belonged to the Nabateans.

Roads and Highways

Six major roads ran through each of the six geographic zones of the southern Levant. The historically most important road was the International Trunk Road, which linked Egypt in the south with Anatolia (Asia Minor) and Mesopotamia by way of Canaan/Israel, Phoenicia, and Aram. The Egyptians called the North Sinai portion of this road the "Ways of Horus." In Exodus 13:17, it is called "the way to the land of the Philistines." One branch of this road continued north into Phoenicia. Another branch passed through the Mt. Carmel range into the Jezreel Valley and Upper Jordan Valley (Huleh Valley). From there, one could veer northeast from Hazor and across the Golan Heights into Damascus or continue northward into the Bekaa Valley. The most common name for this important artery is the Latin expression "*Via Maris*" (Way of the Sea), though this name refers more accurately to a different road linking Damascus with Tyre (Isaiah 9:1).

In the central highlands, a road ran along the watershed line from Beersheba to Shechem by way of Hebron, Bethlehem, Jerusalem, Bethel, and Shiloh. Many call this the "Route of the Patriarchs" since its biblical name is unknown. Local roads passed along both sides of the Jordan Valley, though they were impeded in places by the Dead Sea, whose shoreline touched the base of the hills at several points. The last major north-south artery ran along the western edge of the Transjordanian Plateau. It is called the "King's Highway" (Num 20:17; 21:22). East-west roads also passed through the Jezreel Valley from Acco to Transjordan by way of Megiddo and Beth-shan. In the south, an east-west road ran from Gaza to the key city of Beersheba in the Negev of Judah. The route then turned southeast, passing through the Wilderness of Zin into the Jordan Valley and up onto the Transjordanian Plateau.

International route
Road
Pass
Valley areas
Miles
0 10 20
0 10 20 30
Kilometers
MEDITERRANEAN SEA
Damascus
Mt. Hermon
Tyre
Litani R.
Dan
HULEH VALLEY
International Trunk Road
King's Highway
Hazor
Acco
BASHAN
SEA OF GALILEE
Mt. Carmel
JEZREEL/ESDRAELON VALLEY
Mt. Tabor
Yarmuk R.
Megiddo
Beth-shan
JORDAN VALLEY
GILEAD
TRANSJORDANIAN PLATEAU
Coast Road
International Trunk Road
Shechem
Jabbok R.
Joppa
Shiloh
COASTAL PLAIN
HILL COUNTRY
AMMON
Jordan R.
Bethel
Rabbath-ammon
Ashdod
Ekron
Jerusalem
Gath
Bethlehem
Ashkelon
Via Maris (Way of the Sea)
Hebron
Gaza
DEAD SEA
Arnon R.
Beer-sheba
NEGEV
MOAB
Zered R.
King's Highway
EDOM
WILDERNESS OF SIN
Bozrah

Part 1

Beginnings

Human Occupation in the Levant

According to current estimates, the oldest known members of our genus *Homo* arose in Africa around 2.5 million years ago, and by a million years later, migrated by way of the Levant into Europe and Asia. Ubeidiya in the Jordan Valley, south of the Sea of Galilee, is one of the oldest human habitations outside Africa.

The earliest known member of our own species *Homo sapiens* arose in Africa no less than 150,000 years ago and spread into the Old World along similar pathways. It was in present-day Israel, at the geographical intersection of Europe, Asia, and Africa, that early *H. sapiens* encountered Neanderthal populations who had migrated into the milder Levantine climate from an extremely cold Europe during the Ice Age around 90,000 years ago. Much of what happened afterward is still shrouded in mystery, but by 35,000 years ago, anatomically modern humans (our direct ancestors) were the dominant community worldwide. Most other species, including Neanderthals, became extinct. These early moderns had a skeletal form not so different from our own and shared our intellectual potential. They were the ones responsible for the rich cave art at Lascaux in France and Altamira in Spain, as well as other forms of creativity in art, technology, and innovation.

Excavated site of Jericho, the most famous Neolithic settlement in the Levant. Visible is the rounded Neolithic Tower from about 8000 BCE.

For most of human history, people moved in small bands and engaged in hunting and gathering. The first movements toward agriculture took place during the Epipaleolithic period (22,000–9500 BCE) when people began to supplement hunting and fishing with the herding of wild animals and intensified forms of wild grain collection, production, and storage. By this time the dog had been domesticated. With the dawn of the Neolithic period (9500–4600 BCE)

MIGRATION AND OCCUPATION OF THE LEVANT — map 3

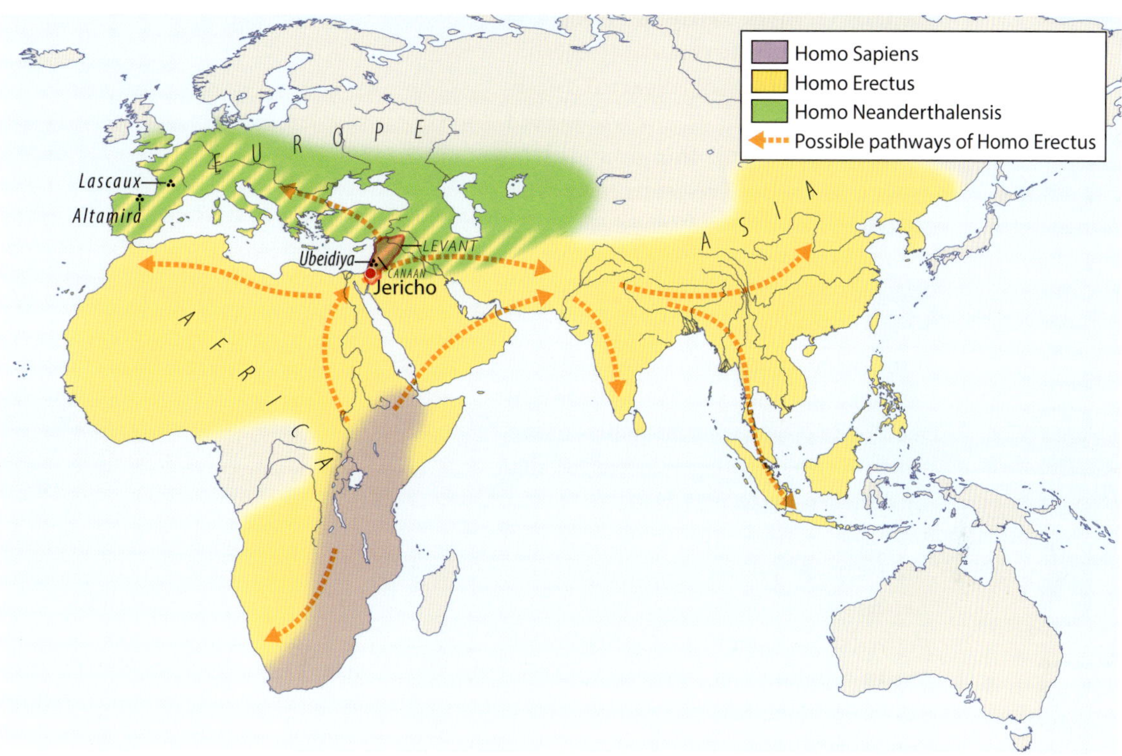

we find domesticated grains (wheat and barley) and animals (sheep, goats, pigs, and the ancestor to the cow). When people can produce their own food, they are better able to manage their resources. The transition to fully developed agriculture and pastoralism was accompanied by changes in social organization. Jericho, with its wall and tower, is probably the most famous example of such a community, though numerous sites in Anatolia, Syria, and northern Mesopotamia are equally as important. Fragments of textiles and basketry are known, and pottery is being used by 6500 BCE. The Chalcolithic period (4600–3600 BCE) witnessed the emergence of cities in southern Mesopotamia and Egypt. Even though urbanization was a long and complex process, Eridu is regarded as the first city in the Sumerian King List, and Cain identified the first builder of a city in Genesis 4:17. Tubal-cain became the first worker in bronze and iron (Gen 4:22). The inauguration of the Early Bronze Age around 3600 BCE witnessed the domestication of the donkey and ox as pack and draft animals, as well as the cultivation of olives, figs, and grapes. By 3000 BCE, we witness systems of writing in Mesopotamia (cuneiform) and Egypt (hieroglyphics), along with complex systems of government, religious institutions, and social hierarchies—the foundations of ancient civilization.

The World of Genesis 1–11

The first eleven chapters of Genesis set the stage for the call of Abraham in Genesis 12. In the Primeval Prologue we learn how an idyllic creation (Genesis 1–2) gave way to disobedience (Genesis 3), murder (Genesis 4), and widespread violence (Genesis 6). This prompted God to destroy and re-create the world through Noah's flood (Genesis 6–8; esp., 7:11; 8:1). In this refashioned world, however, an evil inclination within humans remained (Gen 8:21). God was nonetheless committed to upholding this new creation (Gen 9:1–17), as shown in the divine response to the hubris of the tower of Babel by dispersion rather than by destruction (Gen 11:1–9).

The Primeval Prologue also highlights the human tendency to transgress ordained divine-human boundaries. The first couple ate the forbidden fruit, believing it could "make one wise" and "like God" (Gen 3:5–6). Later, divine beings mate with mortal women (Gen 6:2) and the "whole earth" attempts to build "a city and a tower with its top in the heavens" (Gen 11:4). The Mesopotamian milieu of these stories hints to Israel's setting in Babylonian exile. By engaging the traditions and memories of the past in this strange and foreign land, Israelite theologians formulated a new vision of what it meant to be the people of God. Despite their complex literary history, the first eleven chapters provide a rationale for why humanity needed to be redeemed. Thus, Genesis 11 ends with God calling Abraham out of "Ur of the Chaldeans" (the Neo-Babylonian Empire), since it was through the ancestors and their progeny that God would inaugurate a new plan to repair the world.

THE TABLE OF NATIONS (GENESIS 10)

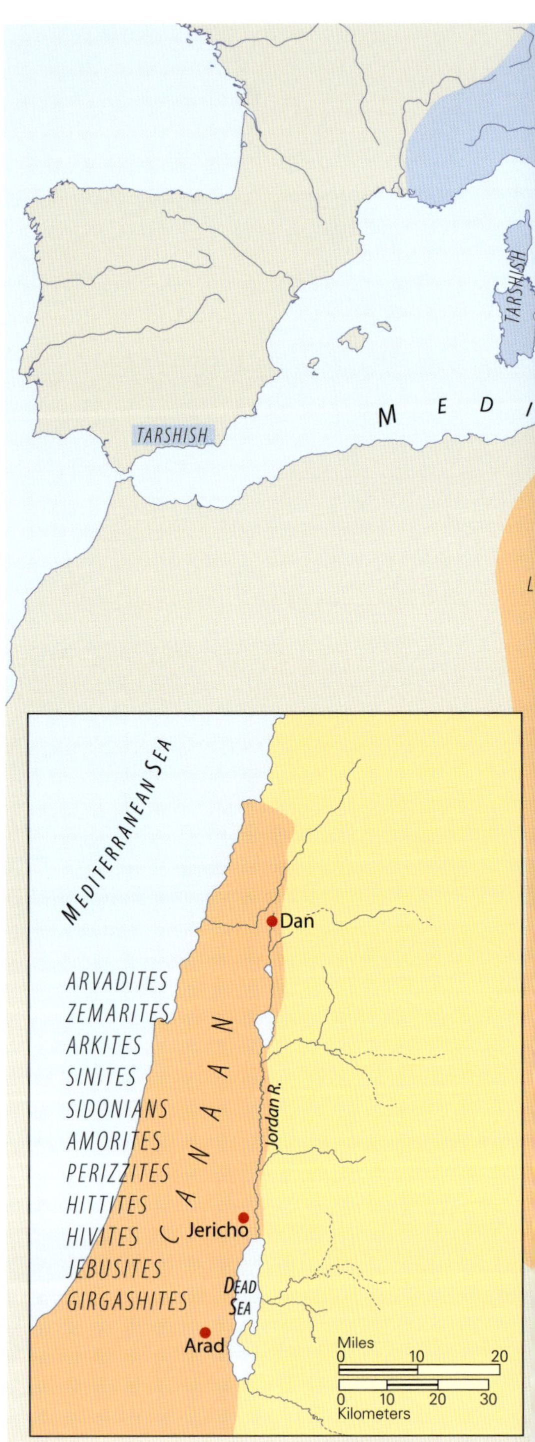

Danube R.
BLACK SEA
CASPIAN SEA
ASHKENAZ
MAGOG
GOMER
LUD
RIPHATH
AEGEAN SEA
TIRAS
MESHECH
Halys R.
TUBAL
TOGARMAH
JAVAN
JAPHETH
Tigris R.
EBER
Nineveh
MADAI
HAMATHITES
PELEG
Calah
RHODANIM
HETH
ASSHUR
Arpachshad
CAPHTORIM
ELISHAH
ARAM
Euphrates R.
KITTIM
UZ
Akkad
PLATEAU OF IRAN
HUL
Babylon
CANAAN
Erech
LEHABIM
PUT
NAPHTUHIM
SHINAR
MASH
CASLUHIM
See enlargement for detail
ELAM
JOKTAN
MIZRAIM
DESERT
HAVILAH
PERSIAN GULF
Nile R.
DEDAN
SHEM
CUSH
RED SEA
PATHRUSIM
ARABIAN DESERT
HAM
JOBAB
RAAMAH
UZAL
SEBA
SHELEPH
HAZARMAVETH
SHEBA
OBAL
SABTAH
HAVILAH
ARABIAN SEA
OPHIR
City
City (location uncertain)
Descendants of Japheth
Descendants of Shem
Descendants of Ham
Miles
0 100 200 300
0 100 300
Kilometers

The Ancient Near East

The Ancient Near East is bounded by mountains to the north and east, and deserts to the south and southwest. Situated in between them is the sickle-shaped corridor of the Fertile Crescent. At either end of the Fertile Crescent lay the two great river valley civilizations of Egypt (Nile) and Mesopotamia (Tigris and Euphrates). The Greek name *Mesopotamia* means "between rivers." Since rivers facilitate trade and the exchange of new ideas, it should not be surprising that civilization started here—in Mesopotamia slightly earlier than in Egypt. Though it lacked major rivers, the Levant—in between Egypt and Mesopotamia—benefited from enough rainfall to allow the cultivation of crops.

Three main phases of Mesopotamian history belong to this period: Early Dynastic, Akkadian, and Ur III. Located in southern Mesopotamia, the city-states of the Early Dynastic period (2900–2350 BCE) shared a unified culture, religion, and language known more commonly today as Sumerian. Three principal Sumerian cities mentioned in the Bible are Uruk (biblical Erech), Akkad (biblical Accad), and Ur. While the roots of the biblical traditions are unknown, Genesis 10:10–12 credits Nimrod with building three cities: Uruk (the city of Gilgamesh), Akkad, and Babel (Babylon) in the land of Shinar (the Sumerian Plain). Nimrod is also credited with two prominent cities in the north, Nineveh and Calah, which became important during the Neo-Assyrian period (1000–612 BCE). The Sumerians also introduced the world's oldest writing system using cuneiform ("wedge-shaped") signs impressed into wet clay tablets with a reed stylus.

Sargon of Akkad, a commoner of Semitic origin, seized control of the Sumerian city-states and established the world's first empire—the Akkadian empire (2334–2160 BCE). The birth legend of Sargon shares details in common with the story of Moses's birth (Exod 2:1–10). The Akkadians spoke and wrote a language related to Hebrew and Arabic. Since the Akkadians had no writing system of their own, they adapted the cuneiform signs to their own language, which continued to be used for another two millennia. A brief revival of Sumerian culture took place during the Ur III period (2119–2004 BCE) when a dynasty of four kings ruled for about a century. The first ruler, Ur-Nammu, created the first law code that would later serve as a model for the Code of Hammurabi and law codes found in Exodus and Deuteronomy. The earliest dates for Abraham generally coincide with the closing decades of Ur III.

The opening phases of the second millennium BCE (more broadly accepted as the time of the Ancestral Narratives) begins with the Old Babylonian period (1894–1595 BCE) when a Semitic king by the name of Hammurabi (1792–1750 BCE) took control in Babylon. His famous law code provides some of the closest parallels to the Covenant Code in Exodus 23–24. During this time in northern Mesopotamia, thriving trade was taking place between Assyria and Anatolia (modern-day Turkey). Tin, wool, and textiles from Assyria were exchanged for timber, silver, and gold from Anatolia. Beginning around 2000 BCE, Indo-European speakers known to history as the Hittites and Hurrians entered Anatolia, most probably from Central Asia. They eventually incorporated the indigenous people of Anatolia into their respective kingdoms. The Hittites settled in central Anatolia, while the Hurrians controlled eastern Anatolia and northern Syria as the kingdom of Mitanni.

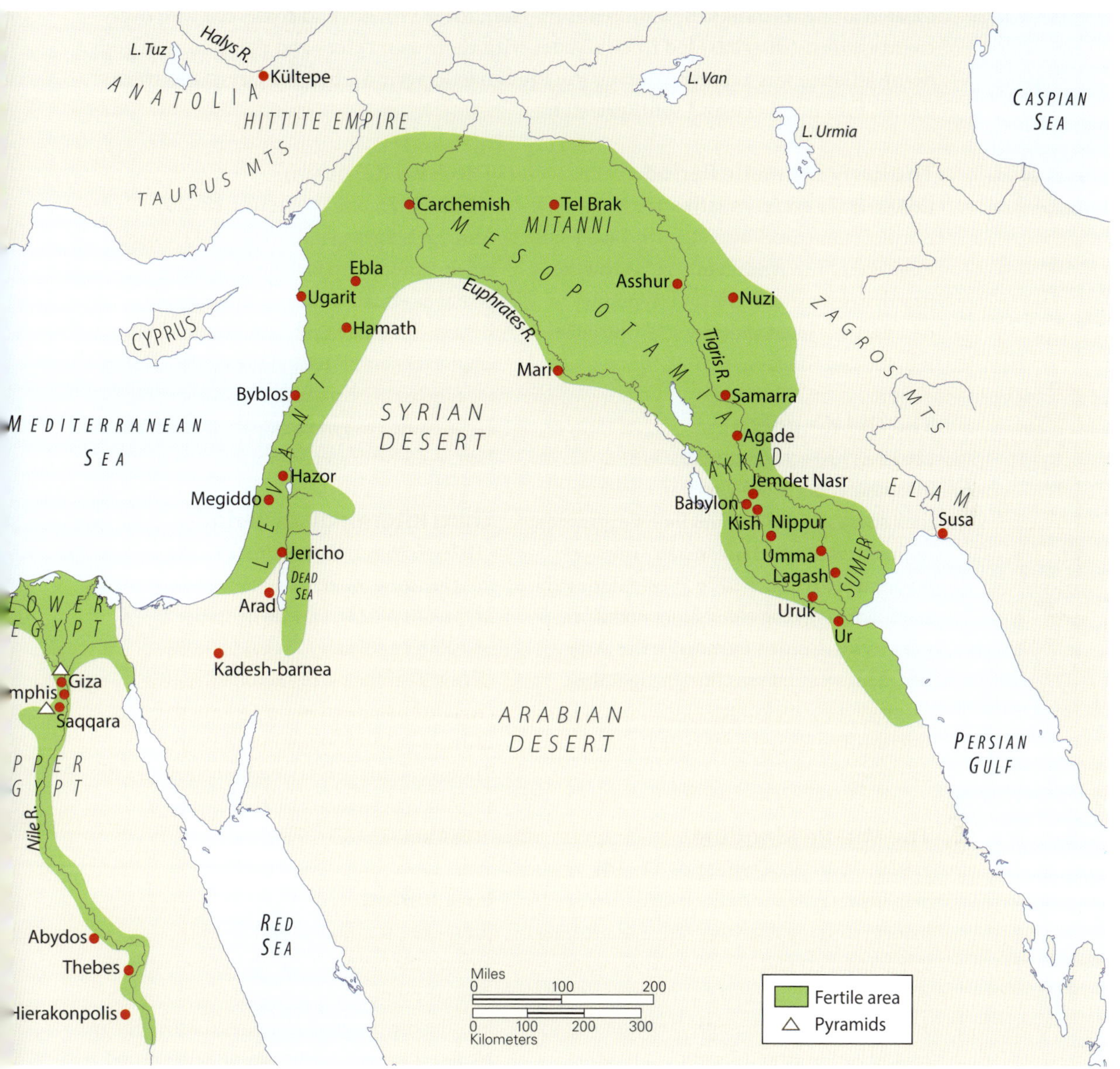
L. Tuz
Halys R.
Kültepe
ANATOLIA
HITTITE EMPIRE
TAURUS MTS
L. Van
L. Urmia
CASPIAN SEA
Carchemish
Tel Brak
MITANNI
MESOPOTAMIA
Ebla
Ugarit
Hamath
CYPRUS
Euphrates R.
Asshur
Nuzi
ZAGROS MTS
Tigris R.
Mari
Samarra
Byblos
SYRIAN DESERT
MEDITERRANEAN SEA
LEVANT
Agade
AKKAD
Hazor
Megiddo
Jemdet Nasr
ELAM
Babylon
Kish
Nippur
Susa
Jericho
Umma
Lagash
SUMER
DEAD SEA
Arad
Uruk
Ur
LOWER EGYPT
Kadesh-barnea
Giza
mphis
Saqqara
ARABIAN DESERT
PERSIAN GULF
PPER GYPT
Nile R.
RED SEA
Abydos
Thebes
Hierakonpolis
Miles
0 100 200
0 100 200 300
Kilometers
Fertile area
Pyramids

The Egyptian Kingdoms

Egypt is largely desert and dependent on the Nile River for water; thus, the earliest farming communities at the end of the Neolithic period, around 5300 BCE, were located along its banks. By a millennium later, these villages had coalesced into over twenty *nomes* (districts) led by city-states with their own rulers and pantheons of gods. Some alliance was achieved during the Predynastic period when the city-states were united into northern and southern states.

The Early Dynastic Period

(3000–2675 BCE; Dynasties 1–2)

Narmer (sometimes also identified as Menes) unified the "two lands" and established the first dynasty around 3000 BCE. Memphis became the capital and retained this status into the Old Kingdom period.

The Old Kingdom

(2675–2130 BCE; Dynasties 3–8)

The basic concepts of Egyptian civilization took shape at this time and found expression in the pyramids and wall reliefs. The step pyramid commissioned by Djoser during the third dynasty is the oldest stone structure of its size in history. Eventually, the Old Kingdom went into decline, inaugurating a time of disunity known as the First Intermediate Period (2130–1980 BCE; dynasties 9–10).

The Middle Kingdom

(1980–1630 BCE; Dynasties 11–14)

Stability returned with the twelfth dynasty, inaugurating a golden age with a flourishing of Egyptian art and literature. This period is also generally regarded as the time of the ancestors (Genesis 12–50). A weakening of central authority and Asiatic (Canaanite) immigration into the Delta brought about the Second Intermediate Period (1630–1539 BCE; dynasties 15–17). The Hyksos established their capital at Avaris in the eastern Delta (the biblical "Land of Goshen"). The Hebrews are often regarded as being among the various West Semitic groups who settled there.

The New Kingdom

(1539–1075 BCE; Dynasties 18–20)

Ahmose I expelled the Hyksos and reasserted Egyptian authority. Eighteenth-dynasty pharaohs extended their control into the Levant, elevating Egypt to the status of an empire for some three hundred years. During the nineteenth dynasty (Ramesside period), Egypt shifted its power base from Thebes to the Delta—the setting of Moses and the exodus.

Third Intermediate Period

(1075–656 BCE; Dynasties 21–25)

Political control alternated between Egyptian (dynasties 21, 23), Libyan (dynasties 22, 24) and Nubian (dynasty 25) rule. Shoshenq (Shishak) of the twenty-second dynasty ruled from Bubastis in the Delta and was a contemporary of Solomon and Rehoboam. The end of this period roughly coincides with the Assyrian conquest of Thebes (Luxor) in 664 BCE.

Late Period

(664–332 BCE; Dynasties 26–31)

During the twenty-sixth (Saite) dynasty, Assyria rapidly declined, and Babylonia became the new regional power. Attempts by Necho II to counter the rise of Babylon and maintain its influence in the Levant resulted in the death of Josiah at Megiddo in 609 BCE and concluded in 605 BCE at the battle of Carchemish. The rest of Egyptian history alternates between Persian and Egyptian control (dynasties 27–31), concluding with the conquests of Alexander the Great.

UPPER AND LOWER EGYPT AND SPHERES OF INFLUENCE map 6

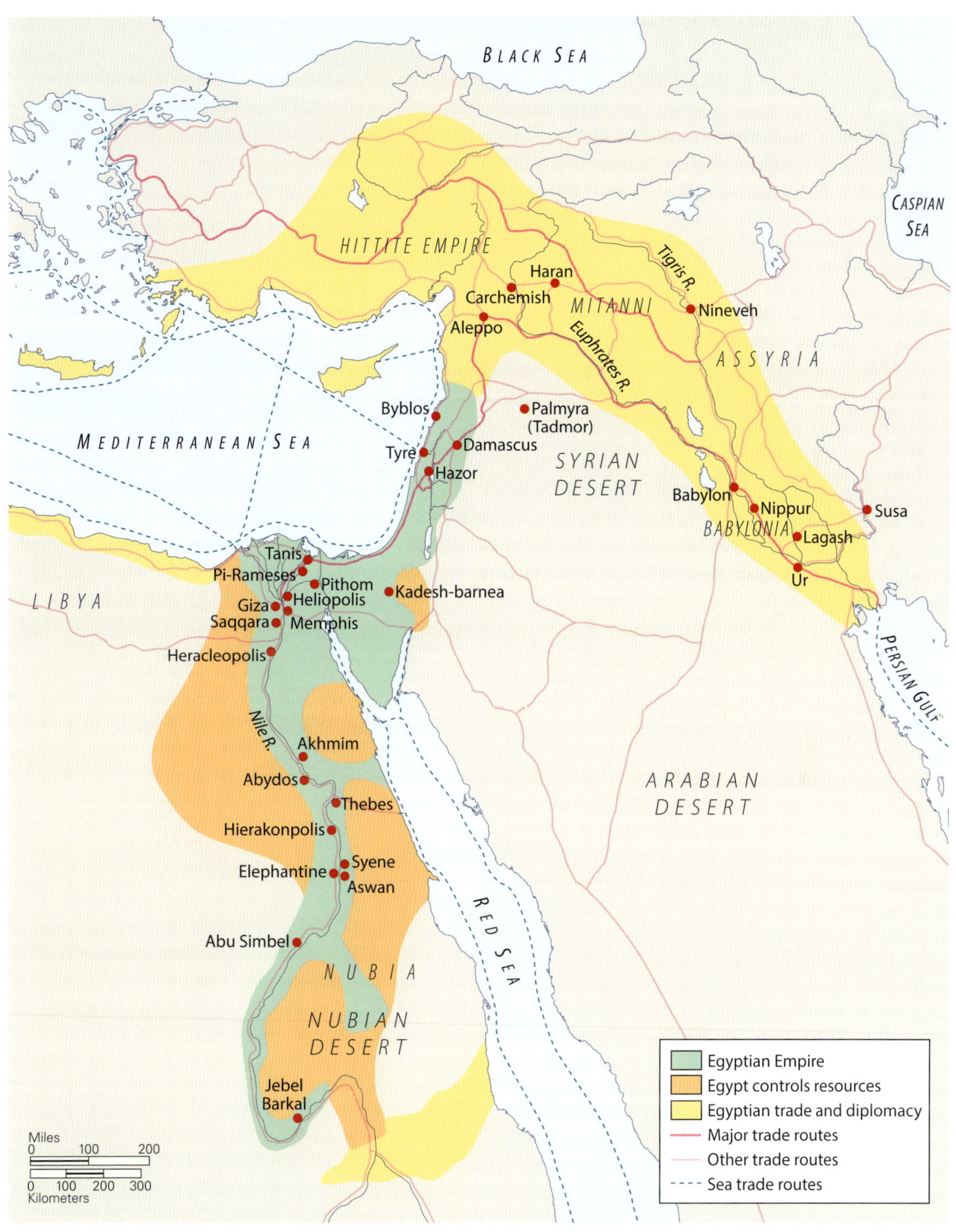

History did not begin with Abraham. By the time he appeared on the world stage, writing had been in use for more than a thousand years and the great pyramids at Giza had been standing for at least four centuries.

The stories of Abram and Sarai (as they were originally called) and the three generations of ancestors that followed them dominate Genesis (ch. 12–50). Though traditionally known as the Patriarchal Narratives, many scholars prefer the more inclusive term Ancestral Narratives, as God also worked through the matriarchs; especially since in many ways, it was the women who enabled God to carry out the divine purpose! Abraham and Sarah were followed by Isaac and Rebekah, and then by the family of Jacob and Leah, Rachel, Bilhah, and Zilpah, and their offspring—the twelve sons of Jacob.

Genesis 11:27–31 and 15:7 places Abraham's origins in Ur of the Chaldeans, usually situated in southern Mesopotamia, though the biblical text also locates the ancestral home some 600 miles to the northwest (Deut 26:5) in Aram-Naharaim (Gen 24:10) or Paddan-Aram (Gen 25:20; 28:2). Islamic tradition locates Abraham's birthplace in Sanliurfa, about twenty-five miles north of Haran, but the evidence supporting this or any other northern site as an alternative Ur is uncertain.

After leaving Haran, Abraham traveled some 470 miles southwest into Canaan, where he sojourned at the Oak of Moreh in Shechem (Gen 12:6). He then passed along the central ridge route to Bethel and Ai (Gen 12:8) and headed into the Negev (Gen 12:9). Following his time in Egypt and separation from Lot, Abraham settled in Hebron at the Oaks of Mamre (Gen 13:18) and subsequently in Beersheba (Gen 22:19). Despite his foibles,

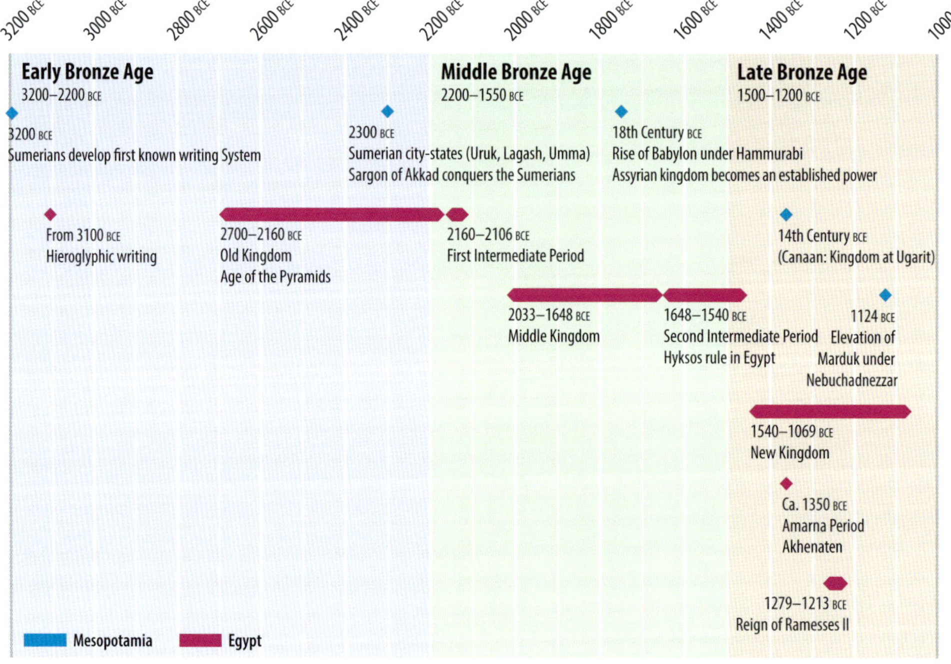

THE ANCESTRAL JOURNEYS map 7

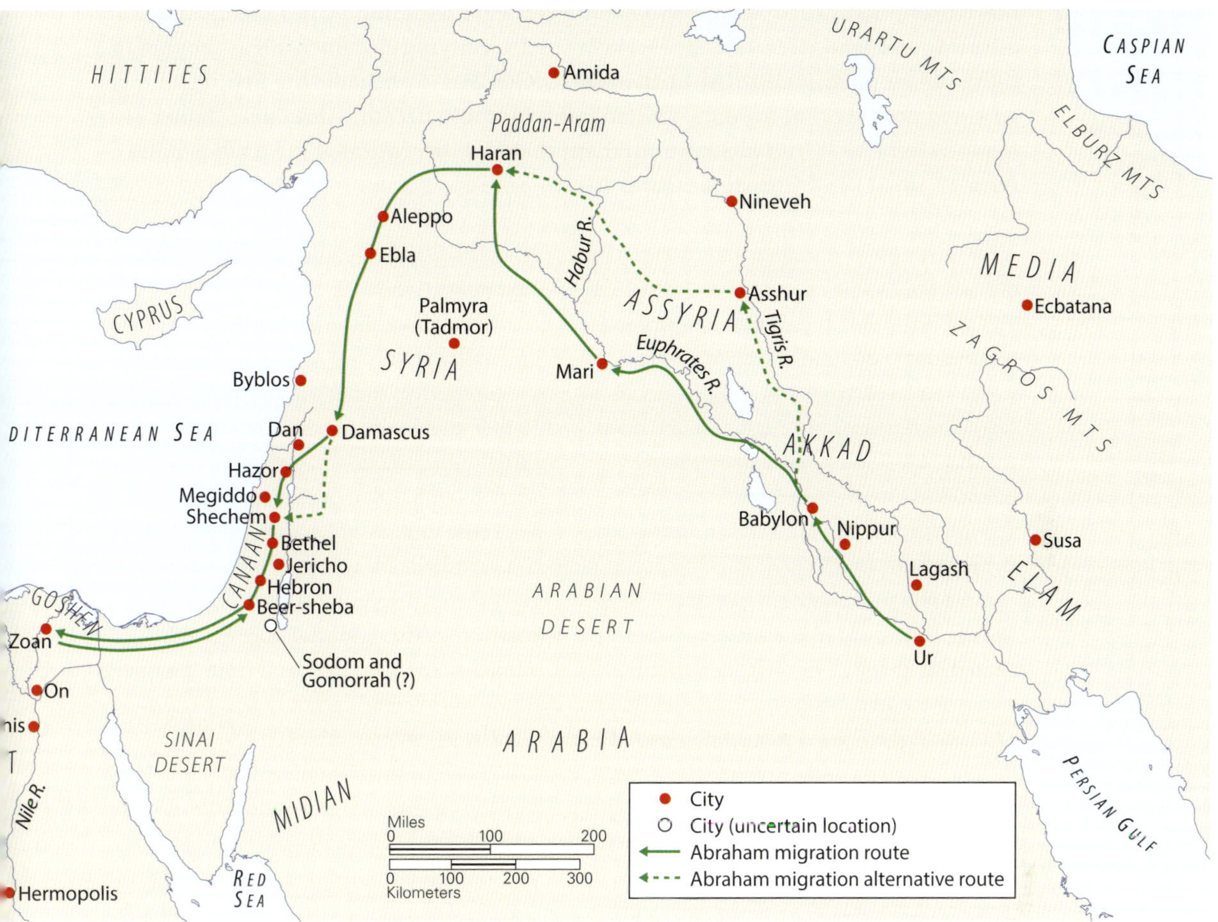

Abraham is remembered for his unwavering obedience. He left Haran at God's command (Gen 12:1; see also Heb 11:8) and did not hesitate when asked to sacrifice his son Isaac in the "land of Moriah" (Gen 22:2), identified by the Chronicler with the site of Solomon's Temple (2 Chr 3:1). Probably the most famous story involving Abraham and his nephew Lot is the twin destruction of Sodom and Gomorrah (Genesis 19).

There is no direct proof for the ancestors or any events associated with them, despite indirect clues like the forms of personal names and the identification of the god of the ancestors as El (see Exod 6:3). The lack of evidence, the schematic nature of the narratives themselves, and the internal evidence for Iron Age composition all have given rise to questions of historicity. A cautious positive assessment would place the ancestors between 2000 and 1000 BCE, with some clues pointing to an earlier time span. Joseph's elevation to a prominent position in the Egyptian court, for example, would not be incompatible with the period of Semitic Hyksos rule over most of Lower Egypt at the end of the Middle Bronze Age (1650–1550 BCE).

The Ancestors in Canaan

The hubris that gave rise to the tower of Babel (Gen 11:1–9) highlighted a stark reality: sin was endemic, and God had to take new steps to redeem humanity. For this reason, God called Abram and made a covenant with him by promising him offspring and land (Gen 12:1–3; 15:18–21) and specifying circumcision as the sign of the covenant (Gen 17:10). The birth of Isaac (Gen 21:1–7) became the first installment on God's promise that *Abram* ("exalted father") would become *Abraham* ("father of many"; Gen 17:5–8), an inclusive covenant that also incorporated the Arab peoples (Gen 17:18–21) and Christians (Rom 4:16).

After the death of Abraham and his burial in the cave of Machpelah at Hebron (Gen 25:8–9), God reaffirmed these covenant promises to Abraham's son Isaac (Gen 26:2–5) and to Isaac's son Jacob (Gen 35:9–13). In Jacob's case, God renamed him "Israel," after Jacob wrestled with God at the Jabbok Ravine (Gen 32:22–30; see also Gen 35:10). The text interprets his name to mean "one who struggles with God."

In a nod to their nonindigenous origins, Isaac and Jacob married women from their ancestral homeland, rather than Canaanite women. Isaac's wife, Rebekah, was handpicked by a servant who noticed the kindhearted young woman who drew water for him and his camels (Genesis 24). By necessity, Jacob fled to Haran after tricking his older twin Esau into surrendering his birthright (Genesis 27). On the way, Jacob stopped at Luz/Bethel, where he dreamed of angels on a staircase between heaven and earth (Gen 28:10–22). Even though Jacob wanted Rachel, whom he had met at a well, Laban tricked him into marrying Leah first. Jacob's subsequent return to Canaan offered him the opportunity to be reconciled to Esau (Genesis 32), eponymous ancestor of the Edomites (Gen 25:25).

Throughout these narratives, the fathers and mothers of Israel are not presented as picture-perfect saints with unwavering faith. Rather, the stories of lying and deception, questioning and doubt, point to a God who carried out his plan over every human failure. For those in Babylonian exile, God's ability to use individuals whose lives mirrored their own struggles must have been highly reassuring. The God who once brought Abram to the promised land from their part of the world could certainly do so again.

The Joseph narrative (Genesis 37–50) explains how the Hebrews ended up in Egypt, and thus sets the stage for the birth of Moses and the exodus. This novella (short story) as it is often classified, focuses on the life of Joseph, who through the treachery of his jealous brothers, was taken to Egypt, where he later rose to prominence in the Egyptian court. According to Genesis 50:22–26, Jacob's family settled in the agriculturally rich land of Goshen in the eastern Nile delta (see Exod 8:22; 9:26), where they stayed and where Joseph eventually died.

ISRAEL'S ANCESTORS IN CANAAN AND EGYPT

map 8

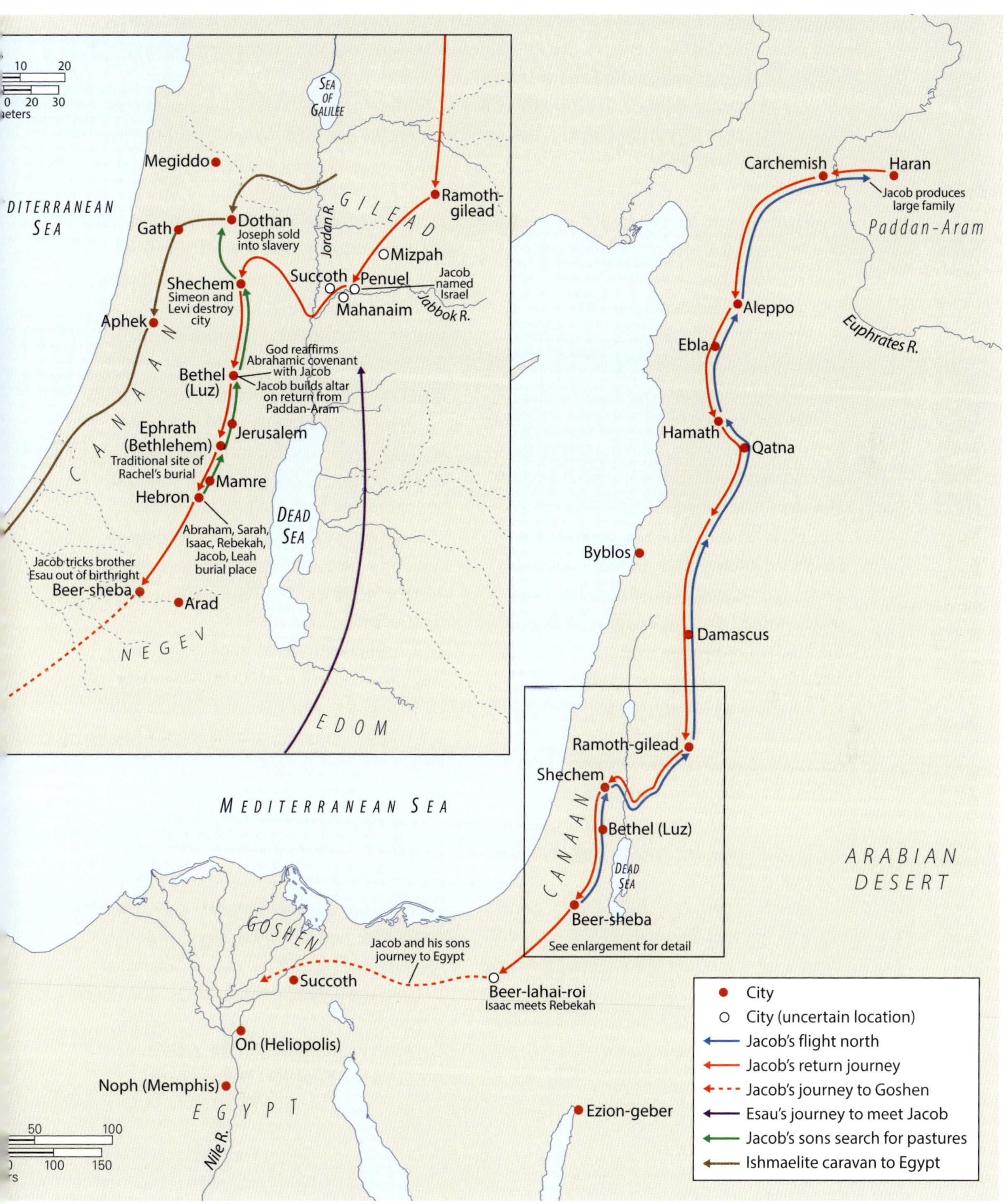

Egypt Invades the Levant

Canaanite (Asiatic) populations from the Levant had been filtering into Egypt for centuries, but toward the end of the Middle Kingdom they took over most of Lower Egypt, established a capital at Avaris (Tell ed-Dab'a) in the northeastern Nile Delta, and ruled for about a century (1650–1550 BCE). Manetho, the early third century BCE author of *Aegyptiaca*, called them *Hyksos* (the Greek form of an Egyptian phrase, "rulers of foreign lands"). Despite their non-Egyptian origins, the Hyksos adopted many aspects of Egyptian culture. As noted earlier, the story of Joseph could fit this period of Semitic rule.

The Hyksos were finally expelled from Avaris by Ahmose I, founder of the eighteenth dynasty. The route by which they fled into Canaan was called the "Ways of Horus" by the Egyptians, while the Bible refers to it anachronistically as the "Way to the Land of the Philistines" (Exod 13:17).

The three dynasties of the New Kingdom (1550–1069 BCE) lasted almost five centuries. Famous eighteenth-dynasty rulers include Hatshepsut, the "heretic" king Akhenaten, and Tutankhamen. The title of "pharaoh" also came into use at this time. It originally meant "great house," but during the reign of Thutmose III, it started to be used in reference to individual kings. The most famous ruler of all, Ramesses II, reigned for sixty-seven years during the nineteenth dynasty and died at age ninety-two. His mummified remains show that he was a redhead. During the twentieth dynasty, Ramesses III famously fought off in 1178 BCE an invasion of Sea Peoples, which included the Philistines.

New Kingdom rule in the Levant grew incrementally. In the time of Ahmose I, the focus was on southern Canaan, but fifty years later Egypt reached the Euphrates River, where new powers in Syria were vying for control of the northern Levant. The major threat during the eighteenth dynasty was the Hurrian kingdom of Mitanni, while during the nineteenth dynasty it was the Hittites. Two pharaohs, Thutmose III and Ramesses II, dealt in turn with these threats. They also happen to be the rulers identified by two different groups of scholars as candidate for the pharaoh of the exodus.

Thutmose III campaigned seventeen times in the Levant. In the first of these battles, he suppressed a Hurrian-inspired revolt of three hundred Canaanite rulers at Megiddo, in 1470 BCE. He consolidated rule in Canaan and set up garrisons to help administer his empire. One of these was at Beth-shan.

Conflict with the Hittites began under Seti I and reached a head with Ramesses II. To help counter this threat, Seti fortified the Ways of Horus. Two monuments from Beth-shan describe military expeditions by Seti, including one in which he declared victory over the Apiru, a group that some have tried to identify with the Hebrews. The major Hittite showdown took place in 1274 BCE under Ramesses II at Kadesh on the Orontes, in central Syria. Although the outcome was a draw, each side boasted victory. The boundaries of Canaan described in Numbers 34:1–12 appear to reflect the Egyptian province of Canaan as defined in the 1258 BCE Egyptian-Hittite treaty.

EGYPT INVADES THE LEVANT

map 9

Egypt in the Levant

Egyptian connections with the Levant go all the way back to the fourth and third millennia BCE. Exported products included raw materials such as copper ore and bitumen from the Dead Sea. In Lebanon, there is evidence from the port city of Byblos for the shipment of cedar logs to Egypt. These trade relations continued into the second millennium and provide a context for the movement of Asiatic (Canaanite) populations in and out of Egypt during the Ancestral period.

It was during the New Kingdom, in the three-hundred-year timespan from 1470 BCE (following the battle of Megiddo) to 1150 BCE (when Egypt withdrew from Canaan) that the Levant came under more direct Egyptian political control. Canaan served as a buffer against Hurrian and Hittite influence and encroachment, while Egypt also benefited from a number of agricultural goods such as grain, wine, and olive oil. Egyptian records between 1450 and 1200 BCE also document the export of Canaanite slaves into Egypt for forced labor projects.

The most revealing information about the Levant at this time comes from an archive of more than three hundred and fifty clay tablets from el-Amarna in Middle Egypt, capital of Akhenaten. About half of these were written by Canaanite kings to Amenhotep III and his son Akhenaten and provide us with a window into the political intrigues taking place among the vassal Canaanite rulers. The letters were written in Akkadian cuneiform, the diplomatic lingua franca of the time, and belonged to a fifty-year period between 1400 and 1350 BCE, when there was relative peace between Egypt and Mitanni. The latter was busy with struggles to the north, and Akhenaten was preoccupied with his political and religious agenda in Egypt. As long as Egyptian rule remained secure in the province of Canaan, the pharaoh cared little for the internal squabbles of the Canaanite kings. The tablets also provide an important backdrop for the emergence of Israel.

At this time Canaan was divided into city-states, where each major city had its own king and controlled a certain amount of surrounding territory. The letters reveal attempts by some of these rulers to expand their territory at the expense of their neighbors. This was particularly true of the central hill country, where settlement was sparse and the territories larger. Labayu, king of Shechem, sought to expand his holdings at the expense of Megiddo to the north and Jerusalem to the south; and Abdi-Heba, king of Jerusalem, accused the rulers of Gezer and Gath of taking territory considered vital to Jerusalem's interests.

Some rulers sought the aid of the Habiru ('Apiru in Egyptian), whom some have sought to equate with the Hebrews of an early date conquest in 1406 BCE. However, the Habiru are a social class, not an ethnic group, and the way they are depicted in the Amarna letters does not conform to the details of the biblical narrative. Even so, it is possible that these Habiru groups coalesced with other indigenous and outside groups to form the basis of later premonarchic Israel.

CITIES CITED IN THE AMARNA LETTERS

map 10

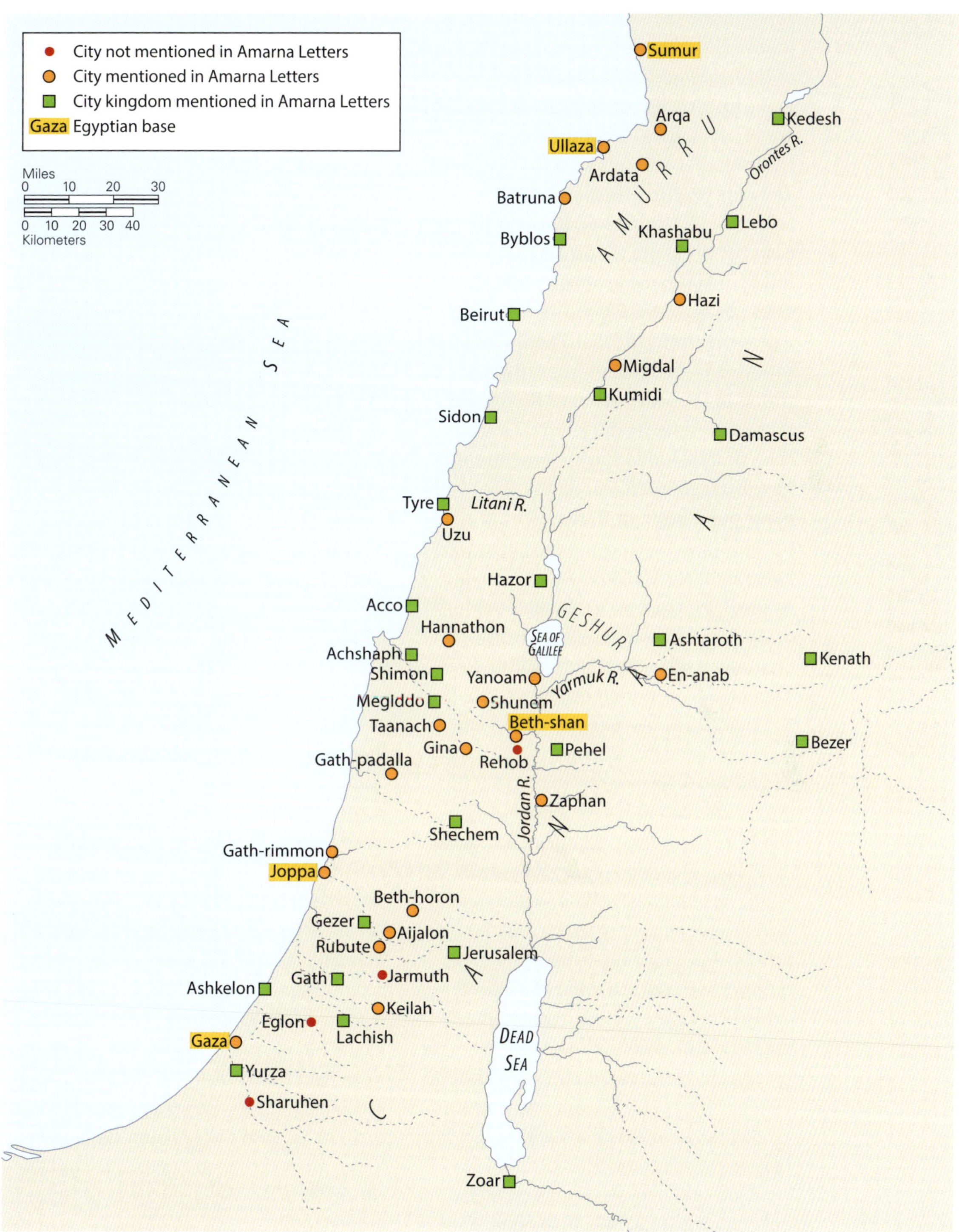

The Exodus and Sinai Route

As with the ancestral narratives, there is no extrabiblical evidence to corroborate the exodus and wilderness wanderings. The Bible also lacks the kind of information that scholars need to make historical correlations—pharaohs are rarely named, and the biblical chronologies are vague and inconsistent. The only precise information is the reference to Pithom and Rameses in the eastern Nile Delta (Exod 1:11), but this might also be anachronistic. Indirect evidence includes Papyrus Leiden 348, which mentions the distribution of grain rations to "the 'Apiru who transport stones to the great pylon of Ramesses." Since the 'Apiru/Habiru were a social class that included slaves, Israelites may have been counted among the forced-labor population in Rameses.

There are three main views for the exodus. Most scholars support a thirteenth-century date under Ramesses II. A smaller group argues for a fifteenth-century date under Thutmose III. A third group views the event as fictional. The first two views appeal to 1 Kings 6:1 and the 480 years between the exodus and Solomon's fourth year; but the groups interpret its meaning differently. "Early date" advocates take it literally. "Late date" supporters view it as a schematic figure, representing twelve generations of forty years. Some try to steer a middle road between historicity and fiction, by arguing for some sort of actual event or series of events, since the exodus is a persistent theme in early poetry (Exodus 15) and other preexilic texts (Amos 3:1–2; 9:7). Whichever view one adopts, the present shape of the exodus narrative was clearly enriched by later theological reflection.

Exod 13:17 reports that the escapees did not leave by the "way to the land of the Philistines" (see p. 16), but along a route leading from Rameses (Qantir) to Succoth (Exod 13:20) where a string of brackish lakes mark the boundary to Sinai. While Lake Timsah is the most obvious candidate for the crossing of the yam suf or "Sea of Reeds" in Exod 13:18 (the "Red Sea" in most translations comes from the Septuagint), the people instead "turned back" and headed north towards Migdol (Exod 4:2). Meanwhile, Pharaoh prepared to intercept them from the west. With Lake Ballah at their backs (a more extensive body of water at the time), this lake becomes the best contender for the Sea of Reeds. Once on the other side, the Israelites either traveled east along the Way to Shur or headed south towards Jebel Musa.

ALTERNATIVE ROUTES FOR THE EXODUS

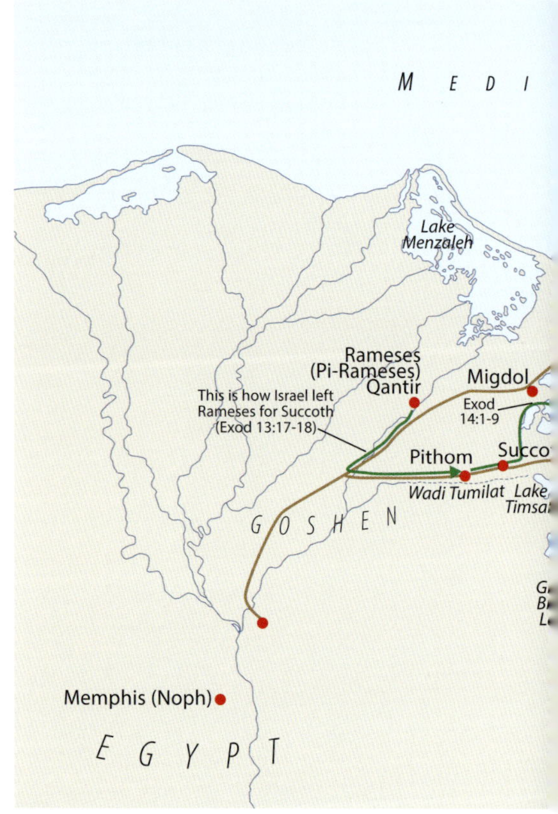

N E A N S E A
Ashdod
Bethel
Jericho
Jordan R.
Shittim
Rabbah
Heshbon
Jerusalem
Mt. Nebo
C A N A A N
PLAIN OF PHILISTIA
Gaza
Hebron
DEAD SEA
Dibon
Raphia
Arad
Beer-sheba
Lake Sirbonis
El-Arish
N E G E V
M O A B
Way to the Land of the Philistines
Bozrah
Punon
W I L D E R N E S S O F S I N
Alternative route (Exod 15:22-16:1)
Jebel Helal
The Way to Shur
Kadesh-barnea
Bir Gafgafa
Bir Haseneh
W I L D E R N E S S O F S H U R
E D O M
Sela ?
King's Highway
W I L D E R N E S S O F P A R A N
Traditional route (Num 10:12)
Ezion-geber
S I N A I
M I D I A N
Dophkah ?
A R A B I A N D E S E R T
Rephidim
Mt. Sinai (Mt. Horeb, Jebel Musa)
Traditional route
Alternative route
Miles
0 10 20 30 40
0 10 20 30 40 50 60
Kilometers
R E D S E A

Wilderness Wandering

Once the Israelites entered the wilderness of Shur, they made their way eastward to the waters of Marah and Elim (Exod 15:22) and into the wilderness of Sin (Exod 16:1), in the central Negev highlands, where God provided both manna and quail (Exod 16:2–36) and Moses brought forth water from a rock (Exod 17:1–7). The place where Moses struck the rock is identified as "Horeb" (another name for Mt. Sinai; compare Deuteronomy 5 with Exodus 19.)

In the light of this, one would expect to find "the mountain of God" (Exod 3:1; 4:27; Num 10:33) in this same general area. Some passages support this notion (Deut 33:2; Judg 5:4–5; Hab 3:3); and Egyptian lists from the time of Amenhotep III and Ramesses II (fourteenth to thirteenth centuries BCE) mention the "Shasu of Yhw," where the Shasu are a pastoralist group that some have identified with the Israelites, and Yhw a geographic or ethnic designation in southern Palestine and Edom that may be vocalized as Yahu, and thus may be a form of the divine name Yahweh. Nevertheless, this region does not fit the eleven-day journey from Kadesh-barnea to Mt. Sinai (Deut 1:2), which—based on a coefficient of 15 miles per day—would be around 165 miles. Such a distance would fit better in the Sinai or northern Arabia, though the composite nature of the biblical texts and their redaction over a long period of time makes it difficult to establish any certain identification.

Understanding of the wilderness wanderings is also complicated by the complete lack of archaeological evidence, even though nomadic groups going back to prehistoric times have been traced in the region. To fit an assumed location in southern Sinai, most maps depict Israel's journey leading out of Egypt deep into the southern Sinai, where Christian tradition has located Mt. Sinai at Jebel Musa (Mt. Moses) since the fourth century CE (see map 11 on p. 37).

According to Exodus 19:1, the Israelites arrived at Mt. Sinai in the third month. Here, God made a covenant with Israel in the form of the Ten Commandments (Exodus 20) and supplementary laws in the Covenant Code (Exodus 21–23). The people also built the ark of the covenant (Exod 25:10–22) and spent a year constructing the tabernacle (Exodus 25–28, 30, 36–40). Israel then set off for the land of Canaan (Num 10:11–12). From Kadesh-barnea they sent twelve spies, one from each tribe, to explore the land of Canaan, but a bad report sparked fear among the people, so God condemned that generation to perish in the wilderness (Numbers 13–14). Eventually, a new generation gathered on the plains of Moab east of the Jordan River opposite Jericho, where Moses reaffirmed the Sinai covenant through a series of speeches in Deuteronomy. Moses then ascended Mt. Nebo to survey the land that God had promised to the ancestors and died (Deuteronomy 34). Whatever date is associated with Israelite presence in the land of Canaan, the Merenptah Stele suggests that there was a recognizable people group known to the Egyptians as "Israel" no later than 1207 BCE.

WILDERNESS WANDERING map 12

Part 2

The People of Israel in Canaan

The Emergence of Israel in Canaan

Three models have been put forth to explain Israel's appearance in Canaan: conquest, pastoral sedentarization, and social revolution. All three attempt to reconcile the archaeological record with the textual evidence.

The conquest model is premised on Joshua 1–12 (esp. 10:40–41; 11:23), together with evidence for the destruction of some Late Bronze Age sites toward the end of the thirteenth century BCE; however, the data does not support a blitzkrieg-style invasion. This impression is largely a result of the narrative's theological shape, which stresses how God gave Israel the land as promised to the ancestors (see Gen 12:7; 28:13; Josh. 21:43–45). Thus, the book of Joshua telescoped what may have been a long and complex process into a single military event.

The immigration, pastoral sedentarization model exists in two main variants—the settlement of pastoralist groups already in the hill country and the infiltration of outside groups. A combination of these views seems plausible, since pastoralists were not limited to the marginal zones. Not only did nomadic groups like the Shasu live in Edom and the southern deserts (see p. 38 and map 12), but texts of Seti I and *Papyrus Anastasi I* locate them in areas linked to the ancestors: Shechem, Bethel, Gerar, and Beer-sheba.

The social revolution model postulates Israel's rise as a predominately indigenous movement. The existing Canaanite city-state system created an oppressive feudalism. Those who refused to participate removed themselves by forming a separate "outlaw" society (Habiru/'Apiru; p. 38). In this scenario, the sociopolitical entity called "Israel" in the Merenptah Stele (dated to 1207 BCE) comprised native Canaanites, who joined forces with a nuclear group of "exodus Israelites" arriving from the desert. One plausible approach might be to regard emergent Israel as composed of diverse groups and embodying a complex interweaving of elements found in all three models.

In the biblical narrative, Joshua and the Israelites used a strategy of "divide and conquer." They first took the Central Benjamin Plateau to drive a wedge between the Samaria and Judean hills (Josh 5:13–10:15). After the covenant renewal at Mt. Ebal (Josh 8:30–35; see Deuteronomy 27), the Israelites were able to more easily take the south (Josh 10:16–43) followed by the north (Josh 11:1–23).

Three cities are most associated with the conquest: Jericho, Ai, and Hazor. Jericho was largely denuded to Early Bronze Age levels by local farmers, who hauled away the nitrogen-rich earth for fertilizer. While there are scattered Late Bronze Age remains on the tel, the cemetery remains indicate that Jericho was a small settlement, occupied only in the Amarna period (fourteenth century BCE), thus falling between the espoused dates for an early or late date conquest. Ai (et-Tell) completely lacks Late Bronze remains, and attempts to find an alternative site are unconvincing. Hazor (Josh 11:10–11) was destroyed in the mid-thirteenth century BCE. Perhaps the Israelites or another group (or groups) that became integrated into greater Israel were responsible, explaining how the memory of this event found its way into the biblical narrative.

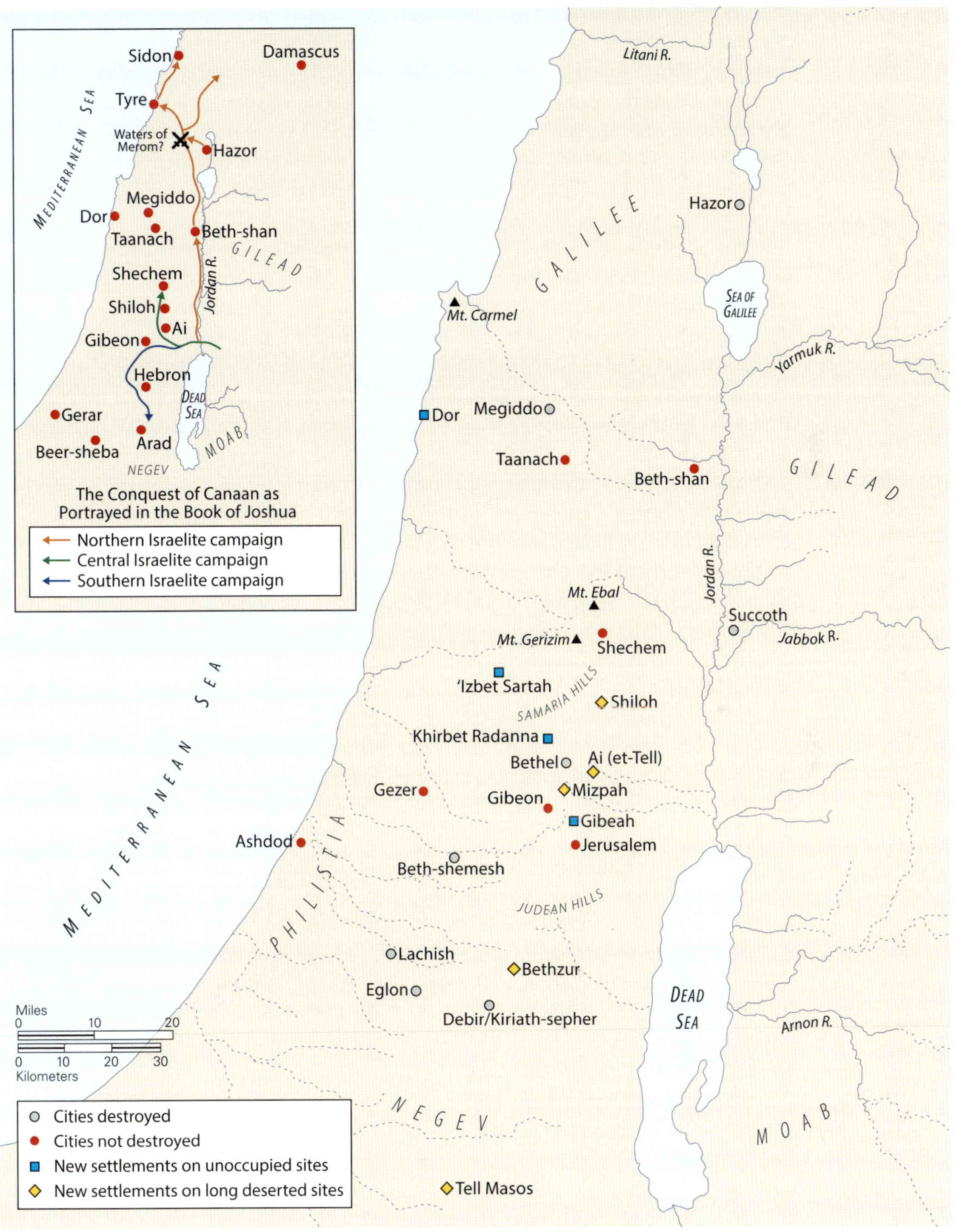
Sidon
Damascus
Tyre
MEDITERRANEAN SEA
Waters of Merom?
Hazor
Megiddo
Dor
Taanach
Beth-shan
GILEAD
Shechem
Jordan R.
Shiloh
Ai
Gibeon
Hebron
DEAD SEA
Gerar
Arad
MOAB
Beer-sheba
NEGEV
The Conquest of Canaan as Portrayed in the Book of Joshua
Northern Israelite campaign
Central Israelite campaign
Southern Israelite campaign
Litani R.
Hazor
GALILEE
SEA OF GALILEE
Mt. Carmel
Yarmuk R.
Dor
Megiddo
Taanach
Beth-shan
GILEAD
Jordan R.
Mt. Ebal
Succoth
Mt. Gerizim
Shechem
Jabbok R.
'Izbet Sartah
SAMARIA HILLS
Shiloh
Khirbet Radanna
Bethel
Ai (et-Tell)
Gezer
Mizpah
Gibeon
Gibeah
Ashdod
Jerusalem
Beth-shemesh
PHILISTIA
JUDEAN HILLS
MEDITERRANEAN SEA
Lachish
Bethzur
Eglon
DEAD SEA
Debir/Kiriath-sepher
Arnon R.
Miles
0 10 20
0 10 20 30
Kilometers
NEGEV
MOAB
Cities destroyed
Cities not destroyed
New settlements on unoccupied sites
New settlements on long deserted sites
Tell Masos

Israel's Tribes are Allotted Land

The emergence of Israel is best seen against the backdrop of the "crisis years" (1300–1100 BCE), when a dramatic change in climate precipitated the movement of the Sea Peoples (including the Philistines). This brought an end to the Late Bronze Age city-state system, and contributed to the demise of the Egyptian empire. In the ensuing political vacuum, various political entities—such as Israel in the highlands, Aram to the north, Ammon, Moab, and Edom in Transjordan, and the Philistines on the southern coastal plain—developed into the tribal kingdoms and fledgling nation-states of the tenth century BCE. Thus, Israel's ethnogenesis is best understood as a *consequence* of the collapse of Canaanite society rather than its *cause*.

The basic alignment of the tribes probably arose at this time, though the late composition of the relevant biblical texts makes it difficult to reconstruct their growing stages of complexity. The tribes probably originated as an amalgamation of various indigenous and immigrant groups, whose boundaries were fixed over time, often as a result of political events, and then later revised into the idealized twelve-tribe configuration.

According to the biblical narrative, Joshua's division and apportionment of Canaan among the twelve tribes began in Transjordan, with a brief description of the boundaries of Reuben, Gad, and the half tribe of Manasseh (Josh 12:1–6), followed by a list of the principal cities (Josh 12:7–24) to be divided among the remaining nine and a half tribes in the west (Josh 13:7). The territorial allotments are repeated in Joshua 13:8–33 for Transjordan and in Joshua 14–19 for the tribes west of the Jordan River. In Transjordan, the half-tribe of Manasseh or "clan of Machir" (Gen 50:23; Num 26:29; 32:39–40; Josh 17:1) took control of the hill country of Gilead, while Gad controlled the territory west of Rabbath-ammon (capital of the Ammonites), and Reuben the Madaba plateau north of the Arnon Gorge.

In Cisjordan, four tribes populated the Galilee—Naphtali, Asher, Zebulun, and Issachar—whose initial letters spell an unfortunate but easy to remember acronym. The most important tribes were in the Central Hill Country. In the highlands of Samaria were the "me" tribes of Manasseh and Ephraim, sons of Joseph, or the "House of Joseph" (Gen 49:22; Judg 1:22). Their geographical position reflects Jacob's blessing (Gen 48:13–14), whereby Manasseh was blessed by Jacob's left hand (north) and Ephraim with his right (south).

Judah (incorporating Simeon) was the largest tribe, situated in the Judean hills and northern Negev. Levi, the third member of the southern triad, did not receive an allotment (Map 15). Benjamin and Dan were situated in a topographical saddle between the higher Samaria and Judean hills. The latter tribe relocated north to the city of Leshem/Laish, which they conquered and renamed Dan (Judges 18; Josh 19:47). Benjamin, whose name means "son of my right hand" (i.e., favored son; Gen 35:18), can also mean "son of the south," reflecting its geographical position as the southernmost of the northern tribes (Judg 5:14). After the division of the monarchy in 930 BCE, Benjamin (Saul's tribe) was compelled to stay with Judah, so the capital of Jerusalem would not be in enemy territory (1 Kgs 11:29–32).

City of refuge
City
Movement of Dan to northern location
Miles
0 10 20 30
0 10 20 30 40
Kilometers
MEDITERRANEAN SEA
Damascus
Ijon
Mt. Hermon
Dan (Leshem/Laish)
ARAM
Tyre
Litani R.
ASHER
NAPHTALI
Kedesh
Hazor
Merom
MANASSEH
CLAN OF MACHIR
Acco
Cabul
SEA OF GALILEE
Rimmon
Golan
Ashtaroth
Mt. Carmel
ZEBULUN
Mt. Tabor
Yarmuk R.
Dor
ISSACHAR
Mt. Moreh
Edrei
Megiddo
Jezreel
Ramoth-gilead
Beth-shan
MANASSEH
Jabesh-gilead
Samaria
Tirzah
Jordan R.
Mt. Ebal
Succoth
Mahanaim
Shechem
Jabbok R.
Yarkon R.
Mt. Gerizim
Aphek
GAD
Joppa
EPHRAIM
Shiloh
DAN
Jazer
Bethel
Mizpah
Gilgal
Rabbath-ammon
Gezer
Gibeon
BENJAMIN
Jericho
Heshbon
AMMON
Ashdod
Ekron
Kiriath-jearim
Bezer
Jerusalem
Beth-shemesh
Mt. Nebo
Gath
Bethlehem
Ashkelon
REUBEN
PHILISTINES
Lachish
Hebron
DEAD SEA
Dibon
Gaza
JUDAH
Eglon
En-gedi
Aroer
Arnon R.
Ziklag
Gerar
Beer-sheba
MOAB
SIMEON
Hormah
Zered R.
EDOM

Levitical Cities and Cities of Refuge

Levi was the third son of Jacob by Leah, and thus one of the twelve sons of Jacob (also called "Israel"). Moses and Aaron were from the tribe of Levi (Exod 2:1). Though all Levites were religious functionaries, only Aaron and his male descendants could serve as "priests" (Exod 28:1). Due to their religious role, the Levites were not allotted territory in the promised land (Num 18:23–24). Instead, the three clans of Levites (Gershon, Kohath, and Merari) received forty-eight towns, on both sides of the Jordan River, and the surrounding pasture lands for their flocks and herds (Num 35:2–3, 7).

Levitical Cities

(Num 35:1–5; Joshua 21; 1 Chr 6:54–81)

Several Levitical towns were originally Canaanite centers, which in some cases did not fall under Israelite control until the time of David and Solomon. Moreover, only twenty out of the forty-five archaeologically known cities reveal occupation during the United Monarchy (tenth century BCE), while during the eighth century BCE, all but one were inhabited. Thus, scholars tend to think that the lists do not predate the eighth century. It is uncertain how the Levites functioned in their allotments, but they were probably invested in religious instruction (Lev 10:11; Deut 31:9–13; 2 Chr 34:30; see also Hos 4:6) and supervised other cult-related activities.

The Levites were also government bureaucrats. During Hezekiah's reforms, local priests and Levites distributed agricultural produce from storehouses built by the king to the towns and cities (2 Chr 31:2–19). Some think the Chronicler may himself have been a Levite, since the writer tends to underscore their institutional role.

Cities of Refuge

(Num 35:6–34; Josh 20:1–9; Deut 4:41–43; 19:1–14)

In the ancient Near East, the prosecution of homicide was generally left to the victim's family. To mitigate against the possibility of immediate and unjustified retaliation, six of the Levitical cities were designated as places of asylum, where a person who had accidentally killed someone could find protection from retribution and get a fair hearing (Exod 21:13; Deut 19:4–10; Josh 20:4–6). However, anyone shown to be guilty of murder on the testimony of witnesses (Num 35:30) could be handed over to the "avenger of blood," usually a close relative of the victim (Num 35:19; Deut 19:11–13). This practice may be an extension, or an alternative, to the use of altars for asylum (Exod 21:14; 1 Kgs 1:50–51; 2:28–34). Three of these cities were located west of the Jordan River (Kedesh, Shechem, and Hebron) and three to the east (Golan, Ramoth-gilead, and Bezer). Their relatively even distribution from north to south allowed any accused person, no matter where they lived, to gain asylum. If the act ended up being judged as unintentional homicide, the slayer remained in the city until the high priest died (Josh 20:6; Num 35:25). Anyone who accidentally killed another was still guilty to a degree, and therefore at risk of being killed by the victim's relatives before the death of the priest canceled the slayer's blood guilt.

Levitical city
Levitical city: location uncertain
City of refuge
City
Miles
0 10 20 30
0 10 20 30 40
Kilometers
Sidon
Damascus
Mt. Hermon
Litani R.
ARAM
ASHER
NAPHTALI
Kedesh
Rehob
Abdon
EAST MANASSEH
Mishal
Nahalal
Rimmon
Kartan
SEA OF GALILEE
Golan
Ashtaroth
Mt. Carmel
Hammath
Daberath
ZEBULUN
Helkath
Mt. Tabor
Yarmuk R.
Kishion
Tabor
Yokneam
ISSACHAR
Jarmuth
Taanach
Ramoth-gilead
En-gannim
Ibleam
WEST MANASSEH
Jordan R.
Mt. Ebal
Mahanaim
Shechem
Yarkon R.
Mt. Gerizim
Jabbok R.
Gath-rimmon
GAD
EPHRAIM
Kibzaim
DAN
Jazer
Beth-horon
BENJAMIN
AMMON
Elteke
Geba
Mephaath
Gezer
Gibeon
Almon
Heshbon
Bezer
Gibbethon
Aijalon
Anathoth
Jerusalem
Mt. Nebo
Beth-shemesh
REUBEN
Kedemoth
Libnah
PHILISTINES
JUDAH
Hebron
DEAD SEA
Jahaz
Gaza
Debir
Juttah
Holon
Eshtemoa
Arnon R.
Jattir
Ashan
MOAB
SIMEON
Zered R.
EDOM
MEDITERRANEAN SEA

Israel in the Time of the Judges

According to the Merenptah Stele, by 1207 BCE the Egyptians were aware of a geopolitical entity called "Israel". Archaeological surveys indicate that in a span of just two centuries this population increased ten-fold. Israel began in the late thirteenth/early twelfth centuries BCE with around twenty-five villages in the territories of Manasseh and Ephraim (the house of Joseph) and spread gradually southward into Benjamin and Judah by the tenth century BCE, when some 250 settlements and 45,000 inhabitants populated the hill country. Since this is too many for natural growth in antiquity, this phenomenon might be the result of various groups settling down during the crisis years (see map 14, p. 44); among them the "seven nations" (Deut 7:1; Josh 3:10).

The diverse groups that made up the Israelite confederation were decentralized and lacked a unifying authority. This raised concern for the biblical writer, who noted, "In those days Israel had no king; everyone did as he saw fit" (Judg 17:6; 21:25; cf. 18:1; 19:1). According to the biblical text, their primary allegiance was to Yahweh, though worship of the native deities continued. Though relatively independent, the tribes were expected to come together and assist the others in times of need. When a serious threat emerged, God appointed a military leader or "judge" to intervene.

The rural highland villages west and east of the Jordan comprised several dozen families and were mainly agrarian, although settlements closer to the arid zones had a larger pastoral component. The lack of public buildings (temples and palaces), the similar size of houses, and the limited range of vessel types consistent with a subsistence lifestyle stands in contrast to the former Canaanite city-state system. A common type of dwelling was the "pillared" or "four-room" house. Some had two stories—the lower one for the animals and cooking, and the upper one for the human occupants. The Iron I pottery assemblage is distinctive, but in the Late Bronze Age tradition. Shiloh appears to have been the principal sanctuary city where the tabernacle and ark were kept (Josh 18:1; 1 Sam 4:3). There were several high places, including one discovered in the Samaria hills near Dothan where a small bronze bull was found.

Israel's primary foe was the Philistines, whose power was centered in five cities (1 Sam 6:17): three on the coast (Ashdod, Ashkelon, and Gaza) and two inland (Ekron and Gath). These sites reflect sophisticated building traditions and a distinctive decorated pottery inspired by Mycenean and Cypriot traditions. Rather than a single group of non-Levantine origin, the Philistines appear to have been a composite culture of groups from various origins. To the east, Israel encountered the Ammonites, Moabites, and Edomites. The absence of Iron I settlements south of Wadi Mujib (N. Arnon) has raised questions about whether Moab and Edom were potent forces at this time, though their existence as nomadic chiefdoms is possible.

Elon Judge of Israel with tribal association
Miles
0 10 20 30
0 10 20 30 40
Kilometers
Sidon
Damascus
Mt. Hermon
Litani R.
Tyre
Shamgar son of Anath
ARAM
ASHER
NAPHTALI
MEDITERRANEAN SEA
Barak son of Abinoam
EAST MANASSEH
SEA OF GALILEE
Elon
Rimmon
Mt. Carmel
Hammath
Golan
Ashtaroth
ZEBULUN
Kedesh-naphtali
Mt. Tabor
Yarmuk R.
Jair the Gileadite
Yokneam
ISSACHAR
Jarmuth
Kamon
Taanach
Ramoth-gilead
Jephthah the Gileadite
Tola son of Puah of Issachar
WEST MANASSEH
Jordan R.
Mt. Ebal
Abdon son of Hillel
Mahanaim
Shechem
Yarkon R.
Mt. Gerizim
Jabbok R.
Gideon son of Joash
Gath-rimmon
Deborah
GAD
Joppa
Shiloh
EPHRAIM
DAN
Jazer
Beth-horon
Ehud son of Gera
AMMON
BENJAMIN
Gezer
Gibeon
Geba
Heshbon
Aijalon
Ekron
Anathoth
Ashdod
Samson
Jerusalem
Mt. Nebo
Beth-shemesh
Gath
Ashkelon
Ibzan
REUBEN
PHILISTINES
JUDAH
Hebron
DEAD SEA
Dibon
Gaza
Debir
Aroer
Arnon R. (Wadi Mujib)
Othniel son of Kenaz
SIMEON
MOAB
Zoar
Zered R.
EDOM

The Judges on the Offensive

When reading the books of the Deuteronomistic History (Joshua, Judges, Samuel, and Kings), it is important to remember that these narratives drew upon memories of Israel's past, which were then shaped into a larger theological message (deeply influenced by Deuteronomy) of how God remained faithful to Israel even when they were unfaithful in return.

The theme is played out in Judges, by focusing on select individuals who are at the center of six recurring cycles of disobedience, oppression, repentance, and deliverance. Judges 3:7–11 exemplifies this pattern. The Israelites break the covenant by turning aside to other gods (3:7), which prompts Yahweh to chastise them by handing them over to foreign oppressors (3:8). But after coming to their senses and turning back to God (3:9a), Yahweh sends a "judge" (in this case, Othniel) to save them (3:9b–10). In some cases, this deliverance was followed by forty years of peace (3:11), after which a new generation would repeat the same mistakes.

There are six major judges (Othniel, Ehud, Deborah, Gideon, Jephthah, and Samson), who have more detail given about them, and six minor judges (Shamgar, Tola, Jair, Ibzan, Elon, and Abdon), about whom little is said. A "judge" is someone appointed by a king (in this case, Yahweh) to administer territory or conduct military campaigns. It does not usually refer to a judicial official, though Deborah partly fulfilled this role (Judg 4:5). Regardless of which tribe a particular judge came from, their battles illustrate how Israel was besieged on all sides by enemies. Othniel (Judg 3:7–11) battled Arameans to the north. Ehud (Judg 3:12–30) fought against King Eglon of Moab, and Jephthah (Judg 10:6–12:7) against Ammon to the east. Gideon (Judges 6–8) engaged Midianites to the south, and Samson (Judges 13–16) Philistines to the west. Deborah (Judges 4–5) fought against the leading Canaanite city-state of Hazor in Upper Galilee.

Of these six judges, three stand out. Deborah is one of the most remarkable people in the Bible. She is described as a prophet, a judge who decides legal cases, and a military leader. Deborah also famously declared to Barak, who requested her help, that the glory of Israel's deliverance would go to an unlikely heroine, Jael, whose actions were not only praised but used to mock the exploitation of women in the ancient world. Gideon is the reluctant warrior who wanted reassurance that God would be with him. Yahweh did so by having Gideon set a fleece on the threshing floor, resulting in a wet fleece and dry ground the first time, and the reverse the second time. Finally, there is the unlikely Samson, whom God used despite his selfish impulses. His tragic death in the Philistine temple at Gaza put an end to the cycle of retaliation that he carried out against them. The Philistine port of Tell Qasile on the Yarkon River contained a small temple, which, like the temple of Dagon in Gaza, used two pillars to support the roof (Judg 16:29).

KEY BATTLES LED BY ISRAEL'S JUDGES map 17

The Capture of the Ark

The dismal note on which Judges closes carries over into the time of Samuel, when "the word of Yahweh was rare and there were not many visions" (1 Sam 3:1). The boy who was dedicated by his mother to serve at the tabernacle in Shiloh (1 Samuel 1–3) would go on later to lead Israel as a priest (1 Sam 2:35), prophet (1 Sam 3:20), and judge (1 Sam 7:15–17).

The ark narrative (1 Sam 4:1b–7:2) unfolds in three acts. Part 1 (1 Sam 4:1b–22) emphasizes two battles between the Israelites and the Philistines. In the first clash near Aphek, some four thousand Israelites were killed. Believing that the ark, as the symbol of Yahweh's presence, would reverse their previous misfortune (Num 10:35; also Josh 3:3–17; 6:6–20), the people brought the sacred relic from Shiloh, around twenty-three miles away, to the Israelite camp at Ebenezer ("stone of help"), a small site tentatively identified with Izbet Sartah on the edge of the Ephraim hills. While it was common practice in the ancient Near East to bring the podium of the deity into battle, to the biblical writers it represented the false theology of "God in a box" (the belief that one can somehow manipulate God). In the second conflict, thirty thousand Israelite soldiers were killed and the ark captured. In part 2 (1 Samuel 5), the Philistines carried the ark to Ashdod and set the venerated symbol of the defeated Yahweh before Dagon in their temple. But on two separate occasions, in the middle of the night, Dagon's statue fell prostrate before the ark, recalling the twin defeats at Aphek. But it took an affliction of tumors (bubonic plague?) to compel the Philistines to return the ark. They moved it to Gath (1 Sam 5:8) and then finally even closer to Israel at Ekron (1 Sam 5:10). In part 3 (1 Sam 6:1–7:2), the Philistines brought the ark along the Sorek Valley to Beth-shemesh, whence it was then taken to Kiriath-jearim in the hill

Sarcophagus of Ahiram, with depiction of the king on a cherubim throne.

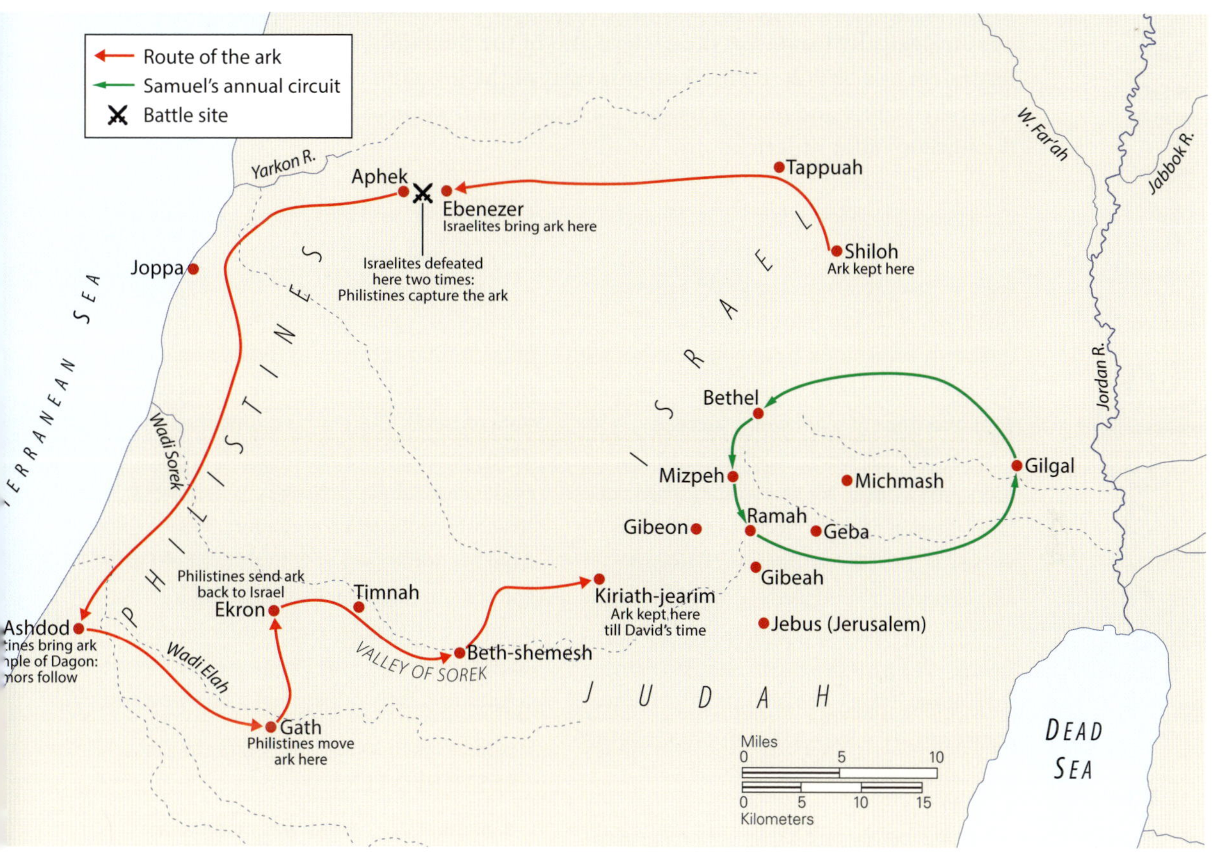

country for about twenty years, until David brought it to Jerusalem.

The ark was a gold-covered box of acacia wood, measuring around 3.75 x 2.25 x 2.25 feet (Exod 25:10–22). The gold lid was surmounted by two gold cherubim, usually depicted as winged human-like figures, associated in the modern mind with "angels", however—based on depictions of cherubim in Israelite art—we know they were actually winged creatures with lion-like bodies and human heads. Yahweh is described in 1 Samuel 4:4 as "enthroned between the cherubim," which suggests that the ark was viewed as the throne for Israel's divine king, the invisible Yahweh (Ezek 10:18). The ark is also described as God's "footstool" (1 Chr 28:2; Ps 132:7). In similar fashion, an ivory knife handle inlay found at Megiddo depicts a Canaanite king seated on a cherubim throne, with his feet resting on a footstool. The storage of the Ten Commandments (Israel's treaty with God) inside the ark finds a parallel in the practice of kings, who would place important treaties and venerated texts at the feet of a deity's image.

Saul: Israel's First King

As a transitional leader who was also Israel's last judge, Samuel reluctantly appointed Saul as the first king (1 Samuel 8–11). The elders approached Samuel while he was at his home in Ramah (1 Sam 8:4). The town, identified with er-Ram, was strategically located at the eastern end of the Benjamin Plateau, between Jerusalem and Shiloh. It stood prominently at the junction of the north-south watershed route and an important east-west road that linked the coastal plain with the Jordan Valley at Jericho.

On a geopolitical level, Israel's incremental rise as a nation state was part of a larger regional pattern of emerging ethnic states (see p. 45, map 14). A growing sense of insecurity brought on by ongoing clashes with the Philistines and the Ammonites, together with questions of who would succeed Samuel after his death (1 Sam 8:5; 12:12), prompted a desire for more established rule. On a theological level, Israel's request was viewed by the Deuteronomistic Historians as a rejection of God as their true king, and part of a pattern that had persisted since the people left Egypt (1 Sam 8:7–8). As in the time of the Judges (see p. 51, map 17), once the people got a leader who won their battles, they felt secure and forgot God (1 Sam 12:9–11).

Following Yahweh's instructions to give the people a king (1 Sam 8:22), Saul was privately anointed by Samuel (1 Sam 10:1) as *nagid* (ruler, leader, captain). He was subsequently confirmed as *melekh* (king) by lot at Mizpah (1 Sam 10:17–24), and then by proclamation at Gilgal (1 Sam 11:14–15). A second coronation followed Saul's rescue of Jabesh-gilead from Nahash the Ammonite (1 Sam 11:1–11), details of which were clarified in a Dead Sea Scroll fragment (4QSam[a]). It is evident now that Saul's rescue was motivated by Nahash the Ammonite's oppression of the tribes of Gad and Reuben, some of whom had escaped to the safety of Jabesh-gilead. Leaving Gibeah, Saul proceeded northward to Bezek, where he prepared the forces of Israel for battle (1 Sam 11:6–8). After crossing the Jordan River, Saul broke the Ammonite siege of Jabesh and defeated them.

Though called a "king," scholars debate whether to regard Saul as a permanent judge/military chief or as the first true king who united the tribes to form the territorial state of Israel. There was rudimentary administration and taxation, but little evidence for drastic changes in the internal structure of the tribal confederacy. Saul ruled from his hometown of Gibeah (Tell el-Ful) and his son Jonathan had a leading role. As military commander, Saul's uncle (or first cousin) Abner (1 Sam 14:50) presided over a voluntary militia rather than a standing army.

RESTORED TEXT

4QSamuel[a] in the NRSV was inserted as the conclusion to 1 Samuel 10:27. This paragraph had been lost from the end of the Hebrew text of 1 Samuel 10, but is now restored from the Dead Sea Scrolls fragment of 4QSamuel[a]. The Hebrew text picks up again with 11:1, "About a month later . . ." The value of this once-missing text is that it gives us the backstory to Saul's rescue of Jabesh-gilead.

"Now Nahash, king of the Ammonites, had been grievously oppressing the Gadites and the Reubenites. He would gouge out the right eye of each of them and would not grant Israel a deliverer. No one was left of the Israelites across the Jordan whose right eye Nahash, king of the Ammonites, had not gouged out. But there were seven thousand men who had escaped from the Ammonites and had entered Jabesh-gilead."

KEY CITIES IN THE LIFE OF SAUL map 19

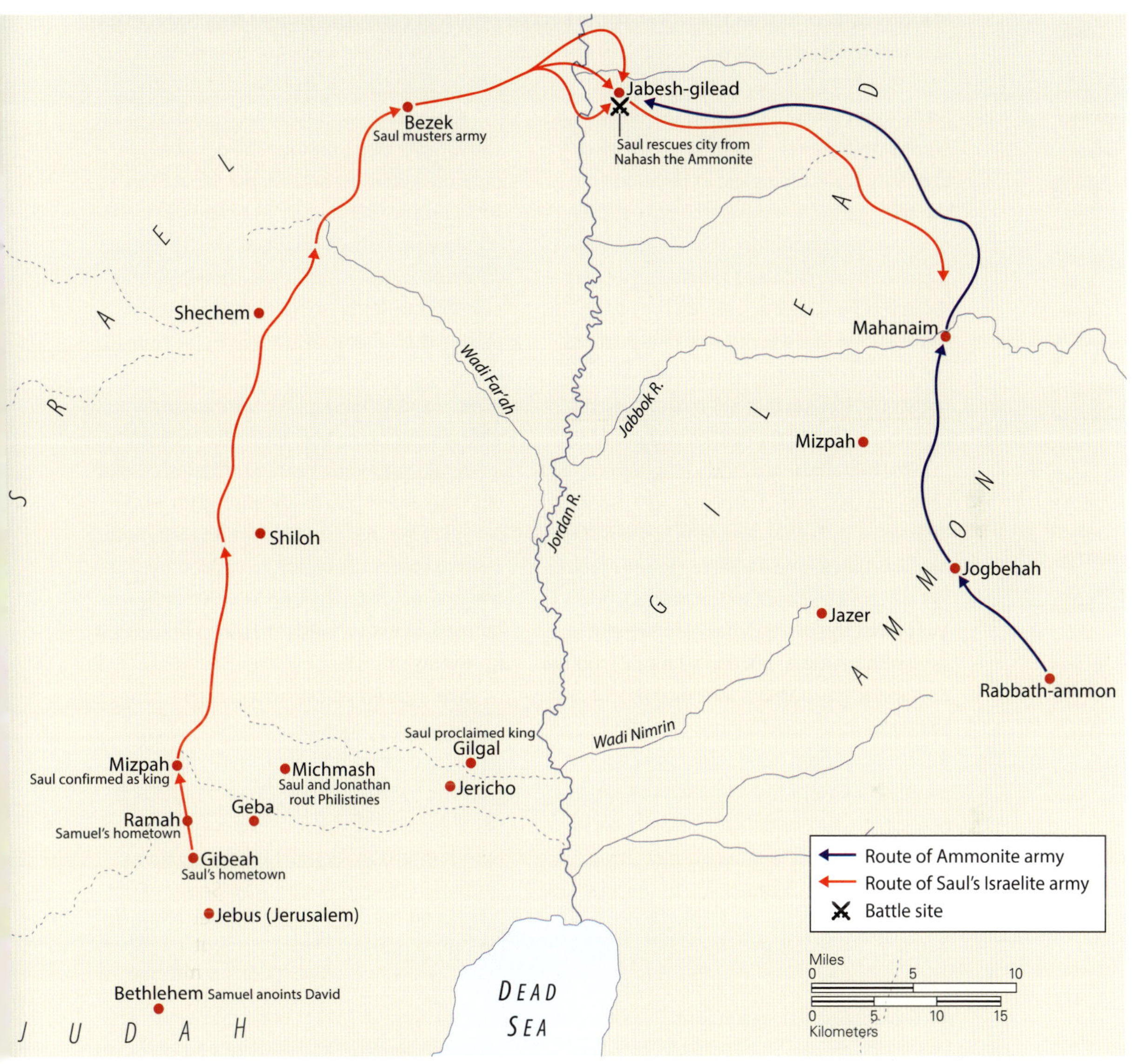

Moreover, Israel's king was not autonomous, as elsewhere in the ancient Near East, but subject to God's law (Deut 17:14–20) and the word of the prophet (1 Sam 10:25; 12:13–15).

The biblical narrative insists that Saul was unable to follow divine directives. On two occasions Saul disobeyed God's commands, which led to his rejection as king (1 Sam 13:14; 15:17–19). This set the stage for Samuel to anoint David in Bethlehem (1 Sam 16:1), the man who would succeed Saul as the next ruler.

The Kingdom of Saul

There is little archaeological evidence for a territorial-political entity fitting the Hebrew Bible's description of Saul's kingdom during the late eleventh century BCE. Still, most accept that there was some sort of political consolidation at this time, even if it was limited in scope.

Saul's hometown of Gibeah (Tell el-Ful) was Israel's first capital (1 Sam 11:4). During the 1920s, archaeological excavations on the hill's summit exposed the corner tower of what was thought to be a square-shaped fortress that served as Saul's headquarters, though others have suggested they were the foundations of a watchtower that guarded the main road leading out of Jerusalem to points further north. Saul most likely ruled from his home in the village (1 Sam 19:9).

The boundaries of Saul's kingdom appear to have been limited to core Israelite territories on both sides of the Jordan. Saul did not control non-Israelite regions, such as Canaanite enclaves in the Beth-shan Valley and the city of Jebus (Jerusalem), but sought to maintain normal relations with the neighboring peoples as long as they did not bother him. The five regions that comprised "all Israel" (2 Sam 2:9) included the hill country of Gilead from the Arnon Gorge (the territories of Reuben and Gad) north to Ramoth-gilead and the Yarmuk River (the half-tribe of Manasseh). To the west lay the territory of Asher in Galilee, the Jezreel Valley, the hill country of Ephraim, and Benjamin. Judah should also be added, since Saul maintained at least nominal control over this territory.

Alphabetic writing, introduced during the Late Bronze Age, continued to develop into the Iron Age; most notably, the 'Izbet Sartah ostracon (twelfth century BCE) and ten incised arrowheads from el-Khadr, near Bethlehem (eleventh century BCE). One arrowhead was inscribed with the name "Ben Anat," the patronymic of an Israelite hero in the time of the Judges. A jar from Khirbet Qeiyafa (see p. 65, map 24), dating to the late eleventh/early tenth century BCE, bore the name "Ishbaal" on its shoulder, the same name as the son of Saul who succeeded him on the throne for a brief period (see p. 63, map 23). The letter-forms are close to the Late Bronze Age proto-Canaanite inscriptions, but a development is discernible on the way to the standardization of the script in Iron Age II.

Saul's life is depicted as a constant struggle against hostile neighbors, who surrounded Israel on every side (1 Sam 14:47–48). There were the tribal kingdoms of Ammon, Moab, and Edom to the east, the Arameans of Zobah (and presumably Geshur) to the north and northeast, the Amalekites who inhabited the desert regions to the south, and the Philistines (Israel's main foe) to the west. The Philistines, who fought against Saul during most of his reign (1 Samuel 13–14), were the people who brought about his death (1 Samuel 31).

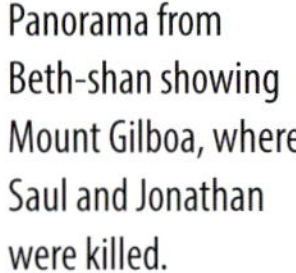

Panorama from Beth-shan showing Mount Gilboa, where Saul and Jonathan were killed.

Saul's campaigns
Miles
0 10 20
0 10 20 30
Kilometers
Mt. Lebanon
Damascus
Mt. Hermon
Ijon
SIDONIANS
Litani R.
Tyre
Dan
ARAMEANS
Kedesh
Beth-shemesh
Achzib
MEDITERRANEAN SEA
Ramah
Acco
Chinnereth
SEA OF GALILEE
GESHUR
Aphek
Hammath
Ashtaroth
JEZREEL
Yarmuk R.
En-dor
Dor
Megiddo
Jezreel
Ramoth-gilead
Taanach
Beth-shan
Ibleam
Hepher
Bezek
Jabesh-gilead
Jordan R.
Socoh
Tirzah
GILEAD
Mahanaim
Succoth
Shechem
Jabbok R.
Aphek
Adam
EPHRAIM
Jogbehah
Joppa
AMMON
Jazer
Bethel
Rabbath-ammon
Mizpeh
Gilgal
BENJAMIN
Gezer
PHILISTINES
Ramah
Heshbon
Ekron
Aijalon
Gibeon
Gibeah of Saul
Ashdod
Jebus (Jerusalem)
Gath
Beth-shemesh
Medeba
Azekah
Socoh
Bethlehem
Ashkelon
Keilah
Hebron
JUDAH
Dibon
DEAD SEA
Gaza
Debir
En-gedi
Aroer
Gerar
Ziklag
Rimmon
Arnon R.
Arad
Beer-sheba
Kir-hareseth
MOAB
Zoar
AMALEK
EDOM

Scenes from David's Early Life

The story of David (1 Samuel 16–1 Kings 2) is assumed to have been composed from two longer narratives (by convention, the History of David's Rise and the Succession Narrative/Court History of David), supplemented by miscellaneous accounts.

We first meet David in 1 Samuel 16, where he was anointed by Samuel after Saul's rejection as king (1 Sam 15:22–34), though David had to wait several years before taking the throne. Meanwhile, David gained access to the court of Saul through his musical ability (1 Sam 16:14–23) and by his defeat of Goliath the Philistine (1 Samuel 17). This latter encounter served the same purpose for David as did Saul's rescue of Jabesh-gilead (see p. 55, map 19). What followed Goliath's defeat was a series of incidents that highlight David's rise and Saul's demise. Fear, treachery, and anger characterized Saul's remaining years, which tragically ended the way he began—fighting the Philistines (1 Sam 31:1–6).

The battle of David and Goliath took place in the buffer zone of the Shephelah (foothills) between the Philistine coast and the hill country of Judah. After leaving Bethlehem for the Elah (Terebinth) Valley to bring food for his brothers, who were fighting alongside Saul, David accepted Goliath's challenge and engaged him in battle, armed with only a sling. The custom of two champions engaging in hand-to-hand combat reflects the Aegean background of the Philistines.

So impressed was Saul by David's heroism that he attached David to his court. He appointed him as commander over a battalion (1 Sam 18:13) and gave him his daughter Michal in marriage (1 Sam 18:27). But with David's popularity rising, as he continued to win battles (1 Sam 18:14–16), Saul became increasingly jealous and paranoid, and actively worked to eliminate David (1 Sam 18:29).

Eventually, David had to flee and seek refuge in a number of different locales. He first went to Ramah, then to Nob, where

Looking north from Socoh to the Valley of Elah, scene of David and Goliath's combat.

SCENES FROM DAVID'S EARLY LIFE map 21

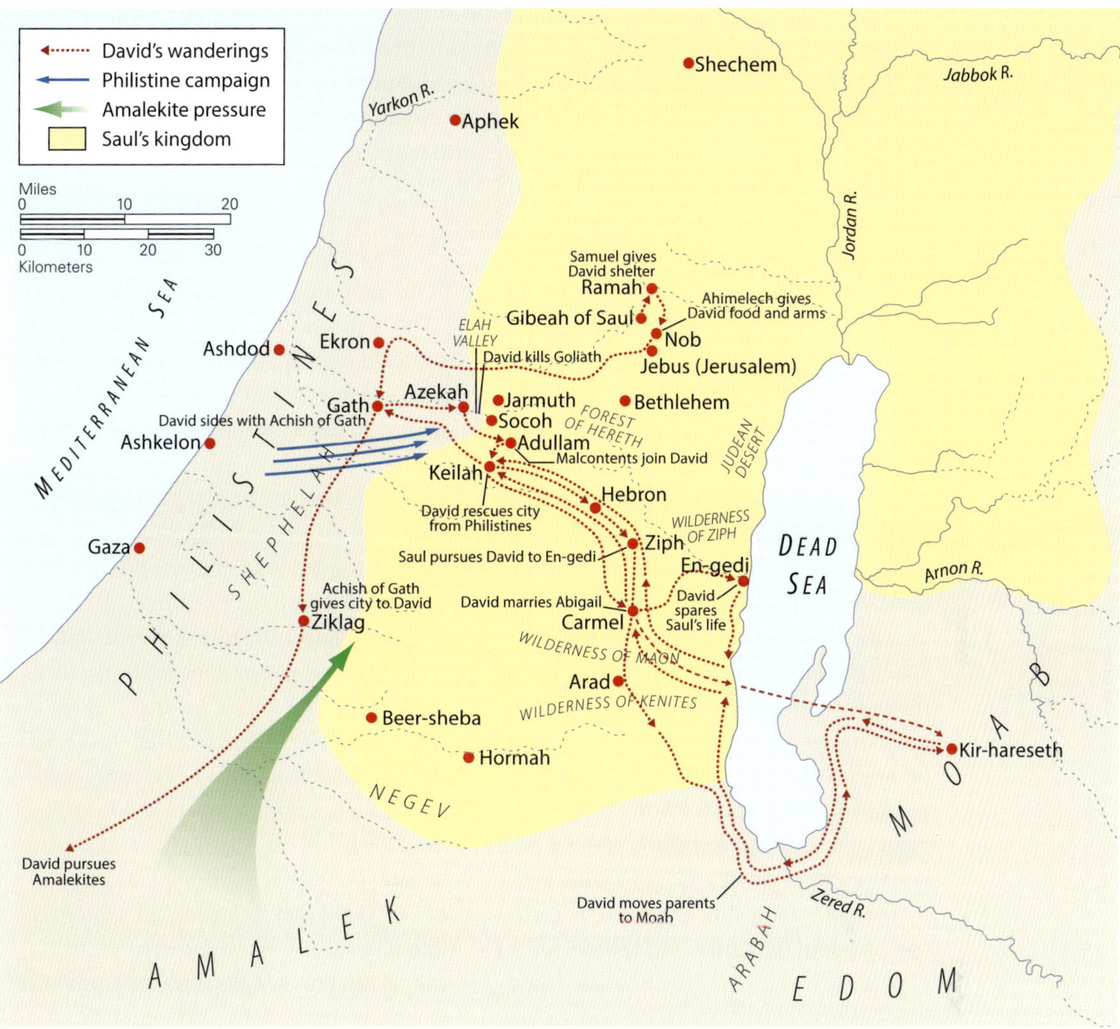

Ahimelech the priest gave him Goliath's sword and consecrated bread to eat (but see Mark 2:25-26 where Jesus identifies the high priest as Abiathar, the son of Ahimelech). David then fled to the Shephelah, where he hid in the caves at Adullam, not far from where he had fought Goliath, and where he gathered his band of malcontents. At times, David sought refuge among the Philistines. Saul even pursued David into the desolate regions of the Judean Desert, where David spared Saul's life on two occasions—the first at En-gedi (1 Samuel 24) and the second in the Wilderness of Ziph (1 Samuel 26). It is between these two encounters that we are told about the death of Samuel and his burial in Ramah (1 Sam 25:1).

The Death of Saul

Despite Saul's relentless pursuit, the biblical writers tell us David did not harm Saul, out of respect for Yahweh's anointed (1 Sam 24:6, 10). In the end, David had no choice but to seek refuge with Achish, the Philistine king of Gath (Tell es-Safi). Achish not only welcomed David but gave him the satellite city of Ziklag as his possession (1 Sam 27:6). This was not out of love for David, but in the hope that David would incite Judah to rebel against Saul. Meanwhile, several warriors and mighty men joined him, forming the nucleus of David's army, and what evolved into a permanent military institution after he became king (2 Sam 23:8–39; 1 Chron 12).

Pressure from the Philistines continued to grow, and Saul was hard-pressed to defend Israel. He tried to make a stand at Mt. Gilboa, in the central part of the Jezreel Valley. As the time for battle approached, Saul was at his wits' end. Samuel was dead, and there was no one to give him counsel or bless the troops. Desperate for a word from Yahweh, who did not answer his earlier plea (1 Sam 28:6), Saul sneaked across enemy lines and approached a medium in En-dor, a small village between Mt. Moreh and Mt. Tabor (1 Sam 28:7–8). At first the medium thought it was a trick, since Saul had earlier outlawed such practices; however, once the woman was assured she would not be punished, she conjured up the spirit of Samuel, who appeared before Saul but only confirmed his earlier rejection. Saul's fate was sealed, and he died the next day on the battlefield. In fulfillment of Samuel's word (1 Sam 28:16–19), the kingdom was taken away, as Saul and his three sons (including Jonathan) died in battle against the Philistines at Mt. Gilboa.

When the Philistine troops came upon Saul's body, they beheaded him, stripped off his armor, and hung his corpse on the city walls (1 Sam 31:8–10) or in the public square (2 Sam 21:12) of Beth-shan for all to see. Upon receiving the news of Saul's death, the citizens of Jabesh-gilead, whom Saul had earlier rescued from the Ammonites (1 Samuel 11), respectfully removed his body and those of his sons and brought them to their city. According to 1 Samuel 31:12–13, the bodies were burned and buried under a tamarisk tree (*eshel*), though the parallel account in 1 Chr 10:12 identifies the tree as a terebinth (*elah*). In another, slightly different, version, 2 Samuel 21:12–14 describes how David took the bones of Saul and Jonathan from the people of Jabesh-gilead and buried them in Benjamin, in the tomb of Saul's father, Kish. Such variations in the received tradition are not unusual; moreover, the editors did not try to suppress or harmonize the inconsistencies, but let them stand.

THE DEATH OF SAUL

map 22

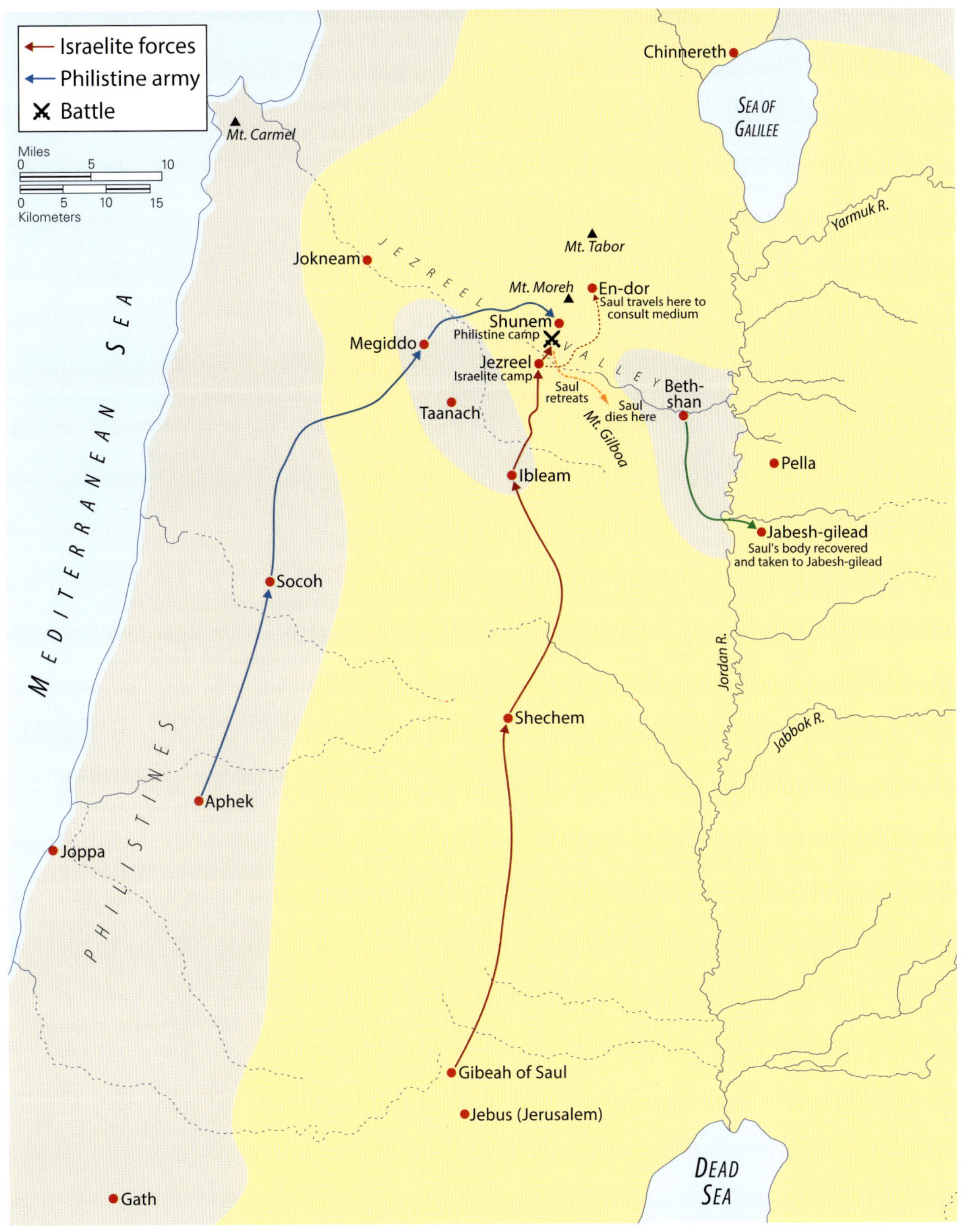

David's Campaigns

Now that Saul was no longer a threat, David left Ziklag for Hebron, where he was anointed king over Judah, and ruled for seven and a half years (2 Sam 2:1–4, 11). Meanwhile, Abner moved the capital from Gibeah to a more secure location at Mahanaim in Gilead, where he crowned one of Saul's surviving sons, Ishbaal (Ishbosheth), as king, though Abner remained the real power behind the throne (2 Sam 2:8–9; 3:6, 11). There followed about two years of skirmishes between the house of Saul (the northern tribes) and the house of David (the tribe of Judah) (2 Sam 2:10). However, the text highlights only one clash, when Joab (David's military commander) routed Abner and his troops at the Pool of Gibeon (2 Sam 2:12–32).

Realizing Ishbaal's weak position (and his own), Abner eventually sealed an agreement with David, designating him as king over "all Israel" (2 Sam 3:17–21). Perhaps sensing a loss of his own prestige, Joab retaliated by murdering Abner before he could complete the arrangements (2 Sam 3:22-30); and soon after, Ishbaal was also murdered (2 Sam 4:1–12). At this point, the elders of Israel came to Hebron and made a covenant with David, anointing him king (*melekh*) over all the tribes (2 Sam 5:1–3).

David's first act was to capture Jebus (Jerusalem), thirty miles north of Hebron, and transform it into his capital, which he renamed the "City of David" (2 Sam 5:6–9). This prompted the Philistines to act, since a unified Israel and Judah posed a threat. They attacked David twice in the Valley of Rephaim, but David managed to defeat them both times (2 Sam 5:17–25).

With the tribes firmly behind him, and Jerusalem established as the new political and religious capital (2 Samuel 5–6), David set out on his wars of expansion (2 Samuel 8, 10). He most likely started out by subduing the old Canaanite centers (Judg 1:27–36), to consolidate his rule. He then set out to conquer the surrounding polities, by defeating the Philistines to the west and the Amalekites to the south (2 Sam 8:1, 12; 1 Chr 18:1, 11). To the east, he subjugated the Moabites (2 Sam 8:2) and the Ammonites (2 Sam 8:12) and set up garrisons in Edom (2 Sam 8:12–14). To the north, he suppressed various Aramean entities and established a garrison in Damascus (2 Sam 8:3–10). The kingdom of Geshur appears to have remained semi-independent due to an alliance sealed by the diplomatic marriage of David to Maacah, King Talmai's daughter, who later became the mother of Absalom (2 Sam 3:3).

David's expansion makes sense as it occurred at a time when the superpowers of Egypt and Mesopotamia were uninvolved, and when neighboring rulers wanted to expand their territory and secure control over lucrative trade routes. Nevertheless, scholars have raised questions about the reliability of these accounts, since there is no archaeological evidence for Israelite presence beyond the borders of Israel proper at this time.

DAVID'S CAMPAIGNS map 23

The Kingdom of David

The growth of the Davidic monarchy from national kingdom (2 Sam 5:5–7) to empire (2 Samuel 8, 10) was nothing short of remarkable, though its boundaries are unclear. David is said to have controlled territory from Dan to Beersheba (2 Sam 3:10; 17:11; 24:2), and from Aroer in the Arnon Gorge to Tyre on the Phoenician coast (2 Sam 24:5, 7). In 2 Samuel 8:3, the northern border is placed on the Euphrates River, while 1 Chronicles 13:5 implies that it stood at Lebo-hamath (Lebweh) on the northern edge of the land of Canaan (Num 34:7). While the Deuteronomist does not specify a southern limit, Wadi el-Arish (the "Wadi of Egypt") is implied by David's conquest of Philistia (2 Sam 8:1). The Chronicler sets the southern border further west in Egypt, at the Shihor River, probably one of the tributaries of the Nile River in the eastern delta.

Managing such a swath of territory would have required an extensive military and administrative apparatus, none of which is evident in the archaeological record. Moreover, the Bible continues to record battles and skirmishes with various enemies closer to the heartland. For this reason, many scholars tend to think that the extent of David's control was inflated for theological reasons (see, for example, the idealized boundaries of the land as given in Gen 15:18). Yet few question David's historicity. His name appears in an Aramean inscription from the mid-ninth century BCE as the "House of David," referring to the southern kingdom of Judah (1 Kgs 12:19), in the same way that the Assyrians alluded to the northern kingdom of Israel by its dynastic founder as the "House of Omri."

The population of "Israel" (the name David chose in deference to the northern tribes) was ethnically, culturally, linguistically, and religiously diverse (Josh 3:10). David also nurtured political and economic ties with neighboring polities such as Hiram of Tyre (1 Kgs 5:1) and the Aramean state of Geshur. The latter even included David's diplomatic marriage to Maacah, daughter of King Talmai (2 Sam 3:3).

Many of David's successes were assisted by the women in his life. His marriage to Saul's daughter, Michal, brought him within the royal family. The "clever" and "beautiful" Abigail (note the order of the adjectives) arbitrated a dispute between David and Nabal (1 Samuel 25), which prompted David to marry her as well. Two other prominent female mediators were the wise women of Tekoa (2 Samuel 14) and Abel-beth-maacah (2 Samuel 20).

During the tenth century BCE, we witness the gradual disappearance of the older Canaanite traditions and emergence of a distinctively Israelite material culture. Khirbet Qeiyafa, a small fortress overlooking the Elah Valley and dating to the late eleventh/early tenth century BCE, displays urban features found in other Judean sites, such as the use of casemate city walls, though not all are in agreement about its ethnic affiliation. An ostracon found inside the city gate bears Phoenician-style letters that may be the earliest preserved example of Hebrew writing, though scholars debate its linguistic identity. While scribes are mentioned among David's officials (2 Sam 8:16–17), the evidence to date indicates that Hebrew writing was still in its infancy.

DAVID'S KINGDOM map 24

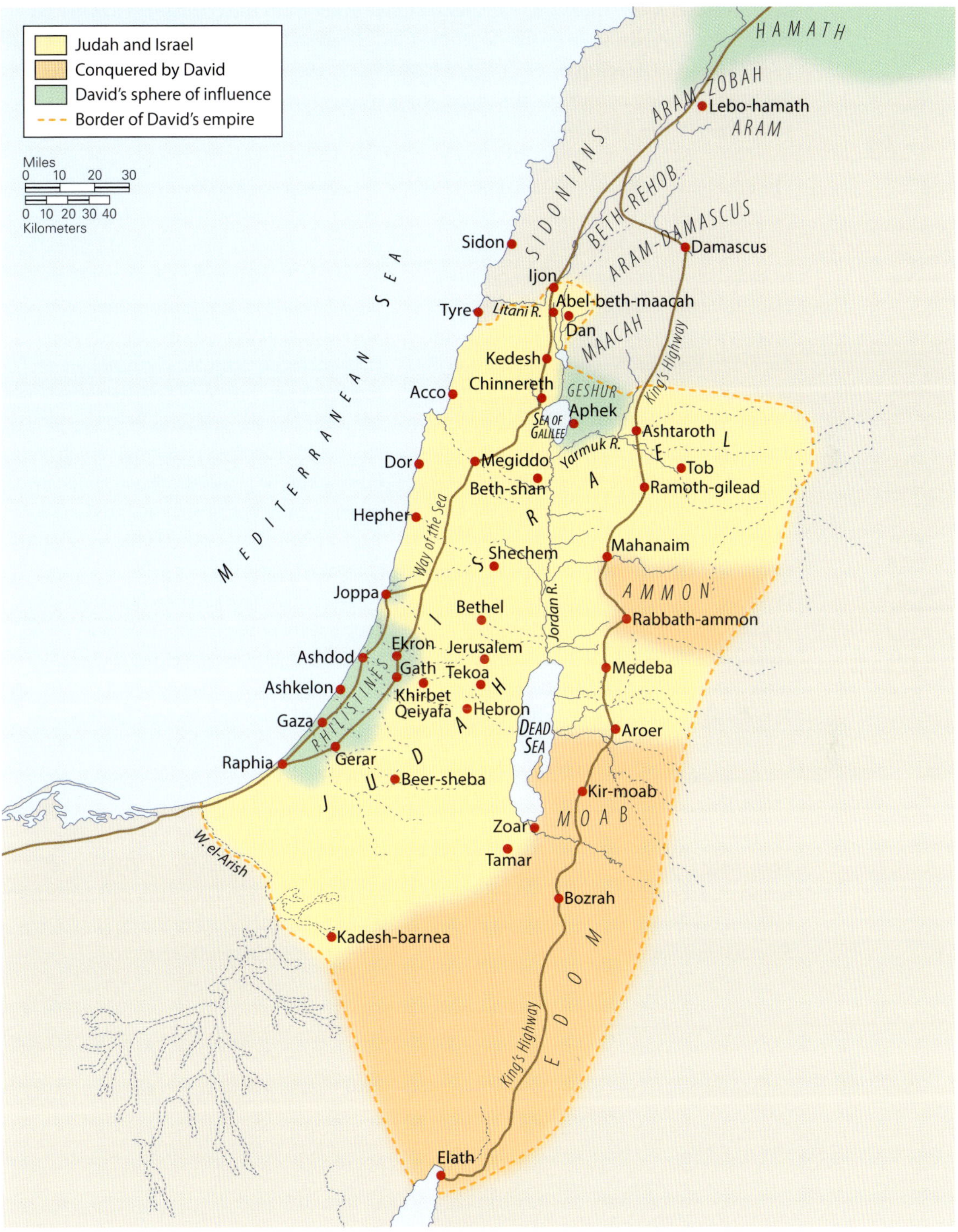

Solomon's Kingdom

Solomon inherited a kingdom that was externally brilliant, but internally tense. David's occupation of foreign territories fueled resentment and a risk of insurgency. Within Israel itself, there was a dramatic move away from the traditional kin-based structures toward a state centered on the king. Even so, David's conquests set the stage for Solomon to develop trade (1 Kgs 10:22, 28–29) and foster diplomatic relations with neighboring countries. His many wives were, at least in part, a result of political marriages (1 Kgs 11:1-3).

The boundaries of Solomon's kingdom reflect the same extensive claims as David's kingdom (see p. 65, Map 24). In his only recorded military campaign, Solomon took Hamath Zoba (2 Chr 8:3), and is said to have dominated everything from Tiphsah on the Euphrates River in the north to Gaza and the border of Egypt (probably Wadi el-Arish) in the south (1 Kgs 4:21–24; 2 Chr 9:26; cf. Num 34:5). There is no archaeological evidence to support Israelite presence north of Tel Dan or west of Wadi el-Arish. Indeed, the language of the text suggests indirect influence through Solomon's vast network of trade and diplomatic relations, rather than direct rule. It is also possible that these outlying territories represented idealized expressions of royal power, as in the case of New Kingdom Egypt—not lands that were actively ruled, occupied, or patrolled.

As in the days of Solomon's father, David, Israel's core settlement remained in the 150-mile long stretch between Dan and Beer-sheba (1 Kgs 4:25). Beyond this lay an economic zone extending 150 miles further south to Ezion-geber on the Red Sea where Solomon maintained a fleet of ships, with the assistance of his father's friend, Hiram of Tyre (1 Kgs 9:26–28). Here, archaeology has revealed a network of fortresses that may have been linked to this trade, which would have incorporated the deserts of Sin and Paran into Solomon's sphere of control. The Egyptian ruler Sheshonq (Shishak) destroyed several of these outposts during his campaign in 925 BCE, five years after Solomon's death (1 Kgs 14:25–28). We can surmise that Sheshonq sought to break apart the monopoly that Solomon held on trade, including the international trunk road on the coastal plain and the spice route along the King's Highway in Transjordan. Solomon may have also benefited from the copper mining and smelting activities carried out by the Edomites at Khirbet en-Nahas (Wadi Faynan).

To safeguard his principal territory, Solomon fortified key strategic cities (1 Kgs 9:15, 17–19) and developed a chariot army (1 Kgs 4:26; 10:26; cf. 1 Sam 8:4). The dating of the three key sites said to have been fortified by Solomon (Hazor, Gezer, and Megiddo) is highly contested, and dependent on complex stratigraphic and chronological issues that are not easily resolved.

THE EXTENT OF SOLOMON'S KINGDOM

Jerusalem

Jerusalem sits in a low saddle in the territory of Benjamin, approximately 2,500 feet above sea level, and is framed by the higher hills of Ephraim to the north and Judah to the south. Part of Jerusalem's appeal was its secluded location, east of the central ridge route that linked Beer-sheba in the south with Beth-shan in the north. The city also sat astride an east-west road through the Benjamin saddle that linked the coastal plain with the Jordan Valley. The more important route passed via Ramah on the Central Benjamin Plateau just to the north of Jerusalem.

Throughout its long history, Jerusalem expanded and contracted according to its political vicissitudes. The city's shape was also determined by the topography, consisting mainly of two hills (Eastern and Western) and four valleys (Kidron, Central, Hinnom, and Transversal).

Jebus (Judg 19:10), named after the Jebusites (Judg 3:5; 1 Sam 5:6) who lived there, was restricted to the ten- to fifteen-acre elongated Eastern Hill, bounded by the Kidron Valley on the east and the Central Valley on the west and south. The Gihon Spring was Jerusalem's primary water source. An underground tunnel from inside the city allowed the inhabitants to gain access to the spring without exiting the city walls, allowing entry in times of siege. This also may have been how Joab captured the city (2 Sam 5:8). At the highest point of the Jebusite city in the north stood a monumental building, whose foundations were buttressed by the "stepped stone structure." One possibility is that this is the "fortress of Zion" (2 Sam 5:7), where David took up residence, calling it the "City of David" (2 Sam 5:9). Another is that the excavated remains are David's royal residence, which he built (or refurbished) with the aid of Hiram of Tyre (2 Sam 5:11). Stepping down from the high point of David's palace on all sides of the hill were supporting terraces called the Millo, on which the houses stood (2 Sam 5:9). At the time of David the population of Jerusalem was around one thousand.

Also in David's time, the summit of the Eastern Hill, north of the city ("Mt. Moriah" in 2 Chr 3:1 and "Mt. Zion" in Psalm 125:1), was occupied by a threshing floor that belonged to Araunah the Hittite. Here David placed the ark of the covenant in a tent after he brought it from Kiriath-jearim (2 Samuel 6). Solomon later incorporated this hillock and the Ophel into his expanded thirty-acre city, as a royal enclosure for his palaces and the temple to Yahweh. Although Jerusalem doubled in size, the population probably remained unchanged, since it was mainly a city for the elite and government bureaucrats.

After the fall of Samaria in 722 BCE, the city expanded onto the Western Hill (see p. 99, Map 38), delimited by the Hinnom Valley on the west and south, and the Transversal Valley in the north. At this time, the city reached 150 acres in area and had a population of around 15,000. Jerusalem remained this size until the Babylonians destroyed the city in 586 BCE. In the time of Ezra and Nehemiah, the city appears to have shrunk back down to its size in Solomon's day.

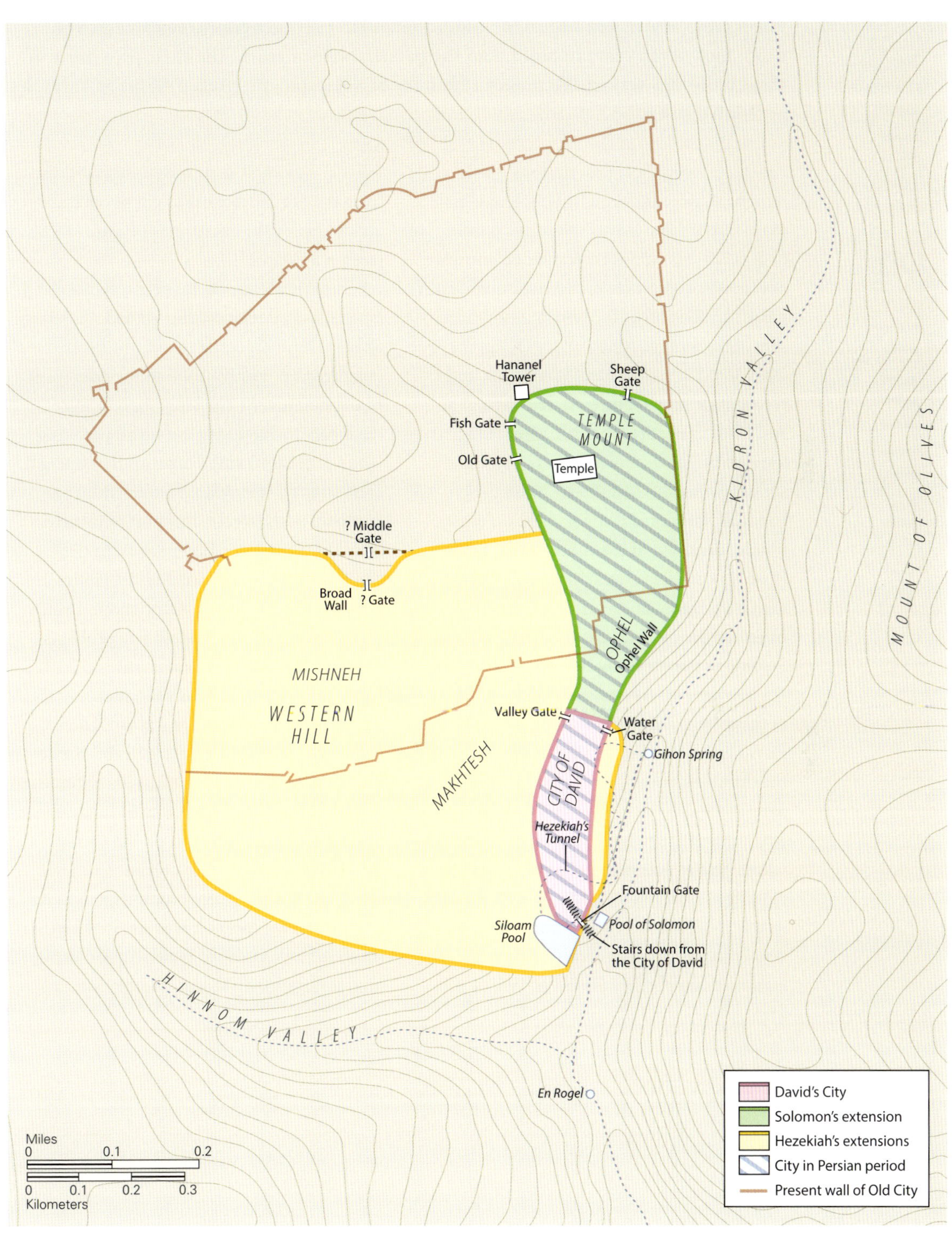

Hananel Tower
Sheep Gate
Fish Gate
TEMPLE MOUNT
Old Gate
Temple
KIDRON VALLEY
MOUNT OF OLIVES
? Middle Gate
Broad Wall
? Gate
OPHEL
Ophel Wall
MISHNEH
WESTERN HILL
Valley Gate
Water Gate
Gihon Spring
MAKHTESH
CITY OF DAVID
Hezekiah's Tunnel
Fountain Gate
Siloam Pool
Pool of Solomon
Stairs down from the City of David
HINNOM VALLEY
En Rogel
Miles
0
0.1
0.2
0
0.1
0.2
0.3
Kilometers
David's City
Solomon's extension
Hezekiah's extensions
City in Persian period
Present wall of Old City

Solomon's Temple

A considerable amount of attention in Kings and Chronicles is devoted to Solomon's two most important building projects—the temple and the royal palace complex. The temple, which was begun in Solomon's fourth year (generally regarded as 966 BCE), took seven years to build, and the palace thirteen years. The close proximity of these buildings served as a potent reminder of Solomon's privileged status as Yahweh's appointed ruler.

Based on the biblical descriptions, these structures were inspired by temple and palace plans in northern Syria. Solomon's palace (1 Kgs 7:1–12) with its colonnaded entrance porch followed the *bit hilani* layout, while the tripartite division of the temple into porch, sanctuary, and most holy place (1 Kgs 6:2–36) was rooted in Canaanite, Phoenician, and Neo-Hittite architecture. At Tell Tayinat and Ain Dara in northwest Syria, archaeologists have excavated temples similar in size and style to Solomon's temple, including its tripartite division and two pillars on the porch, identified in the Bible as Jachin and Boaz (1 Kgs 7:21). The temple at Ain Dara included a multistory corridor enclosing the inner temple on three sides, which is also how Solomon's temple is described (1 Kgs 6:5).

The temple was established on the summit of the eastern hill (see p. 69, Map 26), where David had earlier built an altar to Yahweh on the threshing floor of Araunah the Jebusite (2 Sam 24:18–25). Such a move firmly established Jerusalem as the religious center of the nation, whose destiny was now linked to the Davidic dynasty as declared by the prophet Nathan (2 Sam 7:1–17; esp. v. 16). The craftsmen and the timber for the project (choice cedar and pine logs) were supplied by Hiram of Tyre (1 Kgs 5:1–12). Solomon also conscripted workmen from the northern tribes to cut down the trees and to quarry the limestone (1 Kgs 5:13-18) (see p. 72, Map 27).

The temple and its furniture symbolized Israel's special relationship with God. A large altar for animal sacrifices and the bronze sea (a large water basin) stood in the courtyard. In the sanctuary ("the Holy Place") were ten tables with offerings of bread (evoking God's provision) and ten lamps that burned continuously (expressing God's enduring covenant with Israel). The altar of incense stood in front of the inner sanctum ("the Most Holy Place" or "the Holy of Holies"), which served as God's throne room. Inside, two huge cherubim overlaid with gold sheltered the ark of the covenant.

No traces of Solomon's temple or his palatial compound are known. Later construction, particularly by Herod the Great, permanently altered and most likely removed earlier traces (see p. 142, Map 58); however, the temple probably stood on the summit of Mt. Moriah below the current Dome of the Rock shrine, while Solomon's palace and administrative complex was situated further south in the vicinity of the el-Aqsa mosque on the Haram esh-Sharif (Temple Mount).

VIEW OF SOLOMON'S TEMPLE

Solomon's Administration

The Bible does not tire of telling us of Solomon's wealth and splendor (1 Kgs 4:20–34; 10:23–29), contributing to the long-held belief that the biblical writers consciously magnified the stature of the United Monarchy as an ideal age in fulfillment of the promise made to Abraham (Gen 15:18).

Yet underlying this exaggeration are authentic memories of increasingly centralized control and administrative complexity. David's royal cabinet included a commander of the army, a secretary managing court activities and diplomatic correspondence, a recorder dealing with state records, two priests handling religious affairs (one representing the northern tribes and the other Judah), and a head of the royal guard (2 Sam 8:16–18). To these officials Solomon added a chief priest, a political and religious adviser, a royal steward, an official responsible for the twelve district officers, and a person responsible for the forced (corvée) labor (1 Kgs 4:2–6).

The presence of scribes in David and Solomon's cabinets corresponds with a small but growing corpus of tenth-century inscriptions. These include the Tel Zayit Abecedary (an alphabetic writing exercise), the Gezer Calendar, and the Ahiram sarcophagus from Byblos (Lebanon). Small numbers of stamp seals from the tenth and ninth-centuries BCE used with clay lumps (bullae) to secure rolled-up papyrus documents attest to writing for administrative and other purposes. In the eighth century and later, there is a dramatic and parallel increase in the numbers of stamp seals and bullae alongside inscribed ostraca (broken pieces of pottery with writing on them). One remarkable clay bulla found in 2015 in the City of David bore the following inscription: "Belonging to Hezekiah, [son of] Ahaz, king of Judah.

Solomon's major source of funding for his building projects came from taxation (1 Kgs 10:14–15) and corvée labor (1 Kgs 9:15). While the forced-labor practices were started by David (2 Sam 20:24), they developed into a highly organized state policy under Solomon. To carry it out, Solomon divided "all Israel" into twelve districts led by governors that he personally appointed. Solomon also drew the district lines in a way that ignored the traditional tribal territories and further weakened any sense of tribal identity and independence. Each district provided food for the king for one month every year (1 Kgs 4:7–27), while the compulsory labor gangs worked one month out of every three throughout the year (1 Kgs 5:14). Judah was exempt from this policy, even though it was the largest beneficiary. Given the memory of Israel's slavery in Egypt, this must have been a bitter pill to swallow. Further angering the northern tribes was Solomon's sale of twenty towns to Hiram of Tyre (1 Kgs 9:11), ultimately leading to the secession of the northern tribes under Jeroboam, son of Nebat, one of Solomon's officials (1 Kgs 11:26–40; 12:1–17).

Eventually, Solomon's extravagant lifestyle, oppressive policies, and religious apostasy ignited widespread discontent among the people. Perhaps more than any other king, Samuel's dire warnings about the dangers of kingship were fulfilled in Solomon (1 Sam 8:11–18).

THE ADMINISTRATIVE DISTRICTS OF SOLOMON map 27

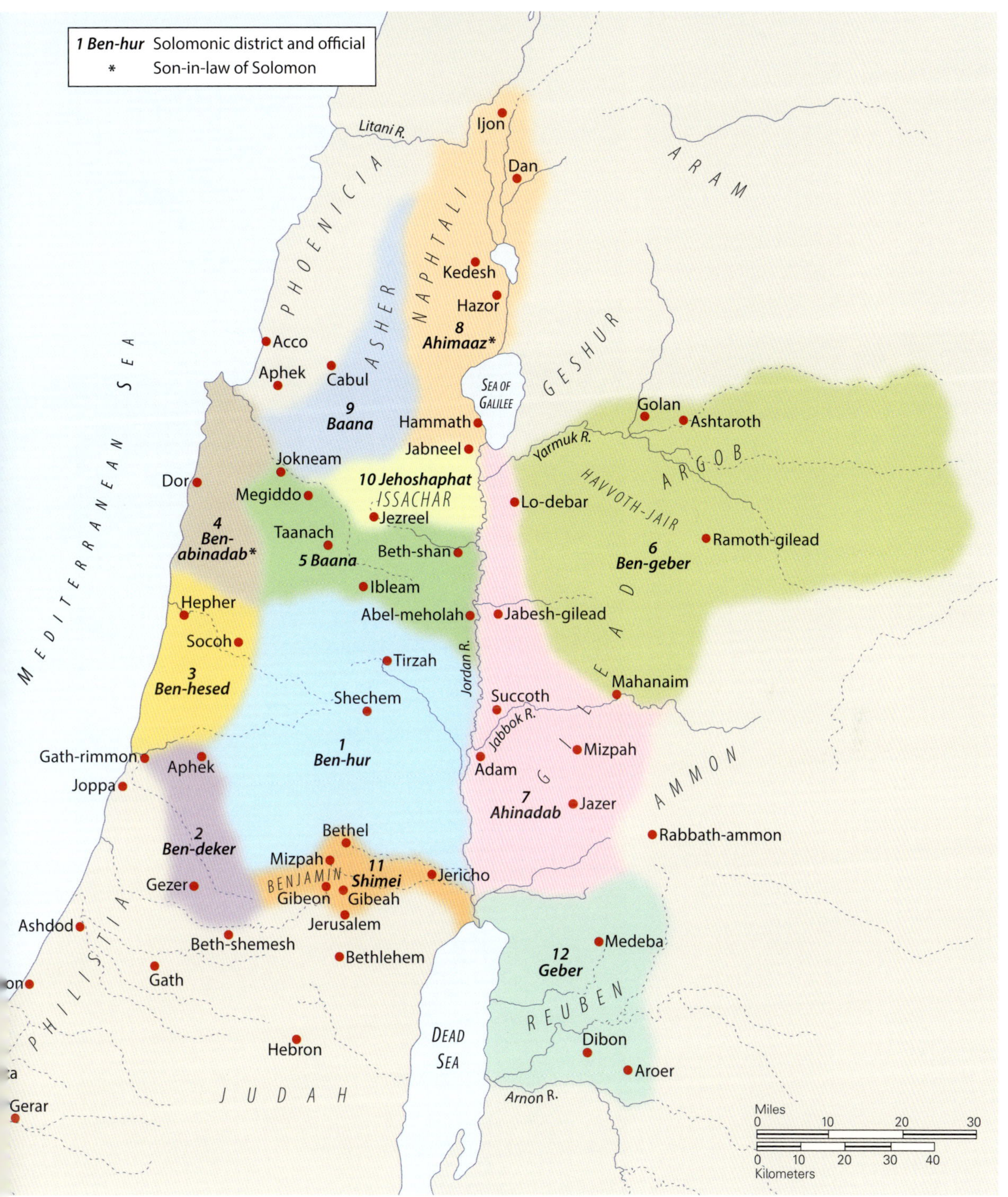

Part 3

A People Divided

A Kingdom Divided

Solomon's plan was to centralize rule in Jerusalem and develop the country, but his policies angered the population to the point that by the end of his reign, Jeroboam, the head of Israelite conscript labor, was organizing resistance. Solomon's son and successor, Rehoboam, faced off with Jeroboam at Shechem, where the people laid out their grievances (I Kgs 12:1–17).

Either Rehoboam was arrogant, or he underestimated their resentment. One gets the impression that there would have been no problem had Rehoboam possessed a little wisdom and tact. Rehoboam's attempt to enforce his demands by sending Adoniram, the official in charge of Canaanite slave labor, only added insult to injury, and the people retaliated by stoning Adoniram to death (1 Kgs 12:18).

At first, Benjamin seceded with the north, leaving only Judah tied to the dynasty of David (1 Kgs 12:20). It was historically a northern tribe and the seat of the house of Saul, but the loss of Benjamin would have left Jerusalem defenseless on the north. By retaining Benjamin (1 Kgs 12:21–23), it was possible to maintain a ten-mile-wide buffer zone between Jerusalem and the border with Israel. We also find a change in the border language from "Dan to Beersheba" (United Monarchy) to "Dan to Bethel" (Northern Kingdom) and "Geba to Beersheba" (Southern Kingdom).

Judah was the smaller of the two kingdoms and more geographically isolated, but it benefited from the stabilizing influence of the Davidic dynasty and the temple in Jerusalem. Israel was the stronger and more populous state, but it was politically unstable and more open geographically, which made it vulnerable to outside influences and the ever-shifting political circumstances of the ninth and eighth centuries. Despite the common tendency to lump Israel and Judah together as a monolithic "Israelite culture," there are clear differences between them in language, material culture, diet, and religious practice.

Jeroboam had two immediate concerns: consolidating power in his new capital at Shechem (1 Kgs 12:25) and establishing alternative places of worship at either end of his kingdom (Dan and Bethel) as rivals to Jerusalem (1 Kgs 12:27–30). Jeroboam also introduced two golden bull-calves as pedestals for the divine presence, in place of the two golden cherubim on the ark of the covenant in Jerusalem, which served as God's throne. The bull iconography should be interpreted not as idolatrous representation (contra Hos 8:5–6) but rather as a return to the older northern traditions unaffected by the royal Davidic and Jerusalemite ideologies. The charge of idolatry was mainly put forward by

BAASHA ATTACKS ASA

For the first fifty years after the split, there were constant border skirmishes between Israel and Judah. Most took place in Benjamin, which was territory that Israel claimed. Among the most notable was the war of Asa and Baasha in 885 BCE (1 Kgs 15:16–22). It began when Baasha, king of Israel, marched across the border and into the heart of Benjamin to fortify Ramah. This gave him control of the strategic Central Benjamin Plateau and routes in and out of Jerusalem. Asa appealed to Ben-hadad I (900–860 BCE) to break his alliance with Baasha and come to his aid. The Aramean king invaded Israel from the north, which forced Baasha to withdraw his troops to defend himself. Asa was then able to take Mizpah and Geba and fortify them with the stones that Baasha used to build up Ramah. The border eventually settled on the Ramallah ridge between Mizpah and Bethel.

THE DIVIDED KINGDOM map 28

KINGS OF ISRAEL AND JUDAH

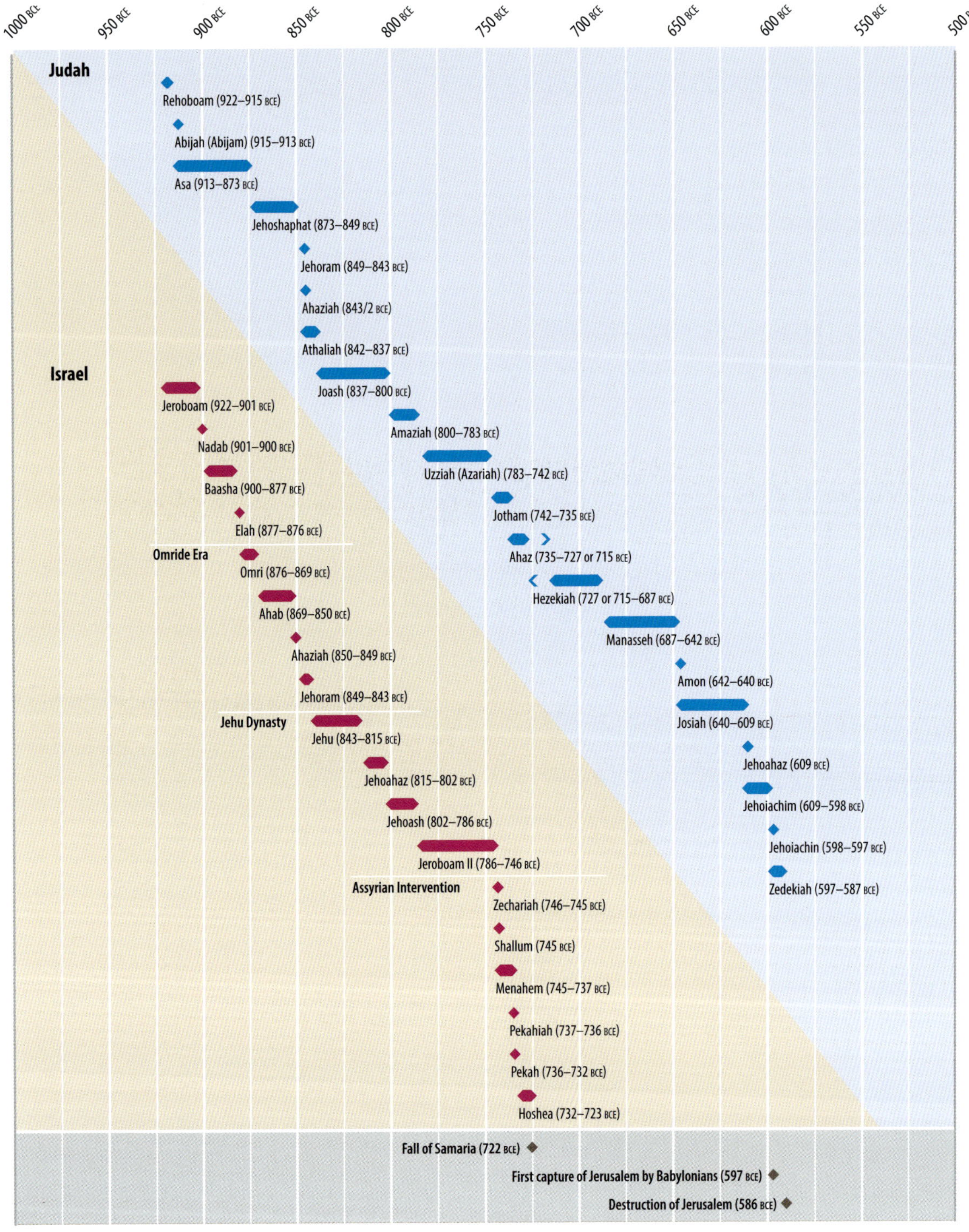

The sacred precinct at Dan with the altar and steps to podium on which a shrine housing the Golden Calf presumably stood.

the Deuteronomists of the seventh century, who viewed the withdrawal of the northern tribes as political and religious treason (1 Kgs 12:19). This interpretation is supported by 1 Kings 13:2, where an anonymous prophet from Judah condemned Jeroboam for carrying out sacrifices in Bethel. In the oracle, he mentions Josiah by name, the Judean king from more than three centuries later whose religious reforms sparked the Deuteronomistic movement (see p. 101, Map 39).

The Invasion of Shishak

Shishak (Sheshonq I) was an Egyptian ruler of Libyan origin who toppled the weak twenty-first dynasty and established the twenty-second dynasty at Bubastis in the eastern Nile Delta. According to the biblical text, Shishak (945–924 BCE) attacked Jerusalem "in the fifth year of Rehoboam" (1 Kgs 14:25; 2 Chr 12:2). Shishak's version appears as a city list on a wall in the temple of Amun at Karnak in Thebes (Luxor). Over 150 cities are said to have fallen victim to his campaign.

The date of Shishak's campaign is disputed, but many tend to favor 925 BCE, which would place Solomon's death in 930. While the lengths of David's and Solomon's reigns—at forty years each —are clearly idealized (1 Kgs 2:11; 11:42), we can still situate these kings in the tenth century BCE. Additional inferences can also be made by correlating archival facts and other details embedded in the biblical narrative with the archaeological and historical data.

Based on the rhetoric of his own monumental inscriptions, Shishak was the great conqueror of the Levant, though the reality appears to have been more modest. Still, his campaign had a devastating impact on his primary targets, who appear to have been the Northern Kingdom and the Negev. Despite the Chronicler's claim that Shishak's invasion was divine retribution for Rehoboam's apostasy (2 Chr 12:1–2), Judah does not appear to have been adversely affected and Jerusalem does not appear in the city list. As a result, some question the historical reliability of the biblical account. One suggested explanation is that after the split, Rehoboam consolidated control over Judah by fortifying fifteen cities along its borders (2 Chr 11:5–12). Such a move would have discouraged attempts by Shishak to invade Judah from all sides but the north, where an absence of fortifications allowed Shishak to approach Jerusalem by way of the Ascent of Beth Horon and the Central Benjamin Plateau. Furthermore, the absence of Jerusalem in Shishak's list may have resulted from his lifting the siege after Rehoboam paid him tribute (1 Kgs 14:26; 2 Chr 12:9).

Shishak then turned his sights toward the Northern Kingdom ruled by his protégé Jeroboam (see 1 Kgs 11:40). While it is difficult to trace his route, Shishak may have marched northward to Shechem and Tirzah, passed down into the Jordan Valley by way of Wadi Farah and across into Gilead. Since Penuel is mentioned in the city list as a target, it may have been this campaign that prompted Jeroboam to move his capital temporarily from Shechem to Penuel (1 Kgs 12:25). The second section of Shishak's inscription describes his conquest of some eighty-five settlements in the Negev, where several small tenth-century fortresses safeguarding trade routes in the Negev and the Wilderness of Zin have been excavated. Archaeological testimony to Shishak's campaign includes a stele fragment from Megiddo and a scarab of Sheshonq from Wadi Faynan (Jordan).

SHISHAK'S INVASION

map 29

The Kingdom of Israel

The Northern Kingdom is known by three names in the Bible—Israel (after the northern tribes), Samaria (after its principal capital), and Ephraim (after its dominant tribe). Unlike Judah, which was ruled by a single dynasty (David), power in Israel shifted among nine dynasties throughout its 210-year lifespan from 930 to 720 BCE. The history of the Northern Kingdom falls into three main phases.

Phase 1: Instability—
The First Fifty Years (930–880 BCE)

To consolidate his kingdom, Jeroboam established his capital at the geographically central and religiously important city of Shechem, followed by brief moves to Penuel (1 Kgs 12:25) and Tirzah (1 Kgs 14:17; 16:23). After Omri took the throne in 880 BCE, the capital was moved to Samaria, where it remained until the Assyrian conquest of the city in 722 BCE. The Northern Kingdom never attained dynastic stability, as is well illustrated by the coups of Baasha (1 Kgs 15:25–29) and Zimri (1 Kgs 16:9–12), and the rival kingships of Omri and Tibni (1 Kgs 16:21–22).

Phase 2: Stability and Prosperity—
The Middle Years: Dynasties of Omri and Jehu (880–752 BCE)

The dynasties of Omri (Omri, Ahab, Ahaziah, and Jehoram) and Jehu (Jehu, Jehoahaz, Jehoash, Jeroboam II, and Zechariah) were largely stable and prosperous. Archaeological remains from the ninth and eighth centuries indicate a rise in sociopolitical complexity—fortifications, administrative buildings, palaces, water systems, stables, and storehouses—as well as evidence for international trade and increased literacy. But Israel's successes also led to religious and social abuses, brought into sharp relief by Elijah and Elisha against the House of Omri, and by Amos and Hosea against the House of Jehu. Israel also found itself enmeshed in struggles with outside powers, most notably Aram-Damascus in the time of Hazael (2 Kgs 8:7–15) and the incremental expansion of Assyria. According to Neo-Assyrian records, Ahab headed a coalition against Shalmaneser III at Qarqar in central Syria in 853 BCE (the Kurkh Stele). Around a decade later, in 841 BCE, Jehu (or an envoy) is depicted paying tribute to Shalmaneser III after the Assyrian conquest of Damascus (the Black Obelisk). There was a brief respite from Aramean and Assyrian pressure during the reign of Jeroboam II, but eventually Assyria returned to the region.

Phase 3: Instability—
The Last Thirty years (752–722/720 BCE)

Four successive coups (Shallum, Menachem, Pekah, and Hoshea) left the last thirty years looking much like the first fifty. An attempt by Pekah to form an anti-Assyrian alliance with Rezin of Damascus culminated in Tiglath-pileser III conquering two-thirds of the Northern Kingdom in 733–732 BCE (2 Kgs 15:29). The Northern Kingdom met its demise a decade later when Shalmaneser V quashed a revolt by Hoshea, the last king of Israel, and captured Samaria in 722 BCE, though completion of the conquest took place by 720 BCE under an energetic new ruler, Sargon II, who seized power and pretentiously adopted the name Sargon from the founder of the kingdom of Akkad some 1,700 years earlier. The kingdom of Israel was now an Assyrian province. The kingdom of Israel was now an Assyrian province and a base for further punitive measures and expansionist goals (see p. 96, Map 37).

Tiglath-pileser III 1st campaign 734 BCE
Tiglath-pileser III 2nd campaign 733 BCE
Tiglath-pileser III 3rd campaign 732 BCE
The campaigns of Shalmaneser V and Sargon II, 724–720 BCE
Bozrah capital
Miles
0 10 20 30
0 10 20 30 40
Kilometers
Sidon
Abana R.
Damascus
Mt. Hermon
Ijon
Litani R.
Abel-beth-maacah
Dan
Tyre
PHOENICIA
ARAM
Kedesh
Hazor
Acco
SEA OF GALILEE
Aphek
Mt. Carmel
Karnaim
Ashtaroth
Yarmuk R.
Dor
Mt. Tabor
Megiddo
Jezreel
Ramoth-gilead
Beth-shan
MEDITERRANEAN SEA
Jordan R.
Samaria
Tirzah
Mt. Ebal
Penuel
Mahanaim
Mt. Gerizim
Shechem
Jabbok R.
Aphek
Joppa
ISRAEL
GILEAD
Adam
AMMON
Rabbath-ammon
Gezer
Jericho
Ashdod
Ekron
Jerusalem
Azekah
Gath
Ashkelon
PHILISTIA
Hebron
DEAD SEA
Dibon
Gaza
Arnon R.
JUDAH
Raphia
Beer-sheba
Arad
MOAB
Kir-hareseth
AMALEK
Bozrah

Ahab and the Arameans

During Ahab's reign (874–853 BCE), Israel was a strong kingdom that enjoyed international prestige and internal prosperity, due in part to increased economic and political benefits from a three-fold alliance established by Omri (Ahab's father) between Israel, Phoenicia, and Judah. It also came from increased taxation and a large work force in the form of corvée labor—the same conditions that provoked the earlier split with Judah. While royalty and nobility benefited from this, life became more difficult for the common folk.

The lot of the poor is seen most vividly in the Elijah and Elisha narratives: Naboth's Vineyard (1 Kings 21) is a dramatic story of upper-class abuse, while the Widow's Oil (2 Kings 4:1–7) illustrates social conditions that Amos condemned nearly a century later. There were religious challenges as well, which the biblical writers attribute directly to the influence of Ahab's Phoenician wife, Jezebel. The most famous story in this regard is Elijah's challenge to the prophets of Baal and Asherah on Mt. Carmel (1 Kgs 18:16–46). Ahab also built a temple to Baal and placed an Asherah pole in Samaria (1 Kgs 16:32–33). Mute testimony to Israelite religious diversity at this time includes inscriptions from the way-station of Kuntillet Ajrud in the central Negev highlands that mention Yahweh and Asherah.

Despite greater security brought about by Omri's alliances with Phoenicia and Judah, and in spite of the Israelite king's expansion into Moab as alluded to in the Mesha Stele (pp. 86-87, Map 32), times remained militarily insecure in the north. Hadad-ezer of Damascus (860–841 BCE), known in the Bible according to his throne name, Ben-hadad (II), subdued other small Aramaean kingdoms in order to expand his control over the region.

The Bible chronicles three Aramaean conflicts with Israel during Ahab's reign. In the first, Ben-hadad unsuccessfully besieged Samaria (1 Kgs 20:1–25). In the second, Ben-hadad mustered his troops at Lower Aphek (modern-day En Gev), but they were again defeated (1 Kgs 20:26–34). The three-year truce that followed (1 Kgs 22:1) may have been to counter the greater enemy of Assyria at the Battle of Qarqar (853 BCE), especially since the Kurkh Stele mentions how Hadad-ezer joined Ahab in the conflict. But the alliance lasted only as long as the Assyrian threat was imminent. In the third and final war, Ahab of Israel and Jehoshaphat of Judah joined forces to recapture Ramoth-gilead from Aram-Damascus, but Ahab was killed (1 Kgs 22:2–40).

Ahab's son, Jehoram (852–841 BCE), continued to suffer the brunt of Aramaean attacks, and late in his reign, he was wounded fighting alongside Amaziah of Judah against Hazael of Damascus at Ramoth-gilead. While recuperating at Jezreel, Jehu, the commander of Jehoram's troops, staged a coup. He slayed Jehoram, the queen mother Jezebel, and the remaining Omride line. He also wounded Amaziah, who later died at Megiddo (2 Kgs 8:28–9:37). This series of events may be echoed in the "House of David" inscription from Tel Dan.

The broken Tel Dan Stele, which mentions the "House of David".

IN THE TIME OF ELISHA AND ELIJAH

The Conquests of King Mesha

The Mesha Stele (Moabite Stone) was discovered in 1868 at Dhiban (biblical Dibon) in Jordan. The slab dates to the mid-ninth century BCE and contains thirty-nine lines of text in a language similar to biblical Hebrew. The author identifies himself as "Mesha, son of Kemosh[-yatti], king of Moab, the Dibonite." Mesha is also mentioned in 2 Kings 3:4. The stele contains the earliest known reference to Yahweh outside the Bible, as well as the name of the Moabite god Kemosh (Chemosh).

While it has been suggested that the phrase "House of David" appears here as well as in the Tel Dan Stele, this view has not been widely accepted. The stele presents scholars with a rare opportunity to compare two versions of the same event, yet it is unclear how the events described in the stele relate to the details given in 2 Kings 3:4–27 and 2 Chronicles 20. The following historical reconstruction is one plausible scenario.

The Reigns of Omri and Ahab
(Early Ninth Century BCE)

According to the stele, Omri had conquered the Medeba plateau north of the Arnon Gorge, occupied it, and imposed tribute on its population. Mesha attributed Omri's actions to the displeasure of Kemosh at his people; circumstances similar to Judges 2:11–14 where Israel provoked Yahweh's anger and suffered the consequences by means of warfare. Mesha began his revolt by leaving Dibon and attacking Ataroth on the western edge of the Medeba plateau, which Mesha states had belonged to the tribe of Gad from time immemorial (see Num 32:34). He then proceeded to slaughter the inhabitants there. Then, on the orders of Kemosh, Mesha conquered the tableland all the way north to Nebo, where he again slaughtered the Israelite population. Ataroth and Nebo both appear to have had Israelite cult centers, since at each spot, Mesha claims to have dragged away cult objects associated with Yahweh and set them before Kemosh. Mesha concludes his text by stating how he settled Moabites in the former Israelite towns, rebuilt many other destroyed cities, and fortified them. According to the stele, Ahab retaliated and tried to regain lost territory at Jahaz.

The Reign of Jehoram
(Mid-Ninth Century BCE)

Following the death of Ahab at Ramoth-gilead, Moab's rebellion intensified (2 Kgs 1:1; 3:5). Ahab's son, Jehoram, aided by Jehoshaphat of Judah, unsuccessfully set out to reassert Israelite authority (2 Kgs 3:6–8). They attacked Moab from the south by way of Edom, to avoid the fortified towns in the tableland and to enlist the help of Edomite warriors. Though he defeated the Moabites and destroyed some cities, Jehoram was unable to capture Kir-hareseth (Kerak). In an act of desperation, Mesha sacrificed his oldest son on the city wall, which prompted Israel and Judah to withdraw (2 Kgs 3:21–27). Later, Moab and Ammon invaded Judah in an attempt to retaliate (2 Chr 20:1–28). They crossed the Dead Sea fords at the Lissan (the tongue of land jutting into the lake from the east) and ascended into Judah at the Ascent of Ziz. The coalition was ultimately defeated in the wilderness east of Tekoa (2 Chr 20:20).

KING MESHA BATTLES ISRAEL AND JUDAH map 32

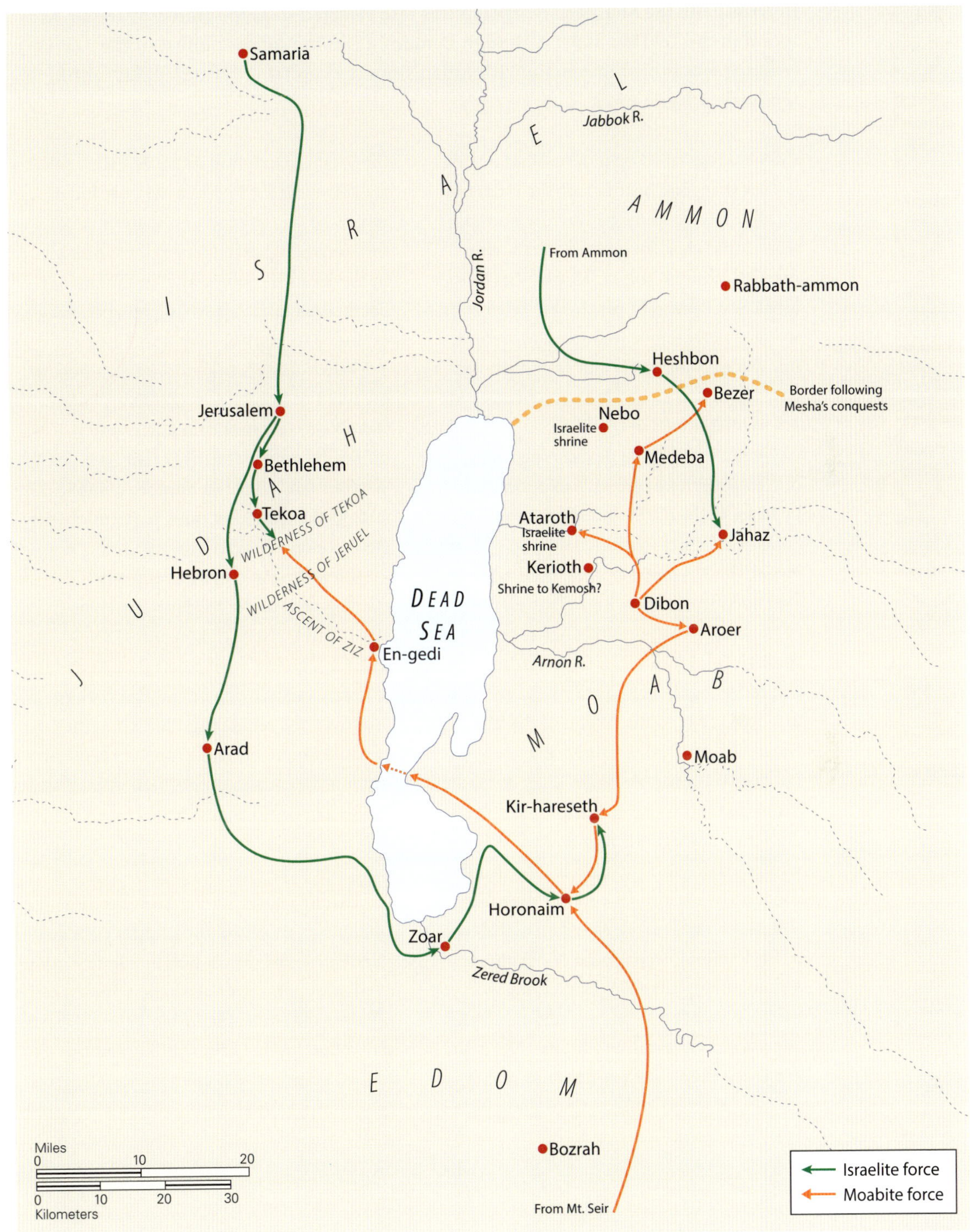

The Kingdom of Judah

The Southern Kingdom of Judah (after the principal southern tribe) is what remained after the secession of the northern tribes. As the continuation of the Davidic dynasty in Jerusalem, the Southern Kingdom was also referred to as the House of David, as found in the Tel Dan Stele. Although Benjamin was the southernmost of the northern tribes, it was forced to remain with Judah since the capital of Jerusalem lay within its territory (1 Kgs 11:32).

Twenty kings ruled from Jerusalem during its 345-year-long history (see the chart on p. 78). All were from the Davidic line apart from Athaliah, a daughter of Ahab who married Jehoram son of Jehoshaphat (2 Kgs 8:18). Seven kings of Judah have been attested to date in extrabiblical sources. Moreover, a number of stamp seals and seal impressions have yielded names of Judean officials and priests mentioned in the Bible.

Judah avoided the devastating impact of Neo-Assyrian aggression experienced by Israel to the north, but after the fall of Samaria, conflict was inevitable. To prepare, Hezekiah (715–686 BCE) enclosed an expanded Jerusalem with a city wall and cut a nearly two-thousand-foot-long tunnel through solid rock to divert water from the Gihon Spring (the city's main water source) to a pool at the southern end of the City of David (2 Kgs 20:20; 2 Chr 32:30).

In 701 BCE, the Assyrian king Sennacherib invaded Judah and destroyed numerous towns and cities (2 Kgs 18:13; see also Map 38). Sennacherib also had the conquest of Lachish (the most important city after Jerusalem) depicted on alabaster reliefs found in his palace at Nineveh. Although Jerusalem was miraculously spared, Sennacherib boasted about having imprisoned Hezekiah in the city "like a bird in a cage." Both sides present contrasting versions of Jerusalem's salvation (compare the Prism Inscription to 2 Kgs 19:35–36; Isa 37:36–37; 2 Chr 32:20–23), yet Judah remained an Assyrian vassal. Over time the Assyrian grip tightened, most notably in the seventh century BCE, in the time of Esarhaddon and Ashurbanipal when Assyria extended its control deep into Egypt.

When Assyria began to weaken during the reign of Josiah (641–609 BCE), Judah was able to reconsolidate power and initiate religious reforms (2 Chr 34:3–35:9). Scholars tend to date a number of biblical texts to this period of time, particularly the Deuteronomistic literature.

The Assyrian empire eventually disintegrated under the Neo-Babylonian assault led by Nebuchadnezzar II (605–562 BCE). Following the defeat of Necho II at Carchemish in 605 BCE, Nebuchadnezzar destroyed the remaining Philistine cities of Ashkelon, Ashdod, Ekron, and Gaza. In 597 BCE, he crushed a rebellion in Jerusalem (2 Kgs 24:10–16) and fully destroyed the city eleven years later, bringing the Southern Kingdom to an end (2 Kgs 25:1–21).

Two tiny silver scrolls from this time that contained versions of the Priestly Benediction (Num 6:24–26) were found in a Judean tomb overlooking the Hinnom Valley. These scrolls preserve the earliest known citations of texts also found in the Hebrew Bible, and the earliest examples of confessional statements concerning Yahweh.

THE KINGDOM OF JUDAH map 33

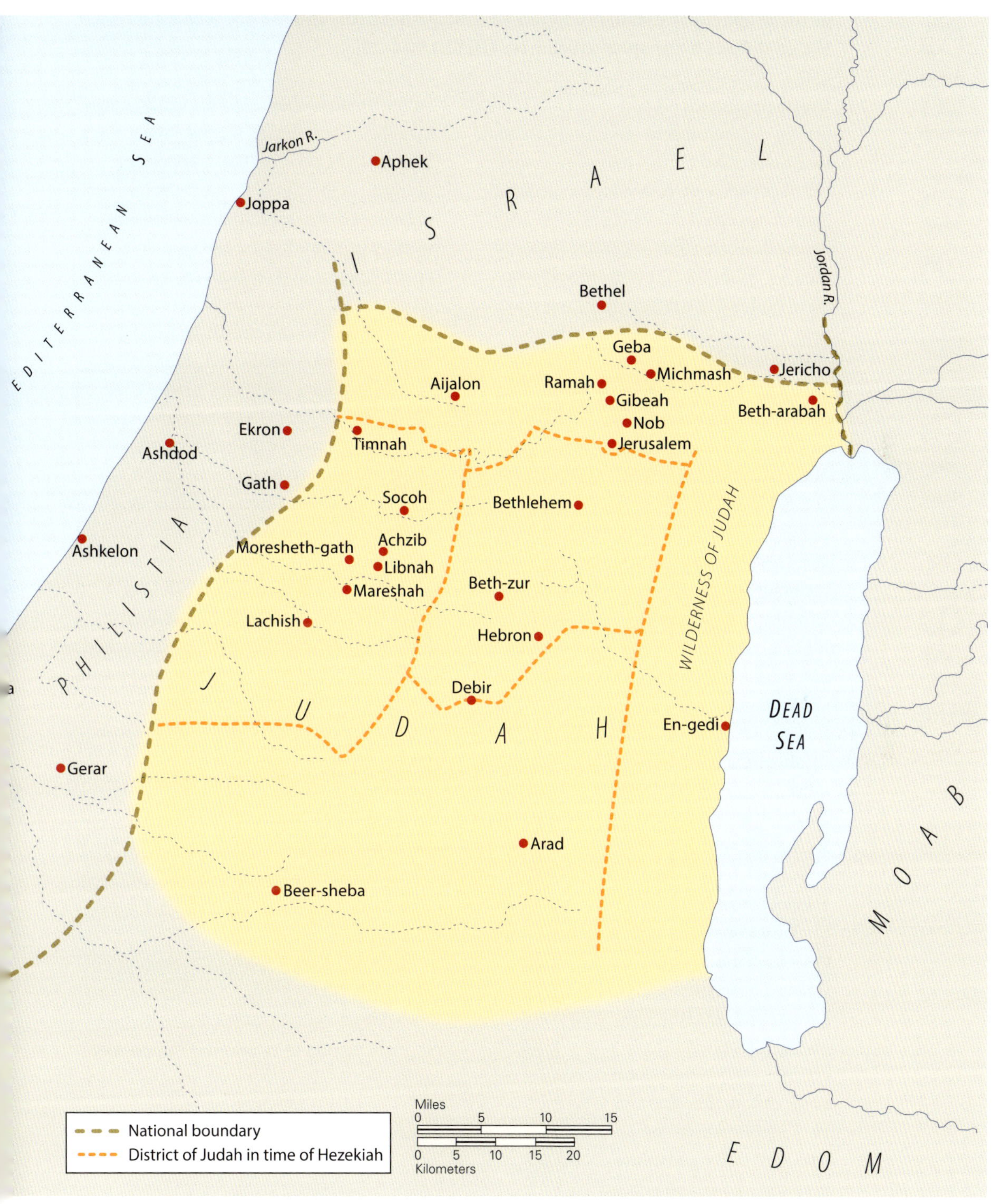

The Prophets of Israel

Prophets were common in the ancient world and not limited to Israel. Though Abraham is called a prophet (Gen 20:7), Israelite tradition has always regarded Moses as the prophet par excellence (Num 12:6–8; Deut 34:10), and the one who established the guidelines for prophetic behavior (Deut 18:14-22).

Unlike the priesthood, where one had to meet certain requirements to serve, prophets could be anyone called for that purpose—young/old, rich/poor, elite/commoner, male/female. Samuel was called at a young age. Jeremiah and Ezekiel came from established priestly families. Amos was a sheepherder. Hosea was a husband and father with a wayward wife. Women prophets include Miriam (Exod 15:20), Deborah (Judg 4:4), and Huldah (2 Kgs 22:14). Some prophets were professionals. Samuel, Elijah, and Elisha were attached to guilds that trained apprentices (1 Sam 10:10; 2 Kgs 2:3; 4:38). Ahijah of Shiloh (1 Kgs 14:2–4) clearly made his living from prophecy. Samuel, Nathan, and Micaiah were court prophets who advised their kings and confronted them when necessary. Jonah may have also been a court prophet to Jeroboam II (2 Kgs 14:25). There are some prophets that we know little about, such as "the man of God from Judah" and "the old prophet from Bethel" (1 Kings 13). The Chronicler also mentions the names and works of prophets not otherwise mentioned in the Deuteronomistic History, such as Iddo the Seer (2 Chr 9:29) and Jehu the son of Hanani (2 Chr 20:34).

The Hebrew Bible organizes Israel's prophets into two main groups—the Former Prophets (the "pre-classical" prophets whose activities and oracles appear in the historical books) and the Latter Prophets (the "classical" major and minor prophets whose rank is based on the length of their collected works, rather than their importance). Despite their diverse backgrounds, personalities, and callings, nearly all of them gave their oracles (poetically structured divine speech) to advocate the worship of Yahweh alone and to institute political, social, and religious change. Some prophets performed symbolic acts to get their point across (Hosea 1; Isaiah 20; Ezekiel 4). They occasionally predicted the future. This gave the prophets credibility, so they could tell their audience what God wanted them to hear.

Isaiah is probably the best known and most influential of the prophets. He lived in Jerusalem and was a confidant of Hezekiah. He witnessed Sennacherib's invasion of Judah in 701 BCE, as did his Judean contemporary, Micah of Moresheth-gath. Jeremiah was from Anathoth, a village on the outskirts of Jerusalem. A contemporary of Josiah, he lived to see Jerusalem's destruction by the Babylonians, as did Ezekiel, who was taken into captivity and became a prophet of the exile, mainly serving the Judean community in Babylon.

THE PROPHETS OF ISRAEL AND JUDAH
Eighth-century Prophets: Period of Assyrian Supremacy
Northern Kingdom: Jonah, Amos, Hosea
Southern Kingdom: Isaiah, Micah
Seventh-century Prophets: Period of Assyrian Downfall
Nahum, Zephaniah, Habakkuk, Jeremiah
Sixth-century Prophets: Period of Babylonian Supremacy
Jeremiah, Ezekiel
Sixth-century Prophets: Period of Persian Supremacy
Haggai, Zechariah, Joel, Obadiah, Malachi

THE PROPHETS OF ISRAEL AND JUDAH

map 34

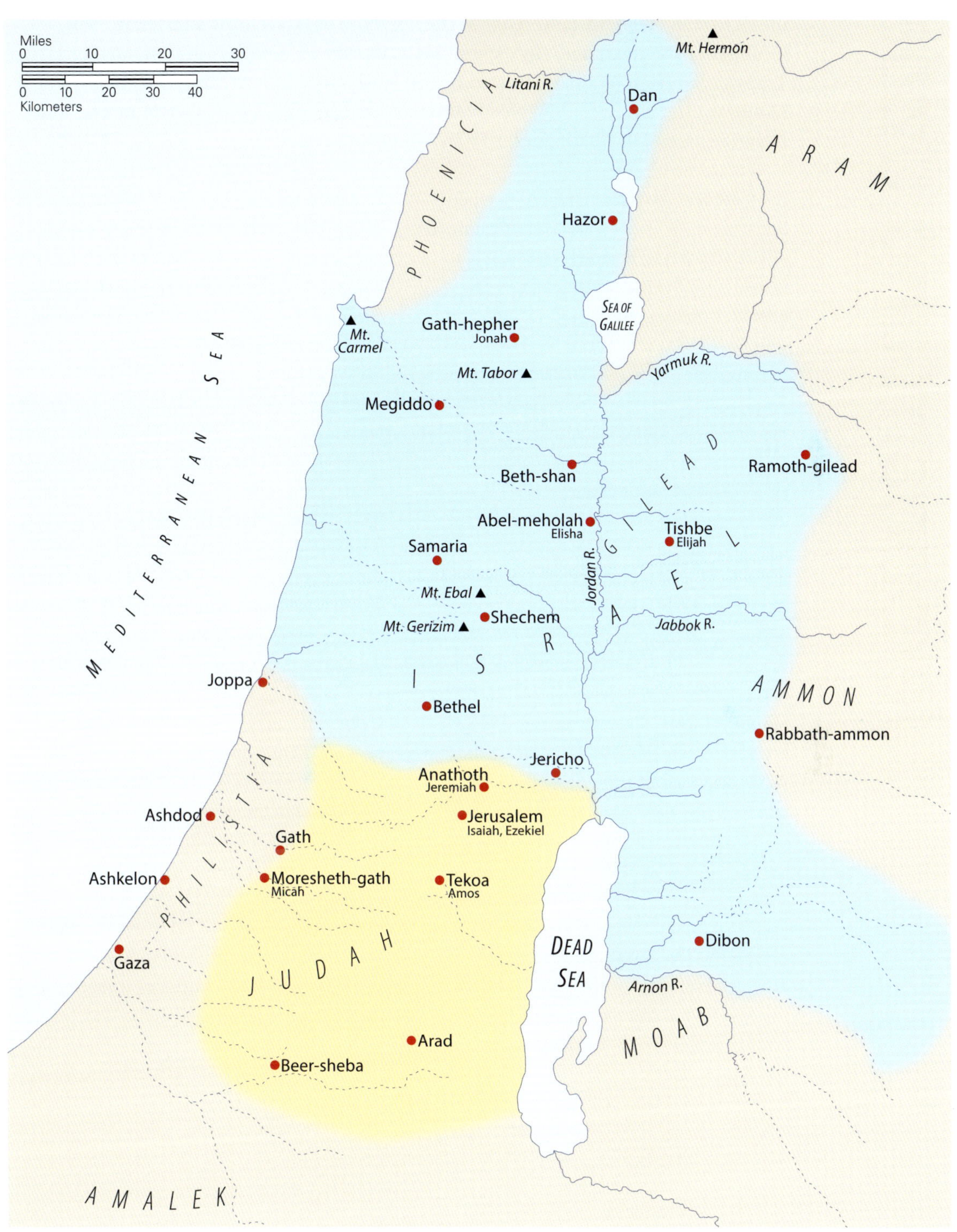

Jeroboam and Uzziah

Assyrian pressure on Aram-Damascus by Adad-nirari III (who carried out a military campaign in 796 BCE and collected tribute from "Joash of Samaria" as mentioned in the Rimah Stele) brought relief to the kingdom of Israel. This allowed his son, Jeroboam II, to incrementally expand his authority. He first recaptured northern Transjordan from Aram-Damascus in two battles fought near Karnaim and Lo-debar (Amos 6:13). Next, he subjugated Damascus, which had been weakened in a second Assyrian assault by Shalmaneser IV in 773 BCE.

A subsequent Assyrian retreat to northern Syria as a result of pressure from the kingdom of Urartu (Ararat) enabled Jeroboam II to extend his influence northward to Lebo-hamath (modern-day Hama) in Syria and south to the Sea of the Arabah (Dead Sea), in accordance to an unrecorded prophecy by Jonah, son of Ammitai, from Gath-hepher (2 Kgs 14:25–28; Jonah 1:1; see also Amos 6:14).

Uzziah of Judah (also called Azariah) also expanded his boundaries (2 Chronicles 26). He reduced Philistine territory in the west and conquered Edom to the east, including the port city of Elath on the Red Sea (2 Kgs 14:22). In the Negev, he initiated settlement activity to strengthen his hold over the Arabian caravan routes and increase his agricultural enterprises (2 Chr 26:10). A number of forts, towers, and outposts have been excavated along trade routes in the wilderness regions from this time. Uzziah also took measures to strengthen Jerusalem.

Expansionist moves by Israel and Judah in the political vacuum created by the absence of Assyria or other domineering regimes ushered in a period of great prosperity. The archaeological record provides evidence for the wealth and socioeconomic complexity of the eighth century BCE through the development of foreign trade, their involvement in regional geopolitics as shown in Assyrian records, and the expansion of cities. In the Northern Kingdom, this can be seen in sites such as Samaria, Megiddo, Hazor, and Dor. Finds from the capital city of Samaria, especially the ivory furniture inlays, indicate the splendor of the royal palace at that time. The ivories were also used by the prophet Amos to point out the conspicuous consumption of the ruling classes at the expense of the poor (Amos 3:15; 6:1–7). Also in the royal compound at Samaria were found sixty-three ostraca (broken pieces of pottery with writing on them), which recorded shipments of wine and oil to Samaria from estates located in the surrounding countryside.

The ostraca inform us about Israelite script at the time and provide us with personal names and clan names from the tribe of Manasseh. Many of these clans are mentioned in the genealogical lists found in Joshua 17:2–3 and 1 Chronicles 7:14–19. In the Southern Kingdom, Judah's growth and prosperity is illustrated by Jerusalem, Beth-shemesh, Lachish, and Tel Sheva (Beersheba). The earthquake mentioned in Amos 1:1 from about 760 BCE left clear traces at several sites such as Hazor, Gezer, and Tell es-Safi (Gath).

IN THE DAYS OF JEROBOAM II AND UZZIAH map 35

The Neo-Assyrian Empire

During the first millennium BCE, Assyria introduced an imperialistic system that was expansive, dominating, and exploitative. Assyria's goal was to drain the surrounding nations of their wealth and divert it to the homeland, mainly through the payment of taxes and tribute. The growth of the Neo-Assyrian Empire (911–605 BCE) occurred in three main phases.

Phase 1: Expansion
(875–824 BCE)

Building on the successes of his predecessors in North Syria, Shalmaneser III (858–824 BCE) moved south, where he was stopped at Qarqar (Tell Qarqur) in Central Syria by "Ahab the Israelite" (see p. 82) and a coalition of local rulers (Kurkh Stele/Monolith Inscription). Three more attempts to advance further south also failed, but during the fifth campaign in 841 BCE, Shalmaneser subdued Damascus and accepted tribute from "Jehu, son of Omri" (Black Obelisk).

Phase 2: Regression
(824–743 BCE)

Internal dissent at home and pressure from Urartu (Ararat) in eastern Anatolia forced Assyria to withdraw and remain largely absent from the region for over eighty years. This ushered in a time of prosperity during the reign of Jehu and his dynasty, which contributed to numerous social abuses addressed by prophets such as Amos and Hosea. The sole Assyrian campaign at this time took place in 796 BCE by Adad-nirari III (810–783 BCE). It ended with the destruction of Damascus and a payment of tribute to Assyria from "Joash of Samaria" (Rimah Stele).

Phase 3: Resurgence
(743–626 BCE)

Tiglath-pileser III (744–727 BCE) transformed Assyria into a world power that cruelly and effectively ruled the region for the next century. In 733–732 BCE, Tiglath-pileser conquered two-thirds of the northern kingdom of Israel, leaving only Ephraim and Manasseh intact. A decade later, in 722 BCE, the capital of Samaria fell to Shalmaneser V (726–722 BCE); but due to his unexpected death, Sargon II (721–705 BCE) completed the conquest of Samaria in 720 BCE. Those who escaped deportation fled to Jerusalem, where they settled on the Western Hill. Though unscathed, Judah was still subject to Assyrian tribute. By 705 BCE, Hezekiah of Judah withheld tribute, prompting a new monarch, Sennacherib, to carry out a punitive military campaign in 701 BCE (see p. 99, Map 38). Assyrian rulers of the seventh century continued their expansionist aims under Esarhaddon (680–669 BCE), whose list of tributaries included "Manasseh, king of Judah." Ashurbanipal (668–627 BCE) extended Assyrian control into Egypt as far south as Thebes (Luxor) in 663 BCE. Following the death of Ashurbanipal, the Assyrian empire, which had ruled western Asia for the last two centuries, started to crack at the seams, setting the stage for the next superpower, Babylon, to arrive on the world stage (see pp. 102-103, Map 40).

THE RISE OF THE ASSYRIAN KINGDOM

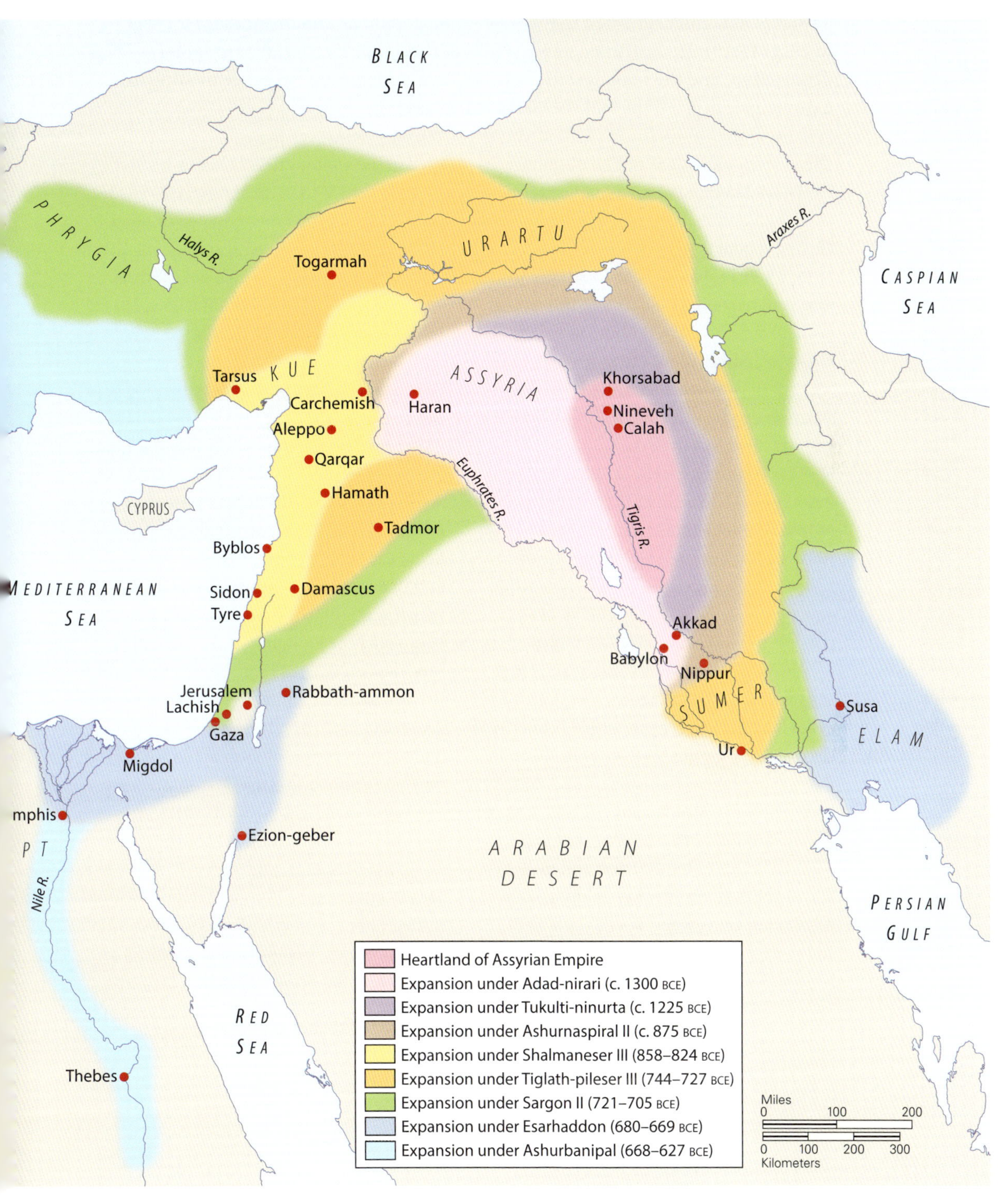

The Downfall of Israel

Following the death of Jeroboam II in 753 BCE, the prosperity and security that characterized the second half of Jehu's dynasty began to deteriorate quickly. A powerful new ruler returned to the west in the person of Tiglath-pileser III ("Pul" in 2 Kgs 15:19). He instituted new policies of conquest, territorial annexation, deportation, and the mass resettlement of population groups in order to mitigate nationalistic aspirations and the chance of revolt.

The western campaigns of Tiglath-pileser III (743–732 BCE) unfolded in four stages and lasted over a decade (see p. 95, Map 36). He first subdued northern Syria (743–740 BCE), where he expelled the Urartians. In 738 BCE, Assyrian annals tell us that he pushed farther south, receiving tribute from several kings, including "Menachem of Israel" (2 Kgs 15:19–20). Four years later, after a brief skirmish involving an alliance of Aramaeans and Israelites against Ahaz of Judah (see p. 82, Map 30), Tiglath-pileser III campaigned in Philistia. He accepted tribute from "Ahaz of Judah", among others. He conquered Gaza and set up a stele on "the brook of Egypt" (probably Wadi el-Arish), where he commemorated his victory and blocked possible military assistance from Egypt.

He conquered Damascus a year later. A fragmentary Assyrian source mentions 13,150 exiles led into Assyria and settled primarily in the district of Gozan on the Habor River. In their place, the Assyrians resettled Aramaean and Chaldean tribes, forming the nucleus of the Samaritans.

Israel's ignominious defeat and the loss of two-thirds of its territory culminated in yet another coup, when Pekah was killed and replaced by Hoshea, the last king of Israel (2 Kgs 15:30). After Tiglath-pileser III died in the winter of 727/726 BCE his son Shalmaneser V took the throne. He exiled Hoshea to Assyria for cozying up to Egypt (Hos 7:11) and laid siege against Samaria (2 Kgs 17:3–6). The city held out for three years, despite the absence of the king, but fell in the winter of 722/721 BCE.

During or shortly after the siege, Shalmaneser died, and a new ruler not directly in line for the throne seized power. He pretentiously adopted the name Sargon after the founder of the kingdom of Akkad some 1,700 years earlier. In a series of swift moves, Sargon II invaded Philistia, where he defeated the Egyptians at Raphiah, and then proceeded against Samaria, which was still in a state of unrest. Sargon completed the conquest of the city in 720 BCE, deported 27,280 inhabitants (Nimrud Prism), and made it the center of a new Assyrian province called Samerina. For the biblical writers, the fall of Samaria was not only punishment for Israel's sins but served as a stern warning to Judah as well (2 Kgs 17:7–41).

In a subsequent campaign in 713-712 BCE, Sargon quelled rebellions in Ashdod. He then turned Philistia into the Assyrian province of Ashdod, which brought imperial control as far south as the Brook of Egypt.

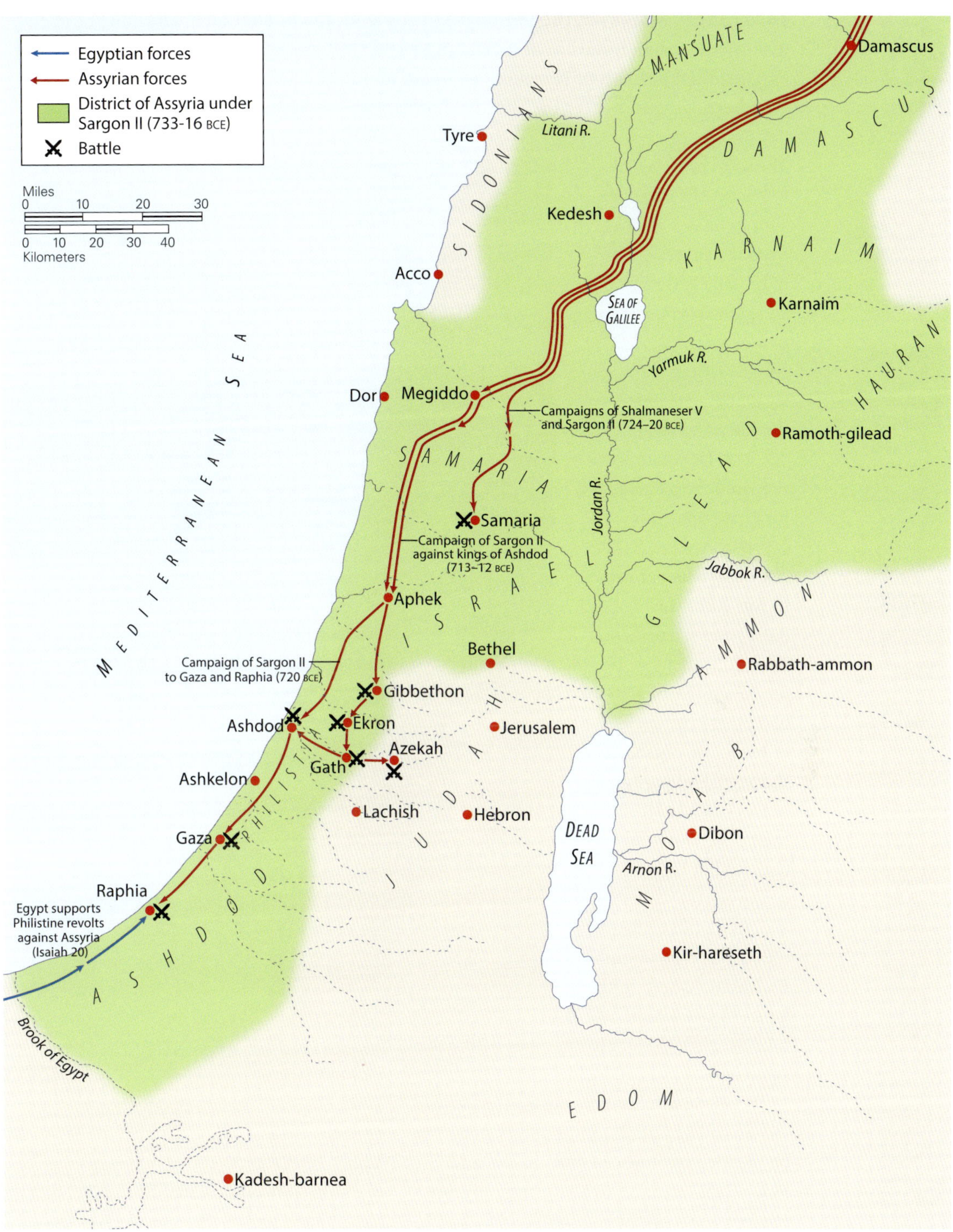
Egyptian forces
Assyrian forces
District of Assyria under Sargon II (733-16 BCE)
Battle
Miles
0 10 20 30
0 10 20 30 40
Kilometers
MANSUATE
Damascus
SIDONIANS
Tyre
Litani R.
DAMASCUS
Kedesh
KARNAIM
Acco
SEA OF GALILEE
Karnaim
MEDITERRANEAN SEA
Yarmuk R.
HAURAN
Dor
Megiddo
Campaigns of Shalmaneser V and Sargon II (724–20 BCE)
Ramoth-gilead
SAMARIA
GILEAD
Samaria
Jordan R.
Campaign of Sargon II against kings of Ashdod (713–12 BCE)
Jabbok R.
ISRAEL
Aphek
AMMON
Bethel
Campaign of Sargon II to Gaza and Raphia (720 BCE)
Rabbath-ammon
Gibbethon
Ashdod
Ekron
Jerusalem
Azekah
Gath
Ashkelon
PHILISTIA
JUDAH
MOAB
Lachish
Hebron
DEAD SEA
Dibon
Gaza
Arnon R.
Raphia
Egypt supports Philistine revolts against Assyria (Isaiah 20)
ASHDOD
Kir-hareseth
Brook of Egypt
EDOM
Kadesh-barnea

Sennacherib's Campaign to Judah

Prior to the Assyrian invasion of Judah in 701 BCE, the Western Hill was settled by a huge population influx, expanding Jerusalem beyond its core settlement on the Eastern Hill. Moreover, the Jerusalem hinterland, the Judean hills, and the Shephelah also witnessed an inflation of urban and rural settlement. This growth was due to the expansionist policies of Hezekiah of Judah and to the overflow of refugees from the Northern Kingdom after the conquest of Samaria in 722/720 BCE.

The reign of Hezekiah represented a complete shift in Judean politics from the appeasement of his father Ahaz to an aggressive policy of rebellion and confrontation. After withholding tribute from the Assyrians around 705 BCE, Hezekiah prepared the country for retaliation. This is probably when he cut Hezekiah's Tunnel (2 Kgs 20:20; 2 Chr 32:30) and strengthened the fortifications of Jerusalem (2 Chr 32:5) and other central cities of Judah. He organized the people militarily (2 Chr 32:6) and built storehouses for agricultural supplies (2 Chr 32:28). Valuable archaeological evidence of Judah's preparations for warfare is seen in the *lamelech* jars, which held food supplies sent out to key cities before the campaign.

Hezekiah's Tunnel starts at the base of the steps where the Gihon Spring originates.

When Sennacherib finally invaded in 701 BCE, he first took control of key ports on the Mediterranean at Tyre, Sidon, and Joppa (Jaffa) in order to secure a supply line. His first target on the southern coast was Philistia. By first taking Timnah in the Sorek Valley, Sennacherib sealed off his main prize of Ekron from any assistance from Judah. He similarly took Gath by sealing off the

SENNACHERIB INVADES JUDAH map 38

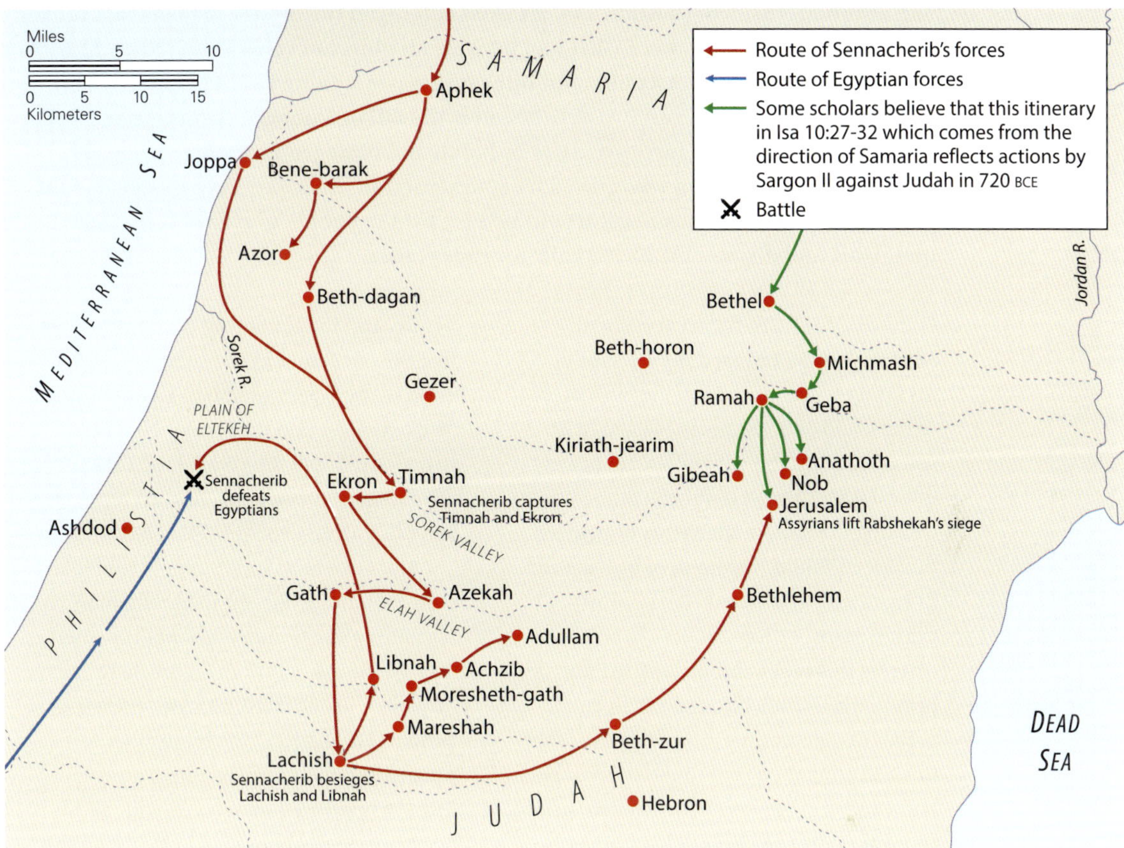

Elah Valley at Azekah. Excavations of the Level III city at Lachish produced evidence for its severe destruction and the impressive remains of an Assyrian siege ramp. Many details in the excavation of Lachish have been correlated with the Assyrian reliefs found in Sennacherib's palace at Nineveh.

In 2 Kings 18:13–16, while Sennacherib was reportedly laying siege to Lachish, Hezekiah tried to buy off the Assyrian monarch by sending him tribute. In response, Sennacherib sent three key Assyrian officials to Jerusalem to persuade Hezekiah to surrender. The siege eventually ended, though the sources differ over what happened. According to the biblical text, the Assyrians went home after an angel struck dead 185,000 soldiers. The Prism Inscription says that the Assyrians were victorious and took home a handsome tribute. They also claim to have captured forty-six cities. Whatever happened, Judah remained an Assyrian vassal, and Judean settlements in the Shephelah—and perhaps other regions as well—were severely curtailed. Many of the sites that were occupied before the campaign were subsequently abandoned.

Josiah's Reforms

Two kings of Judah are praised by the biblical writers for their devotion to God and for their religious reforms. Hezekiah (715–686 BCE) destroyed illicit places of worship in and around Jerusalem (2 Kings 18). He even destroyed the bronze serpent that Moses made in the wilderness, because it had become an object of veneration (Num 21:6–9). He invited Isaiah to counsel him and inform him concerning God's perspective on matters of state. But within two decades after the fall of Samaria, the Assyrians under Sennacherib destroyed forty-six cities in Judah and besieged Jerusalem (see p. 99, Map 38). That Jerusalem was spared from destruction made the work of subsequent prophets more difficult, since it would be easy for the people to regard Jerusalem as inviolable and dismiss prophetic calls for repentance.

Following the forty-five-year reign of Manasseh, who reversed the reforms of his father to the chagrin of the biblical writers, and after the assassination of his son Amon, Judah had another chance at revival under Josiah (640–609 BCE). While cleaning the temple after years of neglect, the priests found "the book of instruction" (2 Kgs 22:8), also called "the book of the covenant" (2 Kgs 23:2). (Chronicles reverses this order and places the reforms prior to the scroll's discovery.) Given the nature of the reforms, it is pretty clear that this text contained laws found in what we know today as Deuteronomy. When Josiah heard the contents, he tore his clothes as a sign of repentance and sought prophetic confirmation from a woman prophet by the name of Huldah (2 Kgs 22:14–20). Her authentication effectively made Huldah the first person to affirm certain writings as sacred scripture and to authoritatively interpret them as God's Word. Thus Josiah began his reforms. These included the destruction of foreign altars built by his predecessors, the destruction of the altar at Bethel built by Jeroboam three hundred years before, and the shuttering of country shrines, like the one found in the Israelite fortress of Arad in the Negev of Judah. Josiah's reforms also extended into the former Northern Kingdom, where the young king took advantage of a weakened Assyria to reassert Davidic rule (2 Chr 34:6-7).

The near-messianic support that Josiah enjoyed among like-minded reformers (including the prophet Jeremiah) earned him specific mention in an oracle by an unnamed prophet from three centuries earlier (1 Kgs 13:2). The biblical writers praised Josiah as a ruler unlike any before him, "who turned to Yahweh with all his heart and with all his soul and with all his might, according to the Law of Moses" (2 Kgs 23:25). Most scholars believe these reforms inspired a religious movement that produced much of the present book of Deuteronomy, large parts of the Deuteronomistic History (Joshua, Judges, Samuel, and Kings), and a few other books. Tragically, Josiah was mortally wounded in a battle with the Egyptians at Megiddo in 609 BCE. In a tribute to him, Jeremiah wrote several laments (2 Chr 35:25).

JUDAH DURING THE REIGN OF JOSIAH

map 39

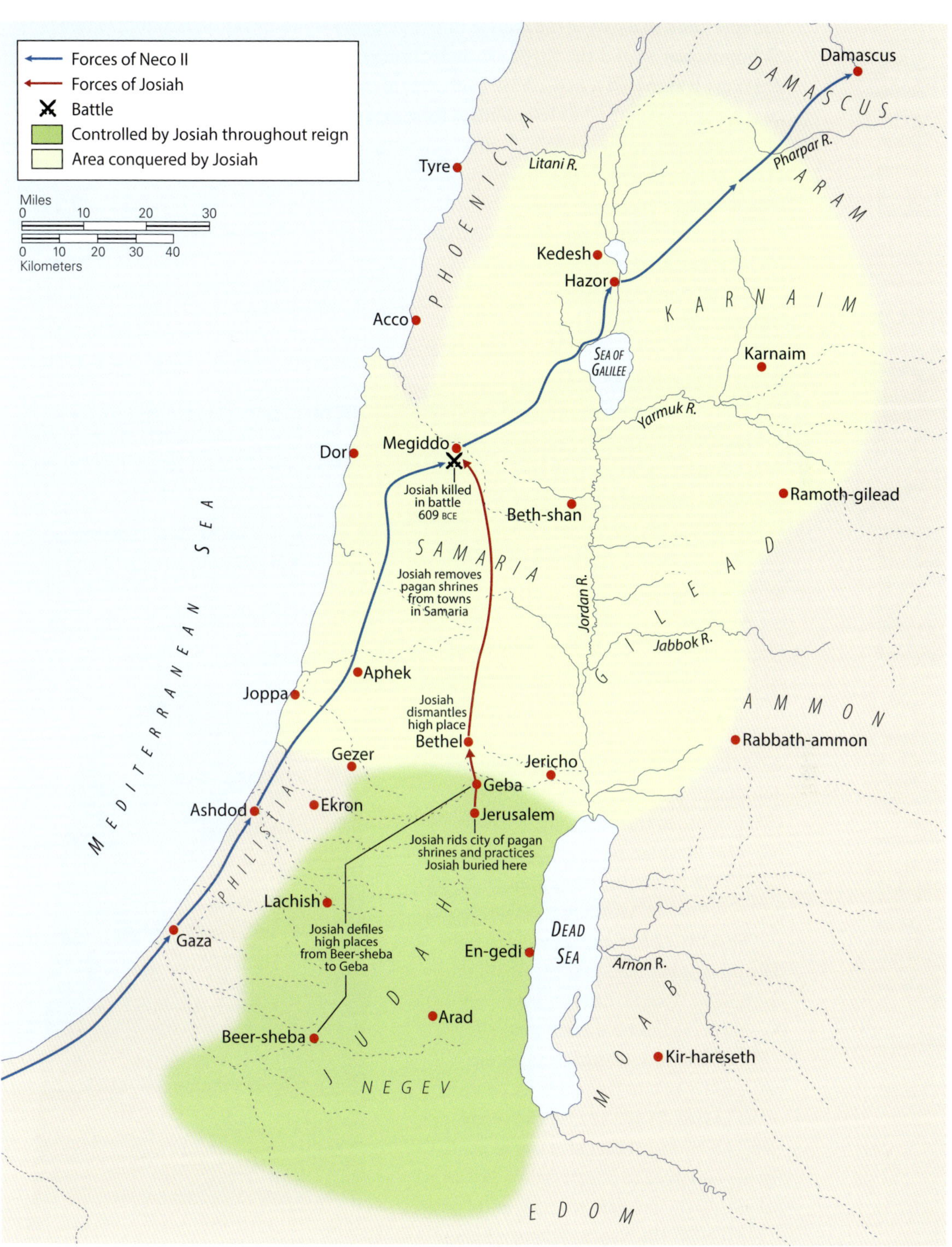

The Neo-Babylonian Empire

Following the death of Ashurbanipal in 627 BCE, the Neo-Assyrian Empire that had ruled western Asia for the last two centuries began to tear at the seams. Its gradual collapse took place over the course of two decades. It all began in 626 BCE, when Nabopolassar seized the throne in Babylon and rebelled against Assyrian domination. This revolt signaled a new phase in Babylonian history that scholars have called the Neo-Babylonian or Chaldean period (626–539 BCE).

In 614 BCE, twelve years after Babylonian independence, the Medes (who occupied what is now northern Iran) invaded Assyria from the east and conquered the old, traditional capital at Asshur. Two years later, Nineveh fell to a combined force of Medes and Babylonians (an event that was celebrated by the prophet Nahum). With Egyptian assistance, a refugee government was set up at Haran in 610 BCE; however, a coalition of Babylonians and Medes captured the city, forcing the Assyrians to cross the Euphrates River and take refuge in Carchemish. The once mighty Neo-Assyrian Empire was now a government in exile.

A year later, in 609 BCE, the Egyptian ruler Necho II of the Twenty-Sixth Saite Dynasty made his way to Carchemish to help the Assyrians retake Haran. Necho probably calculated that a weak but still surviving Assyria would leave Egypt as the dominant power west of the Euphrates. Josiah opposed this move and tried to intercept the pharaoh at Megiddo, but he lost his life in the process (2 Kgs 23:29–30; 2 Chr 35:20–27). Working together, Assyria and Egypt tried to retake Haran from the Babylonians but failed. Ashur-uballit, the last king of Assyria, died at Carchemish, and Assyria ceased to be a world power.

The focus now shifted to a contest between Egypt and Babylonia for control of the Levant. In 605 BCE, Necho II and Nebuchadnezzar II fought at Carchemish, but Egypt was forced to retreat (Jer 46:2), leaving Babylon as the uncontested new world power in the region. The Neo-Babylonian Empire lasted another sixty-six years, until its power was eclipsed by Persia under Cyrus II (the Great) in 539 BCE.

The Neo-Babylonian Kingdom that overthrew the Assyrian Empire was ruled by Chaldean or Aramaean leaders who were not originally part of the Old Babylonian Empire (ca. 1800–1500 BCE). The Neo-Babylonian Empire begins in 626 BCE when Nabopolassar became king. He defeated the Assyrians with the help of his allies, the Medes and Scythians.

The Old Babylonian Kingdom produced the Code of Hammurabi, an ancient law code of Mesopotamia preserved on a basalt stone stele that is over seven feet tall. It contains over 282 laws inscribed on the stele in Akkadian language using cuneiform script.

The top of the Code of Hammurabi Stele, 18th century BCE.

THE NEO-BABYLONIAN EMPIRE map 40

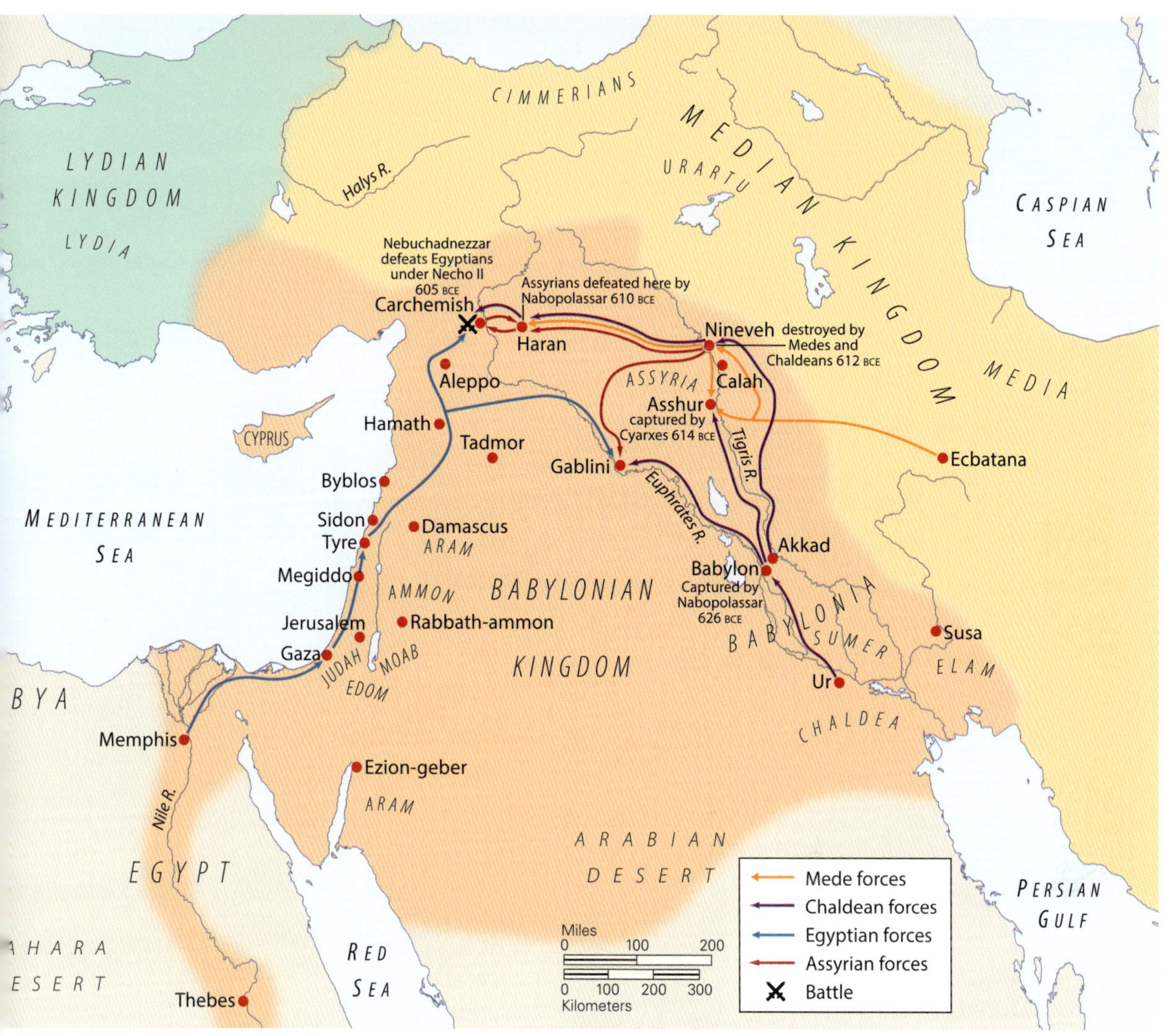

The Neo-Babylonians were the heirs of a long and rich history that included such famous rulers as Hammurabi, known for his law code that found some expression in Israel's legal tradition, and Marduk, the patron god of Babylon. As the greatest ancient city before classical times, Babylon had a population of around 250,000 inhabitants. It was also a center of learning, culture, and the arts. Nebuchadnezzar II, the successor of Nabopolassar and conqueror of Jerusalem in 586 BCE, is credited with building the famous Ishtar Gate and the renowned Hanging Gardens of Babylon, one of the seven wonders of the ancient world.

Part 4

Invasion and Occupation

The Fall of Jerusalem

After the Battle of Carchemish in 605 BCE, when the Babylonians became the new world masters, Jehoiakim was on the throne of Judah. Five years later, he withheld tribute from Babylonia and joined Egypt in a bid for revolt. Babylonian king Nebuchadnezzar's response was quick. In 598 BCE, the Babylonian army besieged Jerusalem.

Jehoiakim conveniently died, or as Jeremiah 36:30 suggests, he may have been murdered. His son Jehoiachin took over and surrendered almost immediately. The new ruler was subsequently exiled to Babylon with several family members and notables of the kingdom, since these were the people most threatening to Babylonian control. Jehoiachin was placed in prison, but released thirty-seven years later by Amel-Marduk (561–560 BCE), who is Evil-Merodach of the Bible (2 Kgs 25:27–30). He was not allowed to return to Judah and died in exile.

In place of the jailed Jehoiachin, Nebuchadnezzar installed one of Josiah's sons, Zedekiah (formerly, Mattaniah) as king. His role as Judah's last king could not have been easy since the legitimate king was still alive. Moreover, the country split into two factions: a pro-Egyptian group, who sought to continue the political line begun by Jehoiakim, and a pro-Babylonian faction begun by Jehoiachin who accepted the sovereignty of Nebuchadnezzar. Zedekiah remained loyal until 589 BCE, when he joined a bid for revolt. Unfortunately, hoped-for allies backed out of the revolt, leaving Judah to fight alone.

The Babylonian reprisal was relentless. Cities of Judah were destroyed one after the other. The last of the fortified towns to fall were Lachish and Azekah. The discovery of a cache of administrative ostraca called the "Lachish Letters" in a chamber of the Level II city gate provides an important parallel to Jeremiah 34:7. They also offer a valuable picture of the daily use of the Hebrew language at the end of the biblical period.

Nebuchadnezzar besieged Jerusalem in December 587 BCE. Eight months later, in August 586, the Babylonians breached the walls and captured Jerusalem. A month later they burned the entire city, including Solomon's Temple, and exiled many people to Babylon. Zedekiah tried to escape, but the Babylonians captured him close to Jericho, along with his family. They killed his family in front of his eyes, blinded him, and then took him to Babylon (Jer 39:4–7). At this point we lose trace of Zedekiah, who probably died in prison.

The Edomites, who had lived for so long under Judean occupation, took advantage of this event to invade Judah and assist the Babylonians. They also occupied the Negev and sacked cities in Judah. Edomite shrines from this period have been excavated at Qitmit south of Arad and at Ein Hazeva in the Arabah. The atrocities carried out by Edom against Judah were denounced by the prophet Obadiah.

JERUSALEM FALLS TO THE BABYLONIANS

map 41

The Babylonian Exile

With the fall of Jerusalem in 586 BCE, Nebuchadnezzar deported 4,600 people (Jer 52:28–30) and settled them along the Chebar River near Nippur and Babylon. Most were from the ruling and skilled classes. While some people escaped to neighboring countries (Jer 40:11), most remained in Judah. To ingratiate the local population and prevent the possibility of revolt, the Babylonians gave land to the poor (2 Kgs 25:12), though this practice created problems later on when the exiles returned to reclaim their property.

To manage local affairs, Nebuchadnezzar appointed Gedaliah (descendant of a renowned Jerusalem family, 2 Kgs 25:22) to head the provincial government at Mizpah. His subsequent assassination by anti-Babylonian extremists generated fear of reprisals and prompted several families to flee to Egypt (2 Kgs 25:23–26). The group that took Jeremiah settled in Tahpanhes (Daphne) in the eastern Nile Delta where he presumably died (Jeremiah 42–44). One distant Jewish settlement was the military colony on the island of Yeb (Elephantine) near Nubia (Sudan). Here, archaeologists found a religiously syncretistic temple dedicated to Yahweh and a trove of documents (Elephantine Papyri) from the fifth century BCE.

Since the Babylonians did not resettle populations as the Assyrians had done, portions of Judah remained depopulated. The Edomites, under pressure from Arabian tribes, seized territory in southern Judah (between Beth-zur and Beersheba), which later came to be known as "Idumea" (Greek for "Edom"; see Map 45). Idumea was the ancestral home of Herod the Great (see Map 49).

For the exiles in Babylonia, the calamity of 586 BCE was divine retribution for apostasy. If they accepted God's judgment and repented, forgiveness and restoration would follow (Isa 54:7–10; Jer 31:2–3). Thus, the crucible of the exile created both the need and the desire for a set of authoritative texts to guide them in matters of faith and practice. One result was the survival and growth of documents that formed the basis of the Hebrew Bible, particularly the laws and narratives of the Torah and the rest of the so-called Primary History (Genesis through 2 Kings). The exile also prompted the development of religious practices such as the observance of Sabbath and the festivals, as well as well as regulations that helped people maintain ritual purity through personal hygiene and diet. The precursor to the synagogue also took shape at this time, giving people an opportunity to gather and pray as a faithful community. Such practices set the people apart from their host country and helped cement a new Jewish identity.

The prophet Ezekiel, exiled to Babylonia with Jehoiachin in 597 BCE, envisioned a reconstituted Israel living around a rebuilt temple enclosed by a square wall consisting of twelve gates—one for each tribe—three gates on each of the four sides (Ezekiel 40–48). However, concrete moves toward the fulfillment of this vision would not occur until Cyrus put an end to Babylonian rule in 539 BCE.

JUDAH IN EXILE

map 42

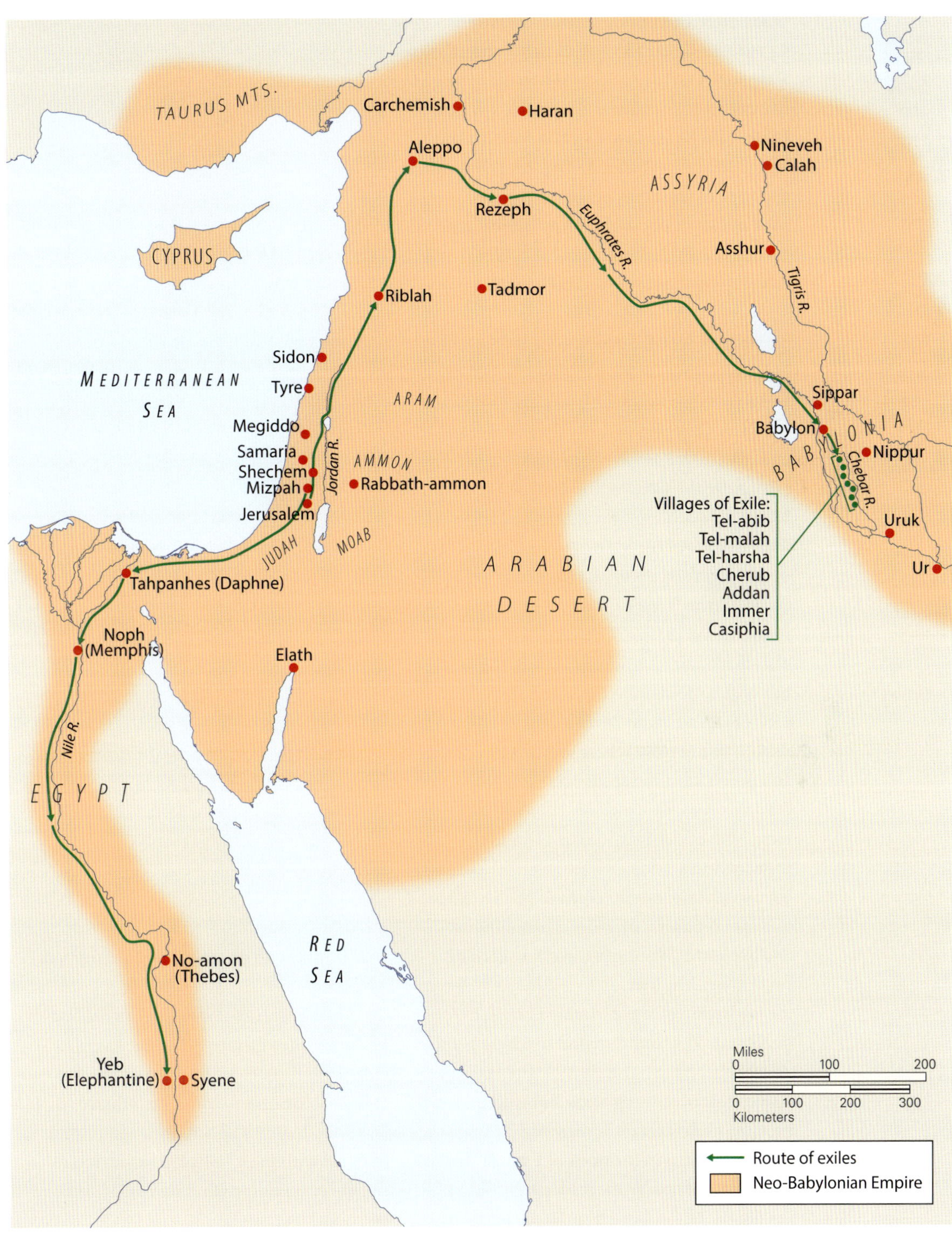

The Persian Period

The Persian or Achaemenid Empire (539–333 BCE) began approximately fifty years after the fall of Jerusalem when Cyrus the Great (559–530 BCE) conquered Babylon. Darius I (522–486 BCE) brought the empire to its greatest extent—from Libya and Macedonia in the west to the Indus River in the east. The Persians were the first to link their empire together by a network of roads. They introduced coinage, established a postal system, and developed a system of courts and judges.

THE PERSIAN EMPIRE

The empire was divided into twenty satrapies (administrative districts). "Yehud" (Judah) was a province in the fifth satrapy, "Beyond the River (Euphrates)." The Persian Empire ended with the defeat of Darius III by Alexander the Great at the Battle of Issus in 333 BCE, which brought about the Hellenistic Period (332–67 BCE).

As recorded on the Cyrus Cylinder, Cyrus II (the Great) allowed all captives to return home (2 Chr 36:22–23; Ezra 1:2–4). This magnanimous act earned Cyrus the honorific title of Yahweh's "Anointed" (Isa 45:1). Even so, many Jewish exiles chose to remain in Babylon, where they formed a large and powerful community whose religious influence was felt centuries later with the formation of the Babylonian Talmud (third to fifth centuries CE).

Shivat Zion, or the return of Jewish exiles to their homeland, mainly occurred in early and late waves. The early wave consisted of two groups. The first left in 538/537 BCE under the leadership of Sheshbazzar (Ezra 1–2; Nehemiah 7), and the second in 525 BCE under Zerubbabel (Hag 1:1; Ezra 2:2). The late wave also consisted of two groups and took place in the time of Artaxerxes I (regarded by some as King Ahasuerus in the book of Esther). The first group left under the leadership of Ezra in 458/457 BCE, followed some thirteen years later by a second group led by Nehemiah in 445 BCE.

Among the great mysteries is the fate of the northern tribes exiled by Assyria (Map 36). Ezekiel 37:16–17 suggests that at least some exiles maintained their Israelite identity and returned to the land of Israel with their Judean compatriots. Others eventually assimilated into the surrounding population.

One of the first challenges faced by the returning exiles was the rebuilding of the temple in the face of external opposition (Ezra 4:1–5, 24; 5:1–6:18), but the project was eventually completed and the temple dedicated in 516/515 BCE. Ezra addressed the threat of assimilation and idolatry, as well as culminating in a spiritual renewal and commitment by the people to follow the Instruction of Moses (Neh 8:1–12). A third challenge was the need to rebuild Jerusalem's fortifications, which Nehemiah accomplished in 445 BCE (Neh 2:11–3:32; 6:15). We know little to date archaeologically about Persian-period Jerusalem, though most scholars assume and evidence suggests that the city returned to the smaller thirty-acre size, as in the time of Solomon.

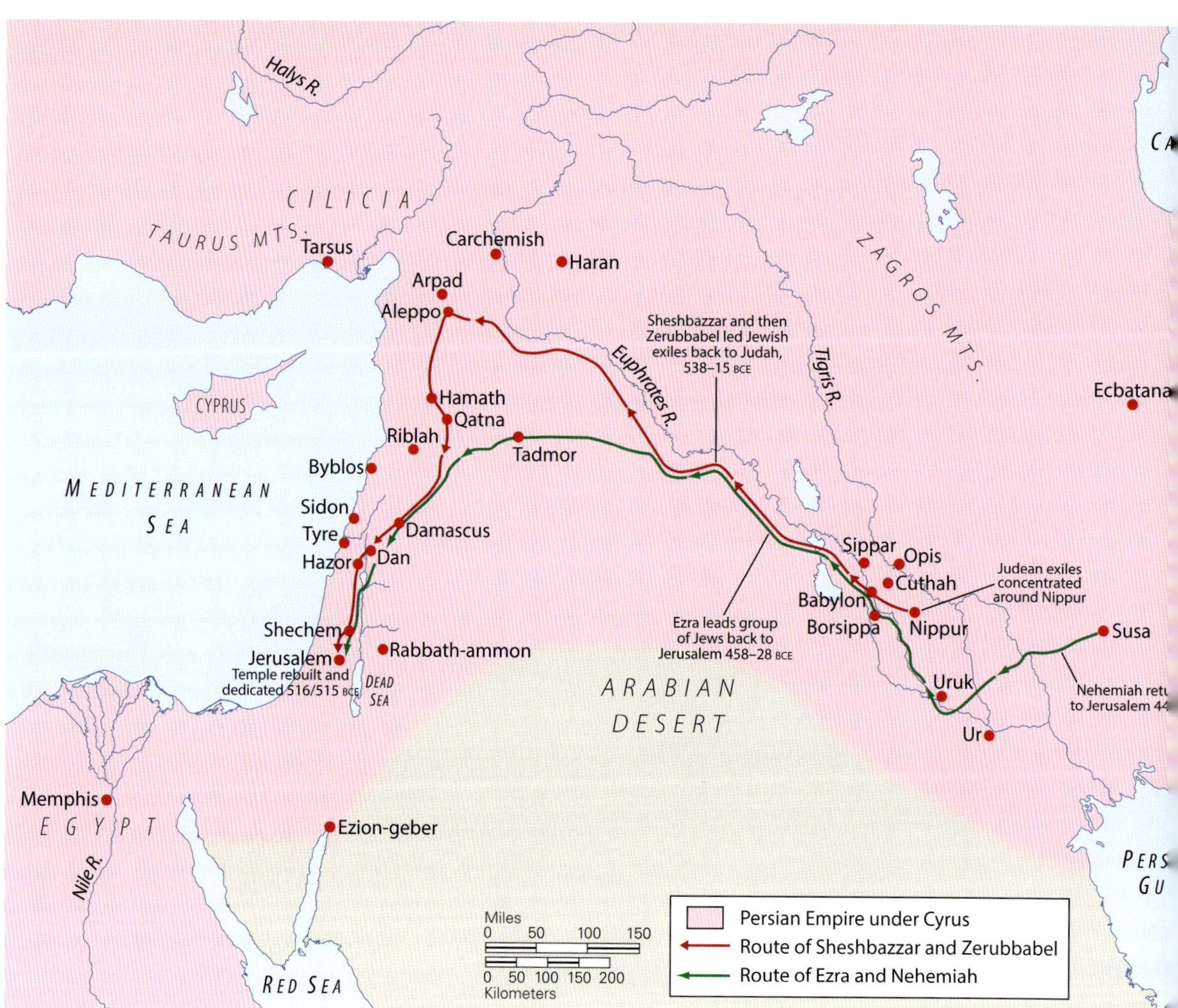
Halys R.
CILICIA
TAURUS MTS.
Tarsus
Carchemish
Haran
Arpad
Aleppo
ZAGROS MTS.
Sheshbazzar and then Zerubbabel led Jewish exiles back to Judah, 538–15 BCE
Euphrates R.
Tigris R.
CYPRUS
Hamath
Qatna
Riblah
Tadmor
Ecbatana
Byblos
MEDITERRANEAN SEA
Sidon
Tyre
Hazor
Damascus
Dan
Sippar
Opis
Cuthah
Judean exiles concentrated around Nippur
Babylon
Borsippa
Nippur
Susa
Shechem
Jerusalem
Rabbath-ammon
Ezra leads group of Jews back to Jerusalem 458–28 BCE
Temple rebuilt and dedicated 516/515 BCE
DEAD SEA
ARABIAN DESERT
Uruk
Ur
Memphis
EGYPT
Nile R.
Ezion-geber
RED SEA
Miles 0 50 100 150
0 50 100 150 200 Kilometers
Persian Empire under Cyrus
Route of Sheshbazzar and Zerubbabel
Route of Ezra and Nehemiah

PERSIAN KINGS

575 BCE
550 BCE
525 BCE
500 BCE
475 BCE
450 BCE
425 BCE
400 BCE
375 BCE
350 BCE
325 BCE
Cyrus II/Cyrus the Great (559–530 BCE)
Cambyses II (530–522 BCE)
Gaumata /Bardiya? (522 BCE)
Darius I (522–486 BCE)
Xerxes I (486–465 BCE)
Artaxerxes I (464–424 BCE)
Sogdianus (424 BCE)
Darius II (423–405 BCE)
Artaxerxes II (404–358/359 BCE)
Artaxerxes III (358–338 BCE)
Artaxerxes IV (337–336 BCE)
Darius III (335–331 BCE)

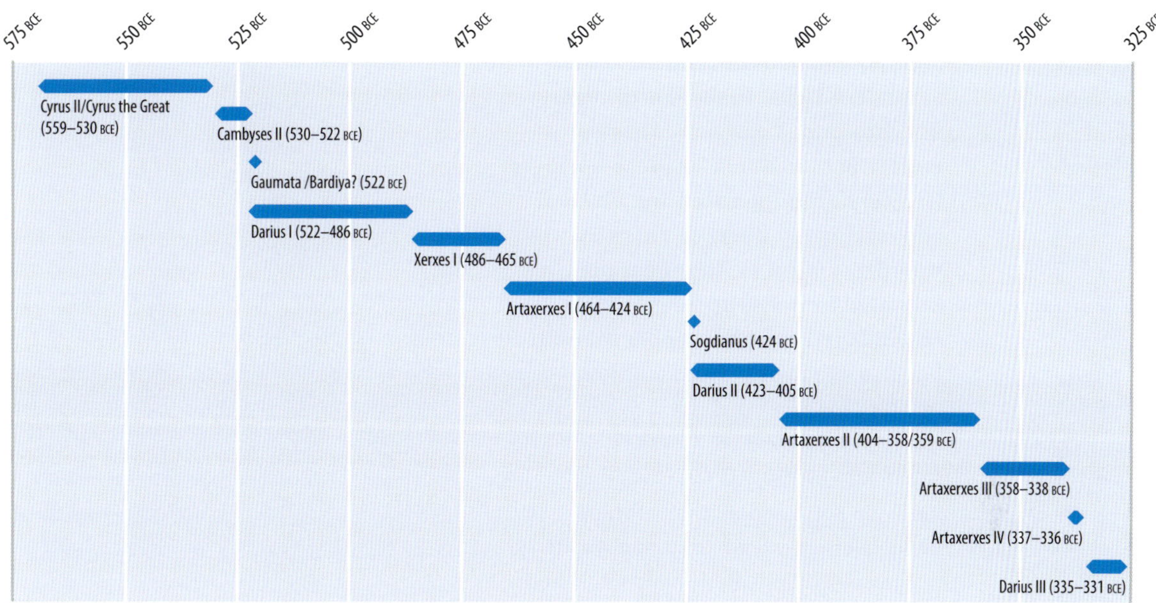

THE PROVINCE OF JUDAH IN THE DAYS OF THE RETURN

map 45

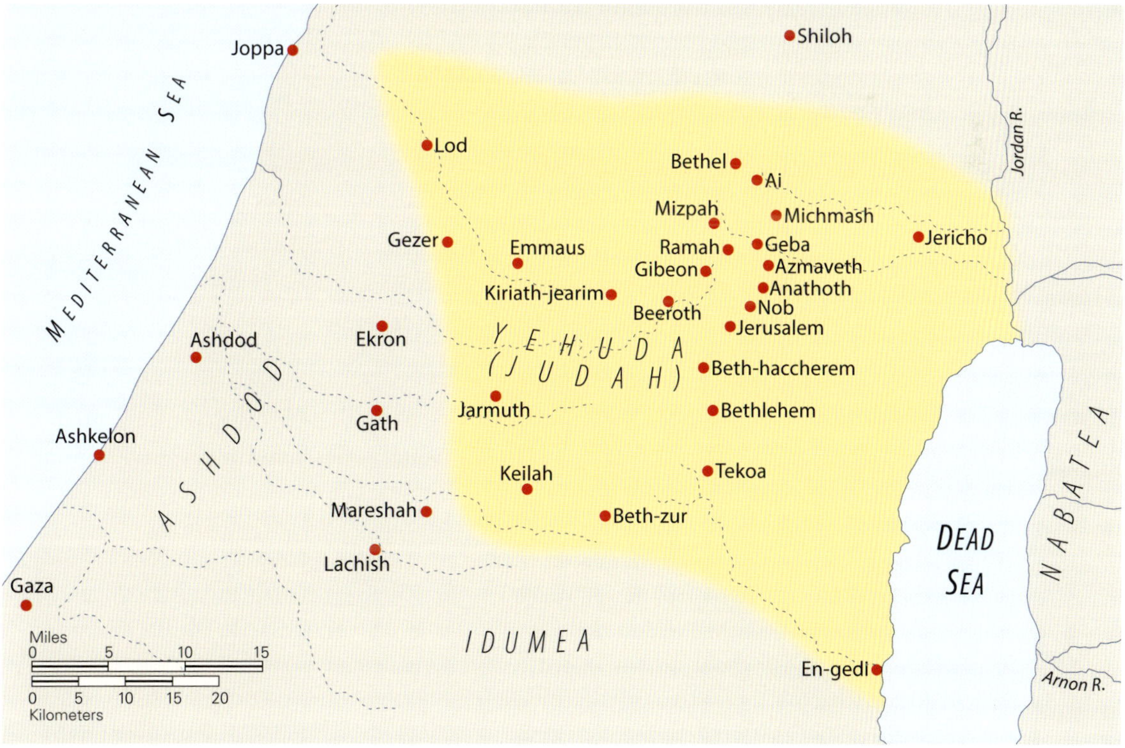

Shiloh
Joppa
MEDITERRANEAN SEA
Lod
Bethel
Ai
Jordan R.
Mizpah
Michmash
Gezer
Emmaus
Ramah
Geba
Jericho
Gibeon
Azmaveth
Kiriath-jearim
Anathoth
Beeroth
Nob
Jerusalem
Ashdod
Ekron
YEHUDA (JUDAH)
Beth-haccherem
ASHDOD
Jarmuth
Bethlehem
Gath
Ashkelon
Keilah
Tekoa
Mareshah
Beth-zur
DEAD SEA
NABATEA
Lachish
Gaza
Miles
0
5
10
15
0
5
10
15
20
Kilometers
IDUMEA
En-gedi
Arnon R.

The Kingdom of Alexander the Great

For over 200 years, beginning in the mid-sixth century BCE, the Persians ruled the eastern Mediterranean, the Mesopotamian basin, and as far east as modern India. In the fourth century BCE, however, a new power began to emerge in Macedonia (modern northern Greece) beginning with King Philip II and reaching its apex with his son, who would be known as Alexander the Great. Educated by Aristotle, Alexander is remembered as a philosopher himself, but also as a brilliant and ruthless military man.

In 356 BCE, as Philip II was expanding his realm north and west into Thrace, he conquered the town of Crenides and renamed it Philippi. Paul would visit it about 400 years later. Also in 356, Alexander was born. According to ancient Greco-Roman historians, on the day of his birth the Temple of Artemis in Ephesus was burned down by arson, and the juxtaposition of these events was interpreted as a prediction of Alexander's future triumphs in Asia Minor.

Alexander assumed control following Philip's assassination in 336 BCE, and moved his troops from Macedonia into Asia Minor, where he routed the Persian forces at the Granicus River. In an important battle in Issus one year later, Alexander and his outnumbered troops soundly defeated the Persian King Darius III and his army. Alexander then moved down the coast and conquered the port cities in order to negate the Persian naval forces. Most cities yielded quickly, though it took a seven-month siege of Tyre and a two-month siege of Gaza before they submitted. Egypt, which had suffered under the Persians, welcomed Alexander as a liberator, acknowledged him as pharaoh, and even attributed divine status to him as "son of Ammon," or Zeus, the king of all the Greek gods. He also founded Alexandria in Egypt, which would become one of the most important centers of learning in the ancient world.

Did Alexander visit Jerusalem? According to Josephus (*Antiquities* 11.317–45) and other later sources, Alexander made a detour to Jerusalem on his way to Egypt in 332 BCE. It is likely the Jewish leadership in Jerusalem met with Alexander to affirm their loyalty

and were granted the same concessions as the Persians had allowed.

By 330, Alexander had captured Babylon, Susa, and Persepolis, and Darius had been killed by some of his own officers. Alexander was proclaimed the ruler of the former Persian Empire. Continuing eastward into modern Pakistan and India, Alexander was only stopped by the exhaustion of his troops. Returning to Babylon, Alexander became ill and died in 323 BCE at only thirty-two years of age.

Alexander created a huge empire and left behind an amazing legacy in the lands he conquered, including the lasting influence of Hellenistic culture. His sudden and unexpected death also sowed the seeds for disruptions that soon followed, particularly in Palestine.

Alexander's Kingdom Divided

"Then a warrior king shall arise, who shall rule with great dominion and take action as he pleases. And while still rising in power, his kingdom shall be broken and divided toward the four winds of heaven" (Dan 11:3–4). Daniel 11:1–45 works out the history of this period, and the "warrior king" is a reference to Alexander the Great. When he unexpectedly died in 323 BCE, his generals, known as the Diadochi, or Successors, divided the empire among themselves.

Thus began a long struggle, including wars for possession, strategic marriages and divorces, deceptions, and murders. Palestine again would serve as a battleground, mainly valuable for its coastal access and the Great Trunk Road connecting Egypt (under a dynasty of Ptolemies) with the powers to the north (Antigonus the "One-Eyed" in Asia Minor) and east (Seleucus in Babylon).

Ptolemy I in 320 BCE quickly ousted the general who had been given the biblical lands now designated as "Syria and Phoenicia." Meanwhile, Antigonus was expanding his empire in Asia Minor and by 311 BCE had pushed back both Ptolemy and Seleucus and had extended his rule into all of Palestine. An alliance among Ptolemy, Seleucus, and others was formed to stop Antigonus, who was decisively defeated at the Battle of Ipsus in 301 BCE. The terms of the alliance had stipulated that Seleucus was to obtain all of Syria and Phoenicia, but Ptolemy refused to hand over the southern portion, Judea.

Over the next one hundred years, Judea was contested property between the Seleucids and the Ptolemies. 3 Maccabees 1:1–7 and Daniel 11:20 recount the Battle of Raphia in 217 BCE, near the border of Palestine and Egypt. Ptolemy IV Philopater defeated the Seleucid king Antiochus the Great, regained Judean territory for Egypt, and then visited Jerusalem. In 200 BCE, however, at the Battle of Paneas (later to be built up as Caesarea Philippi), Antiochus crushed the Egyptians and claimed all Syria and Phoenicia, including Judea.

Within Palestine during this time, a number of things were happening. Administrative districts were established under the Ptolemies, including Idumea, Judea, Samaria, and Galilee. The Samaritans preserved their religious and political identity around Mount Gerizim, often to the consternation of, and in competition with, the Judeans. This matter created rival parties between those

THE HELLENISTIC PERIOD FOLLOWING ALEXANDER IN THE 3RD CENTURY BCE map 47

CASPIAN SEA
ARAL SEA
Jaxartes R.
CHORASMIA
CAUCASUS MTS.
Derbent
Cyrus R.
ARMENIAN MTS.
ARMENIA
Araxes R.
Oxus R.
Alexandria
SOGDIANA
Nisibis
MESOPOTAMIA
Gaugamela
Arbela
Tigris R.
HYRCANIA
Rhagae
Caspian Gates
Ecbatana
Meshed
Bactra
BACTRIA
Drapsaca
HINDU KUSH
Herat
ARIA
Khyber Pass
Taxila
Bucephala
Babylon
BABYLONIA
Susa
PERSIA
Kandahar
ARACHOSIA
MALLI
Pasargadae
Persepolis
PERSIAN GULF
ARABIAN DESERT
Pura
GEDROSIA
Indus R.
INDIA
INDUS VALLEY
Miles
0 100 200 300
0 100 200 300 400
Kilometers

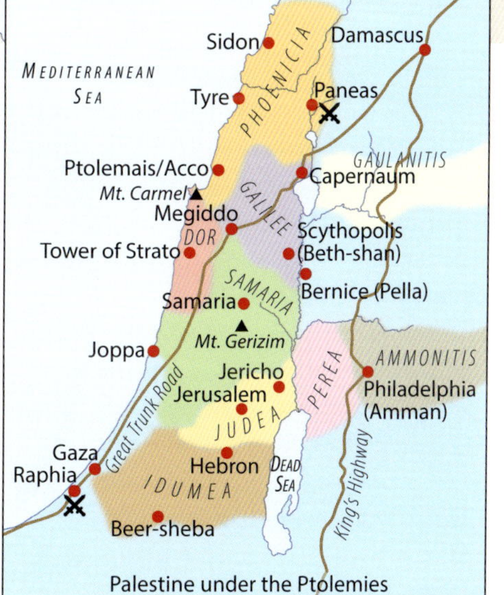

Palestine under the Ptolemies

who supported the Ptolemies and those who welcomed the Seleucids.

This was a political struggle, but also a cultural one. While both the Ptolemies and Seleucids maintained their Greek heritage, the Ptolemies tended to grant more autonomy to the Jews and their practices, while the Seleucids were more aggressive in imposing Hellenistic culture in their realm. So, while most of the Jews of Jerusalem welcomed Antiochus after the Battle of Paneas, the Seleucid program of Hellenization would eventually become a critical problem (see also pp. 118–19).

The Maccabean Revolt

Having control of Judea and Samaria at the beginning of the second century BCE, the Seleucids embarked on two main projects. The first was to extend their power into Asia Minor and Egypt. To the west, their plan was thwarted by the rising Roman Empire, which moved into Macedonia and western Asia Minor. When the Seleucid ruler Antiochus IV Epiphanes came to power in 175 BCE, he successfully invaded Egypt, only for the Romans to force him to withdraw. These military maneuvers were costly. Rivalries in the temple administration in Jerusalem led to an attempt to confiscate the wealth stored in the treasury. That attempt failed (cf. 2 Maccabees 3), but another revenue stream emerged: selling the Jewish high priesthood to the highest bidder.

Here is where the second Seleucid project also comes into view. As heirs of the heritage of Alexander the Great, the Seleucids sought to unify the realm through the imposition of Greek culture, including language, city structure and governance, entertainment, sports, and religion. According to 2 Maccabees 4:7–10, upon the ascent of Antiochus IV Epiphanes, "Jason the brother of Onias [III the high priest] obtained the high priesthood by corruption, promising the king three hundred sixty talents of silver, and from another source of revenue eighty talents. In addition to this, he promised to pay one hundred fifty more if permission were given to establish by his authority a gymnasium and a body of youth for it, and to enroll the people of Jerusalem as citizens of Antioch."

Antiochus IV was happy to accept the money, and to have an ally in the Hellenization of Jerusalem. According to 2 Maccabees 4:13–15, there was such an avid adoption of Greek ways that even the priests neglected their temple duties in order to participate in wrestling and discus-throwing! Jason served only from 175 to 172 BCE before he was ousted by a higher bidder named Menelaus. In 167 BCE, Jason raised an army to depose Menelaus, which Antiochus interpreted as a Jewish revolt. He stormed into Jerusalem, killed tens of thousands, and ransacked the temple, taking the menorah and altar (cf. Josephus, *Antiquities* 12:248ff). To ensure greater religious conformity, Antiochus consecrated the temple in Jerusalem to Zeus Olympias and sacrificed a pig upon the altar. Some Hellenizing Jews had previously reversed their circumcision by surgery, but now circumcision was forbidden, as was Sabbath observance, and Torah scrolls were destroyed.

While Antiochus is usually blamed for attempting to destroy traditional Jewish

Coin of Antiochus IV Epiphanes.

THE BEGINNINGS OF THE MACCABEAN REVOLT map 48

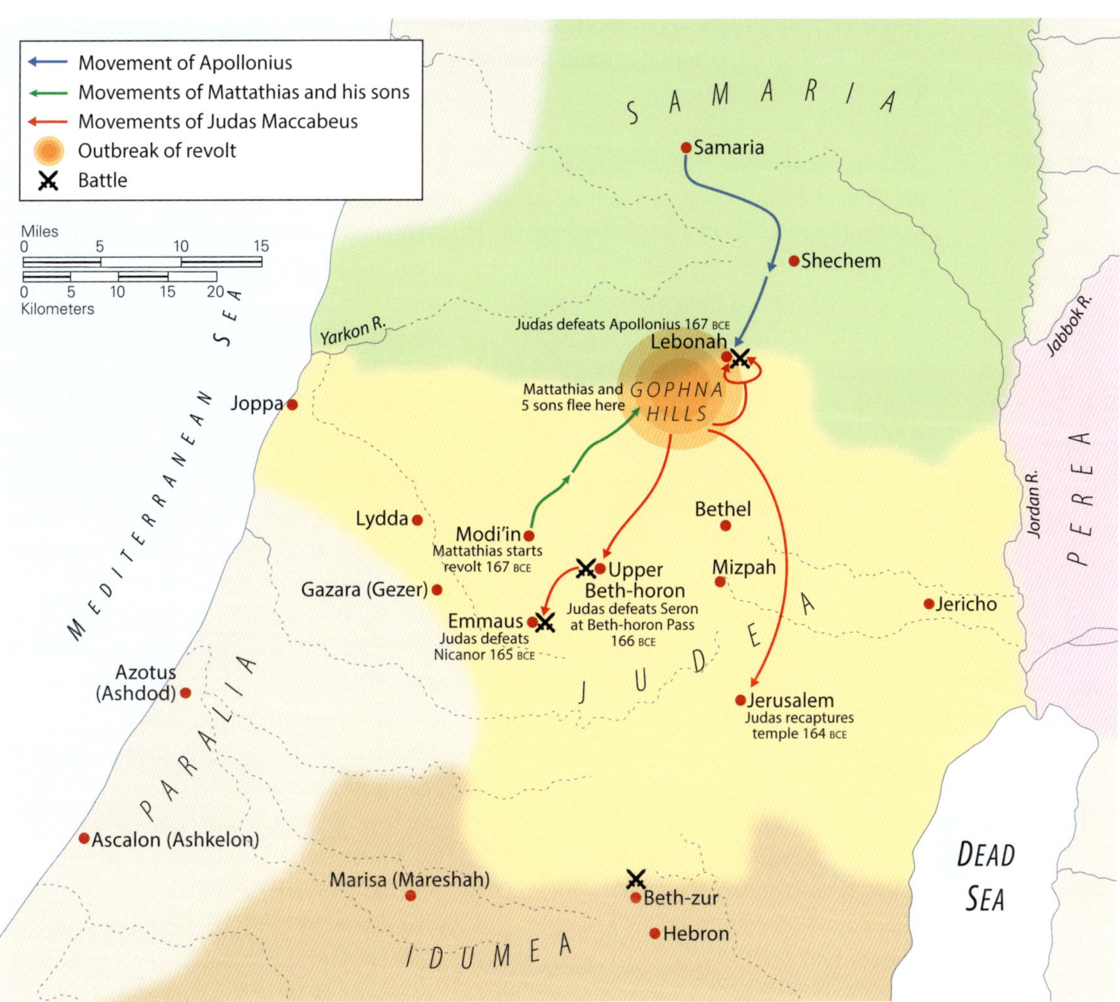

practices, it is apparent that some Jews happily participated in the Hellenistic lifestyle, including many in the high priestly and aristocratic families. But while some Jews now chose to submit, many chose martyrdom. Tensions came to a head in Modi'in in 167 BCE, when Mattathias, a descendant of a priest named Hasmoneus, killed both the Syrian emissary who was enforcing pagan sacrifices and a Jew who was complying. Mattathias retreated with his sons into the Samarian hills. From there they conducted guerrilla warfare, and gathered support from other pious Jews called the Hasidim. Under the leadership of Mattathias's son Judas Maccabeus (or "Hammer"), this Maccabean revolt fought both the Seleucid forces and the Hellenizing Jews. After stunning military victories near Gophna, Beth-horon, Emmaus, and Beth-zur, Judas Maccabeus recaptured Jerusalem in 164 BCE. 2 Maccabees 10 recounts how Judas purified the temple and rededicated it in an eight-day ceremony now known as Hanukkah.

The Hasmonean Kingdom

Though Antiochus IV Epiphanes had died in 164 BCE and Judas Maccabeus had managed to reclaim the Jerusalem Temple, the battle with the Seleucids continued, now fought on military, political, and religious fronts. By 160, Judas had been killed, and his brother Jonathan assumed leadership of the Hasmoneans with the help of another brother, Simon.

While accomplishing military successes, Jonathan and Simon were also able to expand their holdings by manipulating the political tensions between claimants to the Syrian throne, the renewed rivalry between Egypt and Syria, and the increasing influence of Rome. In 152 BCE, Jonathan was appointed high priest and later recognized by the Seleucids as governor of Judea. Jonathan was treacherously captured and killed in 142 by one Seleucid faction. Simon assumed leadership and the high priesthood and switched allegiance to another Syrian rival. As reward for Simon's support, independence was granted to Judea in 142. Simon and his descendants thus mark the beginning of the Hasmonean dynasty that would last until Roman occupation in 63 BCE.

Simon was assassinated in 135 BCE, and Simon's son John Hyrcanus I assumed power and the high priesthood and began an even more aggressive campaign of expansion and Judaizing. He demolished the Samaritan temple on Mount Gerizim.

After Hyrcanus died, his sons Aristobulus I and Alexander Jannaeus continued acquiring land so that by Jannaeus's death in 76 BCE, the Hasmonean kingdom rivaled that of the united monarchy under Solomon. In 40, one of Aristobulus's sons, Antigonus II Matthathias, ruled as the last Hasmonean king and high priest until 37 BCE, when he was defeated and killed at the behest of Herod the Great, with Roman help.

The Maccabean Revolt was initiated by religious fervor and cultural resistance to Hellenization, though gaining religious freedom in 162 BCE only whetted political appetites and enmeshed the Hasmoneans in Hellenistic practices. It was a significant innovation in Jewish polity when Jonathan was appointed both as high priest (even though he was not Zadokite) and political-military head. Since they did not claim Davidic heritage, many Jews were also alarmed when Aristobulus I and his sons took the title of "king."

These irregularities resulted in the birth of the Jewish sects of Sadducees, Pharisees, and Essenes. The Sadducees were from the aristocracy, pro-Hasmonean and supportive of the Hasmonean high priesthood, and open to Hellenization and accommodating to political realities. The Pharisees, on the other hand, were non-priestly and associated with the common people. They became critical of the Hasmoneans for their violation of biblically-defined criteria for high priest and king. Because of their opposition to Alexander Jannaeus, Josephus reports that Alexander ordered about eight hundred Pharisees to be crucified. Such an atrocity helps account for the tension between the groups displayed in Jesus's time.

The third Jewish group to emerge due to the Hasmonean conflicts was the Essenes. They were a priestly group, and along with their leader, the Teacher of Righteousness, they made high priestly claims based on their Zadokite heritage, and so they rejected the Hasmoneans as apostates. Some of them formed a new covenant community in the wilderness at Qumran, on the northwest shore of the Dead Sea. Focusing on purity, they prepared for the apocalyptic coming of the messiah(s) and God's reign that would restore Israel and the Jerusalem Temple.

MACCABEAN-HASMONEAN PALESTINE 166–76 BCE

map 49

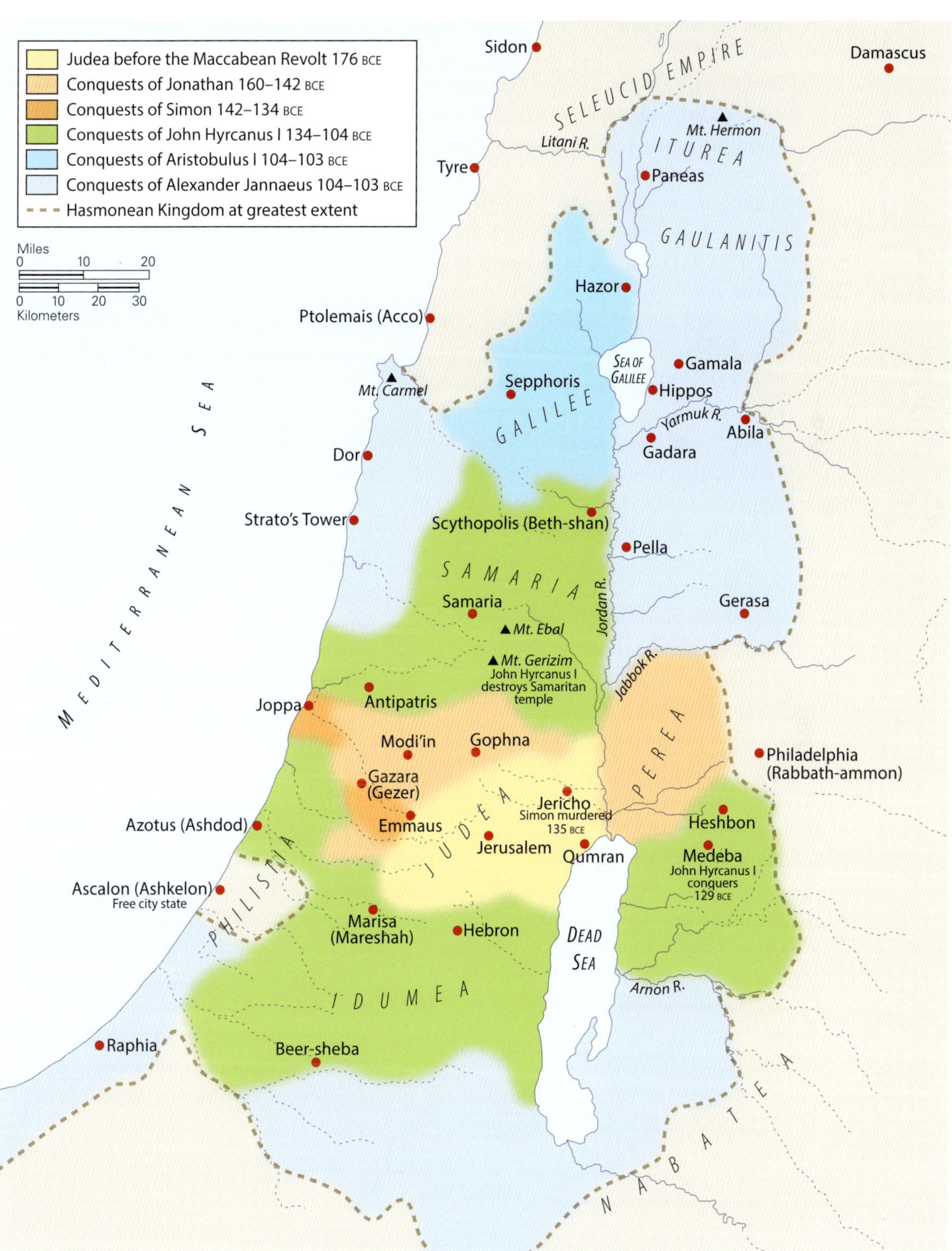

Rome Conquers Palestine 63 BCE

According to tradition, Rome was founded by Romulus and Remus in the eighth century BCE. By 509 BCE the Roman Republic had formed, and by 272 Rome ruled most of Italy. From the mid-third to the mid-second century BCE, Rome fought and won a series of wars against their main rival, Carthage in North Africa. In 198 BCE, the Seleucid king Antiochus III tried to take Greece but was soundly defeated by the Romans, who thus gained a foothold in western Asia Minor and thereafter influenced the politics between the Seleucids and Ptolemies in Egypt.

By 146 BCE, Rome controlled most of the western Mediterranean, including Spain and north Africa, and to the east as far as Macedonia, Greece, and western Asia Minor (or Anatolia, which is modern Turkey). During the early part of the first century BCE, after three wars in Greece and Asia Minor, Roman rule was established over that entire area. By 63 BCE, the Roman statesman and general Pompey (106–48 BCE) had moved south with his troops, occupied Syria and Phoenicia, and ended the reign of the Seleucids.

At this time, there was a civil war in the Hasmonean kingdom between the sons of Alexander Jannaeus, Hyrcanus II and Aristobulus II. Both appealed to the Romans. Pompey eventually decided to support the weaker and more easily manipulated Hyrcanus, and arrested Aristobulus. The Sadducean supporters of Aristobulus retreated to the Temple Mount and burned the bridge leading to the western hill and the Hasmonean palace. Hyrcanus's supporters, however, opened the city gates to the Romans, but it took a three-month siege of the Temple Mount before Aristobulus's supporters were slaughtered. Pompey and his troops entered the temple, and, though they did not destroy anything, they ventured into the Holy of Holies.

The Romans reorganized the entire region and made it part of the province of Syria. The important coastal cities were ruled autonomously by Roman-appointed proconsuls as were ten cities with predominately Hellenistic, non-Jewish populations that became known as the Decapolis. Samaria also became a separate district. The Romans did designate Hyrcanus as high priest and ethnarch, but only of the greatly reduced districts of Judea (which included Idumea and Perea) and part of Galilee. Behind the scenes, Antipater the Idumean, who had earlier come to Hyrcanus's aid in order to provoke the rivalry with Aristobulus and to advance his own ambitions, emerged as the main power-broker. Antipater was appointed procurator, and he in turn set his sons Phasael and Herod as governors over Jerusalem and Galilee.

One of Aristobulus II's sons, Alexander II, escaped Roman imprisonment and returned to Palestine to fight the Romans in 57 BCE. Unsuccessful, he failed again in 55 BCE, even with the aid of his father and brother Antigonus II, who had escaped Rome. In 49 BCE, Julius Caesar freed Aristobulus II and Alexander II and sent them to Palestine in an attempt to weaken Pompey's influence there. Aristobulus was poisoned on the way, and Alexander ended up being beheaded at the command of Pompey through the influence of Antipater's son, Herod (the Great).

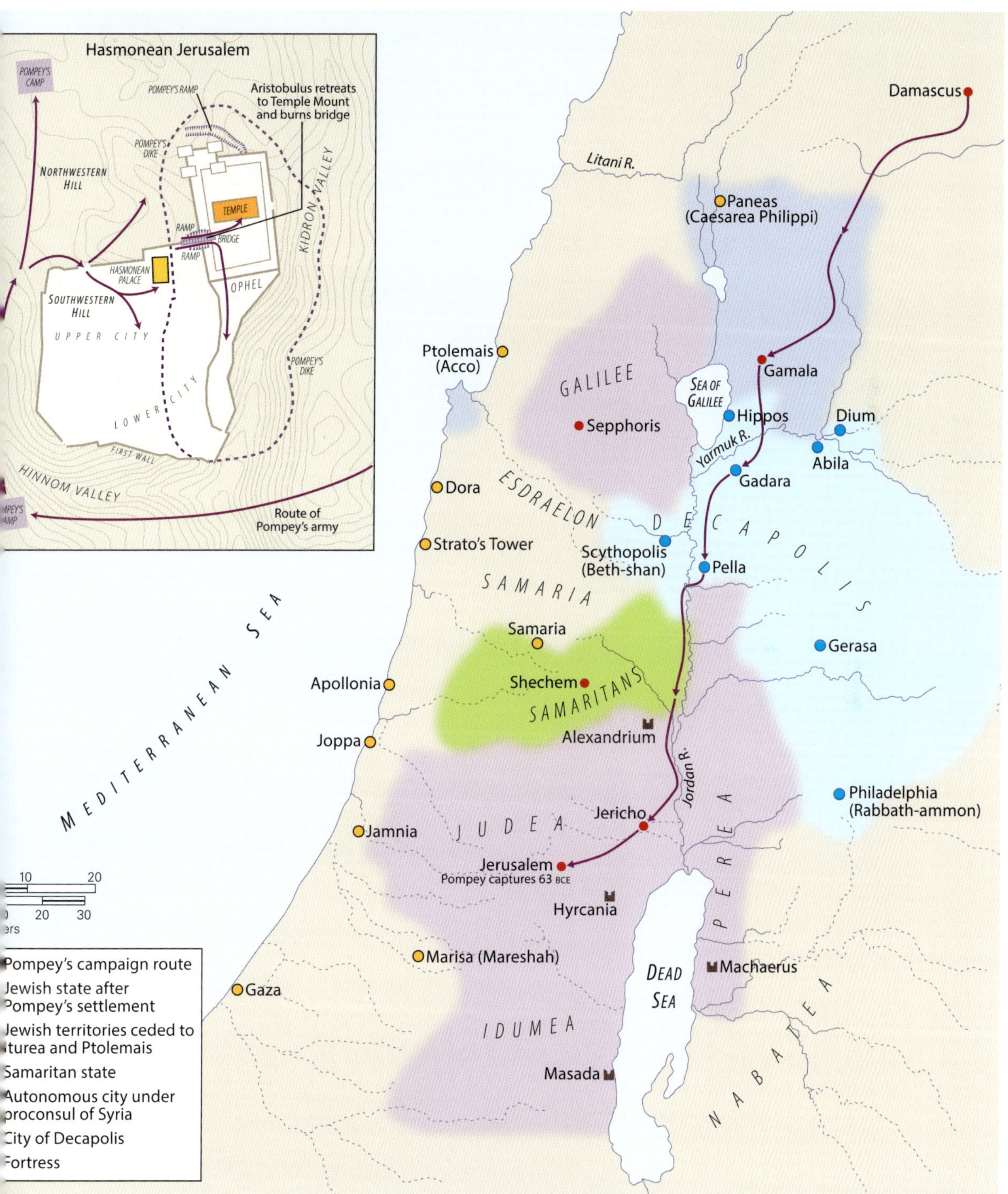

Hasmonean Jerusalem
POMPEY'S CAMP
POMPEY'S RAMP
Aristobulus retreats to Temple Mount and burns bridge
POMPEY'S DIKE
NORTHWESTERN HILL
TEMPLE
RAMP
BRIDGE
RAMP
KIDRON VALLEY
HASMONEAN PALACE
SOUTHWESTERN HILL
UPPER CITY
OPHEL
POMPEY'S DIKE
LOWER CITY
FIRST WALL
HINNOM VALLEY
Route of Pompey's army
Damascus
Litani R.
Paneas (Caesarea Philippi)
Ptolemais (Acco)
GALILEE
Gamala
SEA OF GALILEE
Sepphoris
Hippos
Dium
Yarmuk R.
Abila
Gadara
Dora
ESDRAELON
DECAPOLIS
Strato's Tower
Scythopolis (Beth-shan)
Pella
SAMARIA
Samaria
Gerasa
MEDITERRANEAN SEA
Apollonia
Shechem
SAMARITANS
Alexandrium
Joppa
Jordan R.
Philadelphia (Rabbath-ammon)
Jericho
Jamnia
JUDEA
PEREA
Jerusalem
Pompey captures 63 BCE
Hyrcania
Marisa (Mareshah)
Machaerus
DEAD SEA
Gaza
IDUMEA
NABATEA
Masada
10 20
20 30
Pompey's campaign route
Jewish state after Pompey's settlement
Jewish territories ceded to Iturea and Ptolemais
Samaritan state
Autonomous city under proconsul of Syria
City of Decapolis
Fortress

Part 5

Jesus and the Emergence of Christianity

The Rise of Augustus Caesar

Though the Roman military was mostly successful in expanding the realm, back in Rome, the republic was experiencing difficulties. A slave revolt led by Spartacus had to be quelled in 71 BCE. Due to a variety of conflicting political interests, in 59 BCE Pompey joined with Julius Caesar and Crassus in the First Triumvirate to oversee the republic. In the 50s BCE, the Roman general Julius Caesar (Caesar was his family name) was successfully fighting the Gallic wars and extending the Roman sphere into Gaul and even Britain. Crassus, however, was killed in battle against the Parthians in 53 BCE. When Caesar crossed the Rubicon River in northern Italy with his troops in 49 BCE, civil war erupted between him and Pompey, resulting in Pompey's death in Egypt in 48 BCE while fleeing Caesar.

In February 44 BCE, Julius Caesar was appointed dictator for life, but a month later, on the Ides of March, he was assassinated by a group of senators led by Cassius and Brutus. Three generals emerged to form the Second Triumvirate: Mark Antony, Octavian, and Lepidus. In 42 BCE, Antony and Octavian defeated Cassius and Brutus at the Battle of Philippi. Many of the veteran soldiers were discharged after the battle and remained in Philippi, which became a Roman colony.

Lepidus was never much of a factor in the Triumvirate, and hostilities eventually broke out between Octavian and Antony, who was now closely aligned with his Egyptian lover Cleopatra. At the Battle of Actium in 31 BCE, Octavian emerged triumphant, and shortly thereafter, Antony and Cleopatra committed suicide. By 27 BCE, Octavian was granted the title of Augustus Caesar.

Augustus was an honorific and religious title. As the grandnephew and adopted son of Julius Caesar, he claimed the name of Caesar, which would be used as a title for subsequent emperors. Since Julius Caesar had been posthumously deified by the Roman senate in 42 BCE, Octavian could also claim that he was *Divi Filius*, "Son of the Divine One." The era of the *Pax Romana*, the Roman Peace, had begun, and Rome now controlled the entire Mediterranean basin.

In general, when the Romans conquered new lands, they were quite tolerant of

THE ROMAN EMPIRE

diversity and happy to integrate local religions into the Greco-Roman pantheon. The Romans acknowledged the antiquity of Judaism, and its monotheism was attractive. Special concessions were made to the Jews so they could practice their ancestral religion. Roman military and political power was omnipresent, and their securing of the Mediterranean Sea for commerce and their tireless construction of roads had a profound economic and cultural impact. Rome maintained control through its chain of command and by the bestowing of privileges—for example, right of citizenship, land, honorific titles, offices—that kept subordinates constantly beholden to their superiors. Threats to the Roman peace would not be tolerated.

The Herodian Dynasty

Although there was turmoil in Roman leadership in the 50s and 40s BCE, matters in Palestine were relatively quiet. Hyrcanus II was functioning as high priest and ethnarch, but Antipater the Idumean was the real power. He negotiated his allegiances between Pompey, Julius Caesar, and Cassius, but his pro-Roman stance led to his being poisoned and dying at the hands of a Jewish rival in 42 BCE. Antipater the Idumean's main legacy, however, was his son Herod, who became known as Herod the Great.

Herod proved to be even more politically adept and resourceful than his father. Appointed governor of Galilee in 47 BCE, Herod brutally removed those who resisted Rome and rebelled against his rule. Exploiting Roman weakness after Julius Caesar's assassination, the Parthians invaded Palestine and removed Hyrcanus II—whom Herod supported—from office. Herod fled to Rome, who entrusted him to repel the Parthians and appointed him king of Judea in 40 BCE. It took three years of bloody conflict before Herod and the Romans succeeded. During the war, Herod married Hyrcanus II's granddaughter Mariamne I in order to gain royal credentials and priestly connections.

Herod faced many threats to his power. First, he had no claim to the priesthood so was pressured into appointing Mariamne's popular and respected brother, Aristobulus III, to the high priesthood. Herod arranged for him to "accidentally" drown. Eventually Herod also accused Hyrcanus II of treason and had him executed, thereby removing any further Hasmonean threats.

Second, Herod was beholden to his benefactor Mark Antony, and thus also to Antony's paramour, Cleopatra. Octavian's triumph over Antony and Cleopatra allowed Herod to break free of Cleopatra's ambitions.

Herod then had to convince Octavian he would be faithful to him. In 30 BCE, Octavian restored all the lands Cleopatra had and added land in Gaza, Samaria, and on the southeastern shore of the Sea of Galilee. By 20 BCE, Octavian, now Augustus Caesar, granted additional land to the north and east of the Sea of Galilee: Gaulanitis, Batanea, Trachonitis, and Auranitis.

Having solved these various problems, Herod embarked on an ambitious building program that became the trademark of his reign. He built winter palaces at Cypros and at Machaerus. Masada was refortified. Herodion, a hilltop fortress and Herod's future burial place, was built up high enough for it to be visible from Jerusalem. Sebaste (Samaria) was built up as a Roman city, with all the usual structures for commerce, government, civil religion, the military, and entertainment. The harbor at Caesarea Maritima was an incredible construction achievement, utilizing the recent discovery of underwater concrete made with ash from Mount Vesuvius.

Herod was not considered to be truly Jewish, he usurped royal power and manipulated priestly authority, he was complicit with Roman goals and Hellenistic practices, and imposed a heavy burden of taxation to support his building programs. How, then, did he maintain control? The answer lay in Herod's crowning achievement: the temple in Jerusalem, which was known as one of the most beautiful structures in the entire Roman world. It became the focal point of Jewish piety and the economic center of Herod's kingdom, and largely accounts for his title "Herod the Great." Herod was beholden to his benefactor Mark Antony and his paramour, Cleopatra, whom Antony had helped expand her Egyptian empire by granting her all the Judean coastline plus land around Jericho.

THE GROWTH OF HEROD'S KINGDOM

map 52

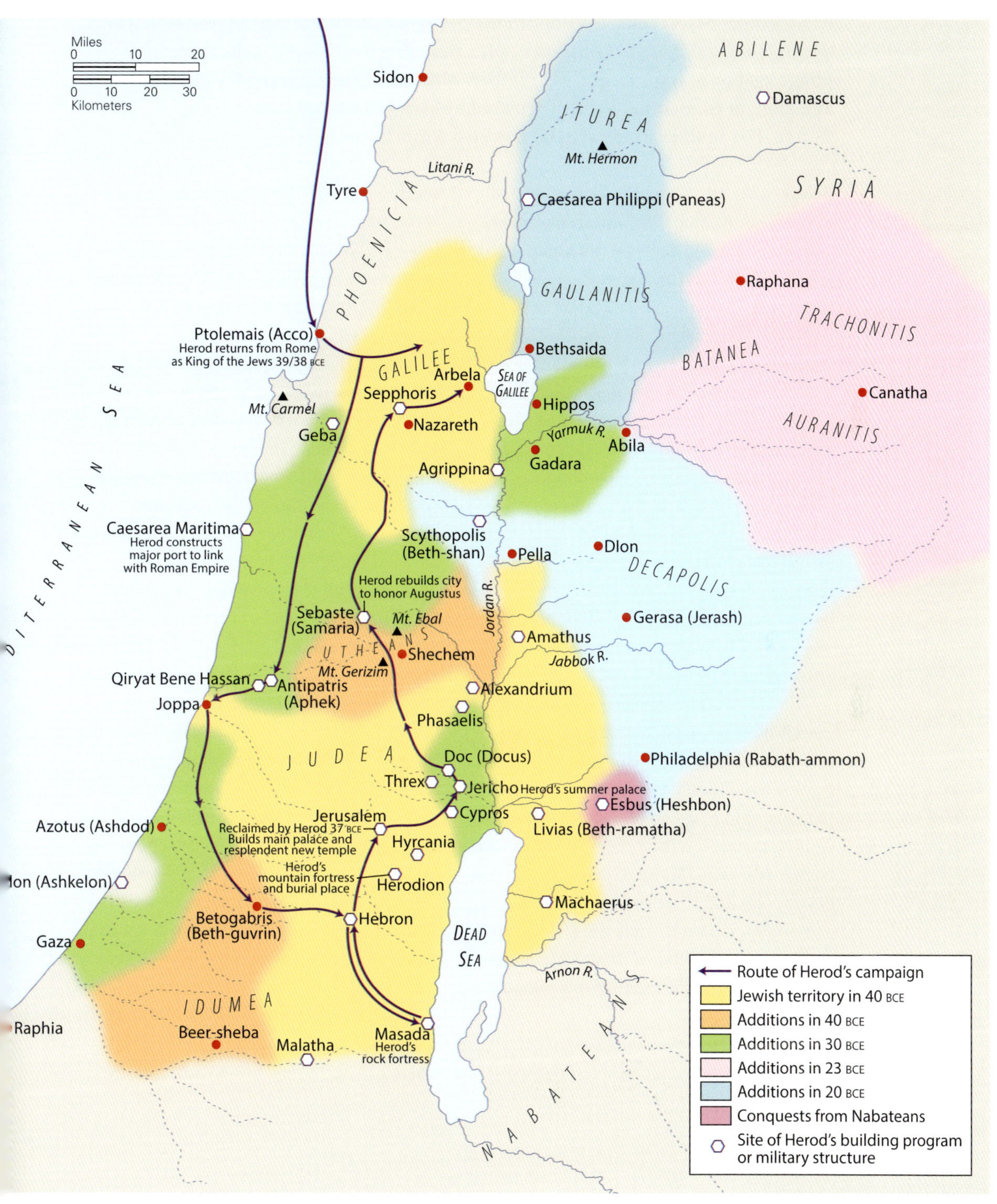

Herod's Kingdom Divided

Herod the Great knew how to manage a kingdom, but he could not manage his family. In 37 BCE he divorced his first wife, Doris, in order to marry Mariamne I, daughter of Alexander Maccabeus, to establish his credentials with the Hasmonean line. The dysfunction and intrigue continued, with Herod's sister Salome maneuvering for power against Mariamne and her mother. Although Herod apparently had deep affection for Mariamne, she was betrayed by her mother, and Herod executed her in 29 BCE. Her mother would also be executed a short time later.

Before her death, Mariamne had given birth to two sons, Aristobulus IV and Alexander, who were raised in Rome as potential successors. By this time, all the descendants from male Hasmonean lineage had been removed, so for people still nostalgic for the Hasmoneans, these sons of Herod from the female Hasmonean line were a logical and popular choice. Herod, however, had ten wives, with other sons potentially in line for his throne. In 28 BCE, Herod married Malthace, a Samaritan. Besides a daughter, she bore two sons: Herod Archelaus and Herod Antipas. Also about that time, he married Cleopatra of Jerusalem, by whom he had two sons, the more important of whom was Herod Philip II. Herod's first wife, Doris, also had a son by him, Herod Antipater II.

During all these intrigues, Herod had to keep Augustus happy, and deferred to him to settle some of the disputes. After Mariamne's death, Herod recalled Antipater II, the son of Doris, whom he had previously dismissed. In 17 BCE, Herod went to Rome and brought back Aristobulus IV and Alexander, but Salome opposed these sons of Mariamne. In 13 BCE Herod named Antipater II as his heir, and in 7 BCE Aristobulus IV and Alexander were executed on the grounds of attempting to depose Herod.

By this time Herod had become quite ill. Antipater II, whom Salome also opposed, was too eager as heir apparent, and so in 4 BCE—just five days before Herod died—he too was executed with the permission of Augustus. Herod then chose Herod Antipas as his heir, but Salome's influence once again was felt, and—in his final will—Herod appointed Herod Archelaus as ethnarch over Idumea, Judea, and Samaria; Herod Antipas as tetrarch over Galilee and Perea; and Herod Philip II as tetrarch over the regions north and east of the Sea of Galilee (Batanea, Trachonitis, Gaulanitis, and Auranitis). Salome was given a small toparchy around Jamnia and Azotus.

Herod ruled successfully but harshly. He remained a friend of Rome but was not popular among his Jewish subjects. The Sadducees lost power during his reign. The Pharisees opposed his many violations of the Torah. Those who had admired the Hasmoneans were dismayed by Herod's removal of that line. The common people suffered under the heavy taxation needed to finance his battles and building projects. Aware of his unpopularity, Herod ordered a large group of leading men to be killed when he died to guarantee that there would be plenty of mourning in the land. When Herod died in 4 BCE in Jericho, this order was not carried out, though there was an elaborate funeral procession to Herodion, where he was buried.

THE DIVISION OF HEROD'S KINGDOM

map 53

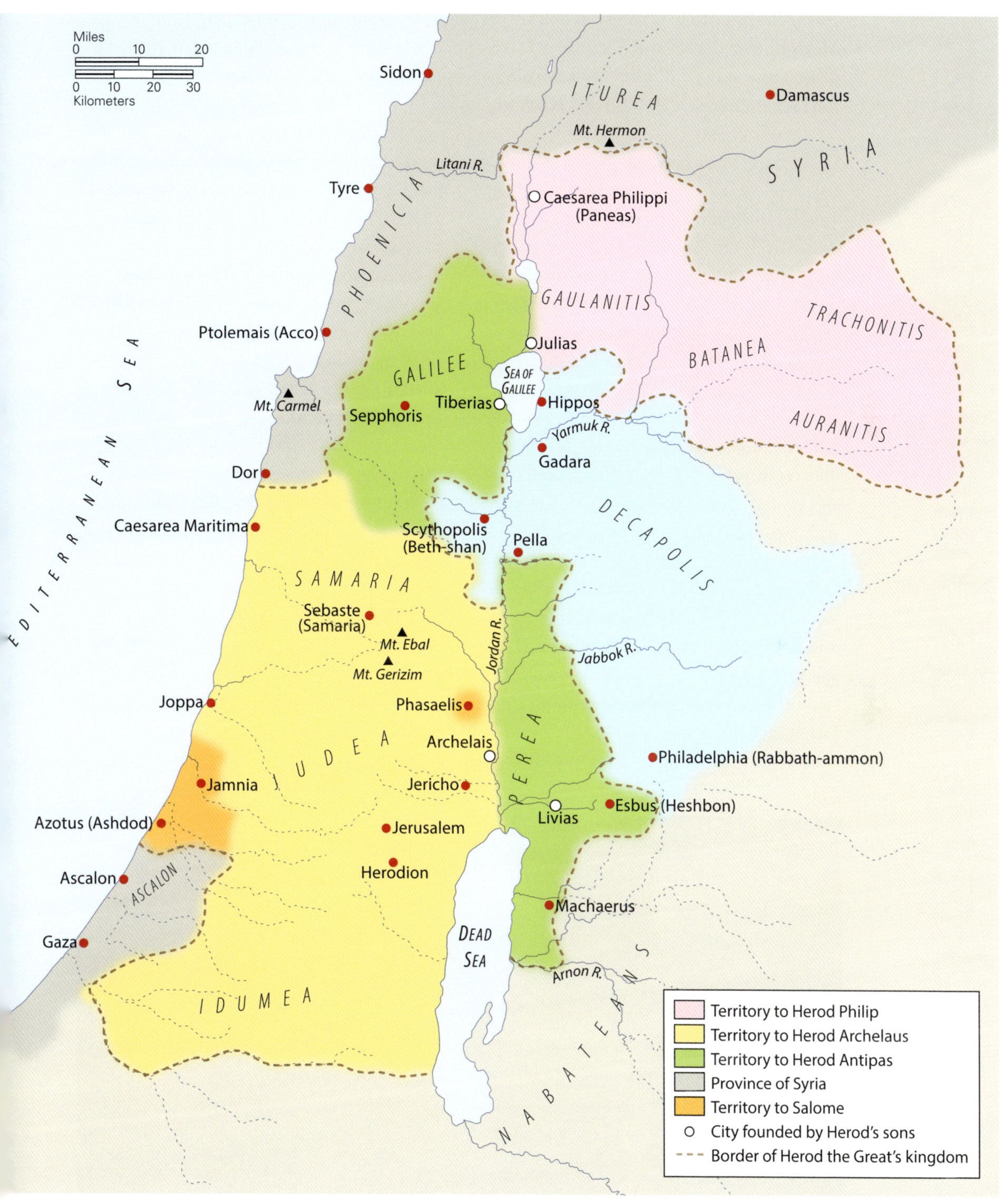

The Birth and Childhood of Jesus

Narratives about the birth of Jesus only appear in Matthew's and Luke's Gospels, although all four Gospels call Jesus the "Nazarene" and identify his hometown as Nazareth. Matthew is interested in a "theological" geography connecting Jesus as Messiah with Israel and Scripture. Luke appears to have a vague sense of the physical geography, but highlights the key role of Jerusalem and points to Jesus's birth in Bethlehem because it connects Jesus to David.

In Matthew, Mary becomes pregnant, and an angel appears to Joseph assuring him of her virginal conception and that the child is to be named Jesus, Emmanuel. This apparently takes place in Bethlehem of Judea where they lived and where Jesus was born. Wise men (magi) from the East—probably Parthia in ancient Mesopotamia—then come to Herod the Great, having seen an astronomical/astrological sign indicating that the king of the Jews was born. With the aid of Scripture, they are directed to Bethlehem and find Mary and the baby Jesus. Warned in a dream, the wise men return home via an alternative route. Joseph is similarly warned in a dream to flee with his family to Egypt to avoid Herod's wrath. No specific location in Egypt is identified, but part of Matthew's intent in telling this incident is to connect Jesus with Israel's exodus experience and to fulfill Hosea 11:1— "out of Egypt I have called my son." After Herod's death, Joseph is instructed to return the family to Israel, but upon learning that Herod Archelaus now rules Judea, he is directed to Galilee and settles in Nazareth.

Luke begins with an annunciation to Zechariah the priest in the Jerusalem Temple regarding the birth of his son, John the Baptist, by his aged wife Elizabeth. The angel Gabriel then appears to Mary in "a town in Galilee called Nazareth" (Luke 1:26) and declares she will experience a virginal conception and bear Jesus, the Son of God. Mary then journeys to "a Judean town in the hill country," a trip of about 100 miles (160km), to visit her relative Elizabeth. About three months later, Mary returned to Nazareth.

After John the Baptist's birth, Luke reports that "a decree went out from Emperor Augustus that all the world should be registered. This was the first registration and

Shepherds' Fields, Bethlehem.

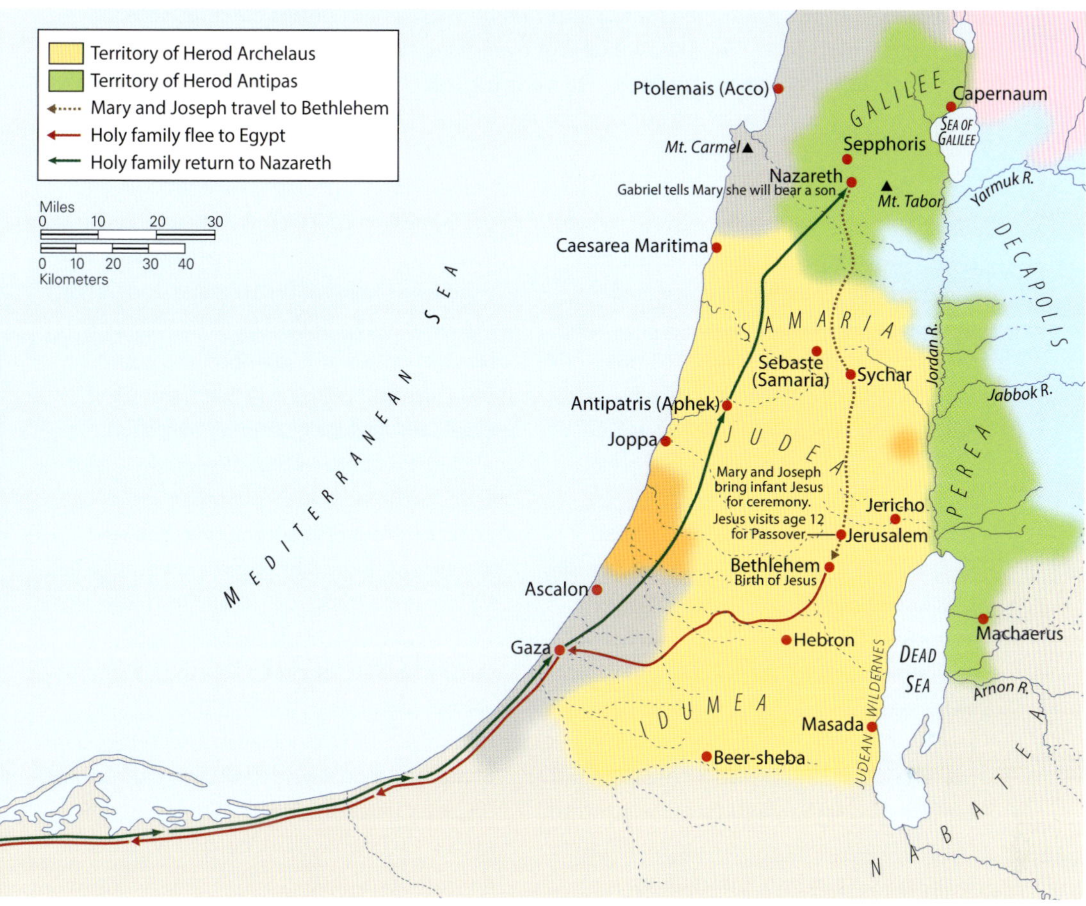

was taken while Quirinius was governor of Syria" (Luke 2:1–2). This statement reflects a typical way of setting dates in antiquity, but raises considerable problems. There is no evidence that Augustus ever conducted such a census, and the census by Quirinius occurred in 6/7 CE, yet according to Matthew, Jesus was born during the reign of Herod the Great, who died in 4 BCE. In any case, Luke uses the census as an explanation for why Joseph and Mary go to "the city of David called Bethlehem" (Luke 2:4), since Joseph belonged to the Davidic line.

After Jesus is born and the shepherds hail the event, the family apparently stays in Bethlehem until Mary's purification, which occurs forty days later according to the law of Moses. Then at the temple, Jesus is presented and acknowledged by Simeon and Anna, and the family returns to Nazareth. There is no additional information about Jesus's childhood, except for the account in Luke 2:41–51 when the family goes up to Jerusalem for Passover and the twelve-year-old Jesus stays behind to converse with the teachers in the temple.

The Beginning of Jesus's Ministry

"In the fifteenth year of the reign of Emperor Tiberius, when Pontius Pilate was governor of Judea, and Herod [Antipas] was ruler of Galilee, and his brother Philip ruler of the region of Ituraea and Trachonitis, and Lysanias ruler of Abilene, during the high priesthood of Annas and Caiaphas, the word of God came to John son of Zechariah in the wilderness. He went into all the region around the Jordan, proclaiming a baptism of repentance for the forgiveness of sins" (Luke 3:1–3)

Luke's description sets the beginning of John the Baptist's ministry at 26 or 29 CE. When Jesus was baptized at this time, Luke 3:23 states his age as about thirty years old. As Luke notes, John was in the region around the Jordan that stretches about 65 miles (105 km) from the Sea of Galilee to the Dead Sea. Mark's observation (1:5) that "the whole Judean countryside and all the people of Jerusalem" were being baptized suggests a southern site, now known as Bethany beyond the Jordan, across from Jericho. John 1:28 locates the Baptist here, but Origen in the fourth century CE did not know of such a place. Some scholars, therefore, have suggested that Bethany actually refers to the region of Batanea beyond the Jordan, to the northeast in Philip's territory. There is another baptismal site at Yardenit, near the south end of the Sea of Galilee, where the Jordan River exits, that connects to this tradition.

Matthew, Mark, and Luke report that, following his baptism, Jesus was tested by the devil in the "wilderness." Tradition locates the spot west of the Jordan in Judea—there is a Mount of Temptation just west of Jericho—but there is "wilderness" on both sides of the Jordan, and "wilderness" is also important as a concept to connect Jesus with Israel's wandering in the wilderness.

After John is arrested, Jesus begins his ministry in Galilee. (It is later reported in Matthew, Mark, and Luke that John was imprisoned by Herod Antipas and beheaded. Josephus, *Antiq.* 18.119, notes that he was killed at the Herodian fortress of Machaerus, east of the Dead Sea.) Though Jesus is consistently identified as coming from Nazareth, it appears that Capernaum eventually became his base of operation.

The Jordan River and the Sea of Galilee, known as Kinneret today, mark the eastern border of Galilee proper. The sea is mentioned in the Old Testament as the Sea of Chinnereth (Num 34:11; Deut 3:17; Josh 12:3, 13:27). Matthew, Mark, and John call it the "Sea of Galilee," but Luke uses the technically correct term *lake* and calls it the Lake of Gennesaret (5:1), associating it with the plain of that name on the northwestern shore. John 6:1 notes that the Sea of Galilee is also called the Sea of Tiberias, associating it with the most prominent city on the western shore.

The Gospels repeatedly record Jesus and the disciples going to "the other side" of the sea. This does often indicate travelling to a geographically opposite side. Since the Jordan River was the boundary between the territories ruled by Herod Antipas and Philip, however, "the other side" can simply refer to moving from one side of the Jordan to the other.

Miles
0 10 20
0 10 20 30
Kilometers
ABILENE
Sidon
ITUREA
Damascus
Mt. Hermon
Litani R.
SYRIA
Tyre
Caesarea Philippi (Paneas)
PHOENICIA
GAULANITIS
TRACHONITIS
GALILEE
Ptolemais (Acco)
Capernaum
Bethsaida (Julias)
BATANEA
Gennesaret
Sea of Galilee
Cana
Sepphoris
Tiberias
Hippos
Mt. Carmel
AURANITIS
Nazareth
Yardenit
Yarmuk R.
Mt. Tabor
Gadara
Dor
Bethany beyond the Jordan (?)
Scythopolis (Beth-shan)
Caesarea Maritima
Pella
Aenon
DECAPOLIS
SAMARIA
Salim
Sebaste (Samaria)
Jordan R.
Jabbok R.
Joppa
Phasaelis
PEREA
Archelais
Philadelphia (Rabath-ammon)
Jesus tested for 40 days
Mt. of Temptation
Possible site of Jesus' baptism
Bethany beyond the Jordan
Jamnia
Jericho
Azotus (Ashdod)
JUDEA
Livias
Esbus (Heshbon)
Jerusalem
Mt. Nebo
JUDEAN WILDERNESS
Ascalon
ASCALON
Herodion
Machaerus John imprisoned and executed
Gaza
Dead Sea
Arnon R.
IDUMEA
NABATEANS
Territory of Herod Philip
Territory of Herod Archelaus
Territory of Herod Antipas
Syria
Salome's territory
Possible route to Jesus' baptism

Jesus's Ministry in Galilee

John refers to Jesus's ministry occurring over three different Passovers. In the Synoptics, Jesus's initial ministry takes place exclusively in the northern part of Palestine, especially Galilee, and is centered around Jesus's adopted hometown of Capernaum. In John, Jesus repeatedly travels to Jerusalem for the pilgrimage festivals.

Nazareth was a small Jewish town in Jesus' time. According to Luke 4:16–30 (cf. Matt 13:54–58, Mark 6:1–6), Jesus inaugurated his ministry by speaking in the Nazareth synagogue. His message was rejected, which may explain his relocation to Capernaum.

Nain, about 5.5 miles southeast of Nazareth, was where Jesus restored the widow's son to life according to Luke 7:11–17.

Cana was the site of Jesus's first miracle according to John 2, home of Nathanael (John 21:2), and the place from which Jesus heals by his word the son of a royal official in Capernaum (John 4:46–54). There is a church commemorating Jesus's changing water into wine at Kfar Cana about four miles northwest of Nazareth, but scholarly consensus now locates the actual site as Khirbet Cana, about eight miles north of Nazareth.

Magdala is presumed to be the home of Mary Magdalene. It was known as a fish-processing center in antiquity, and recent excavations have revealed a first century CE synagogue. It is likely the place named Magadan in Matthew 15:39, and at least near the place called Dalmanutha in the parallel passage in Mark 8:10.

Gennesaret was both the name of a city and of the plain on the northwest shore of the Sea of Galilee (Lake of Gennesaret according to Luke). Jesus did many miracles here (Matt 14:34–36; Mark 6:53–56).

Tabgha is a traditional site on the northern shore of the Sea of Galilee. The Heptapegon (Seven Springs) Church there commemorates Jesus feeding the five thousand (see Matt 14:13–21; Mark 6:30–44; John 6:1–15). By the shore is another church which marks a traditional site where the resurrected Jesus appeared to the disciples, according to John 21.

The Mount of Beatitudes, a hill overlooking the Sea of Galilee between Tabgha and Capernaum, is a traditional site celebrating Jesus's Sermon on the Mount (Matt 5:3–7:27).

Capernaum was the home of Jesus's first disciples, according to Matthew, Mark, and Luke. It would not have been surprising to find a tax office to monitor the transportation of goods and a Roman outpost near the **Jordan River**, which separated Herod Antipas's and Herod Philip's territories. Matthew (Levi) the tax collector is called to follow Jesus at Capernaum, and the Roman centurion who invokes Jesus's help for his slave is identified as a contributor to the synagogue there (see Luke 7:1–10.) Jesus is reported to have stayed at Simon (Peter) and Andrew's house in Capernaum (Matt 8:14; Mark 1:29; and Luke 4:38). Excavations have revealed a house that dated back to the first century CE, with other churches built around and over it.

Chorazin was 2.5 miles inland north of Capernaum. Together with Bethsaida and Capernaum, Jesus pronounced woes on these cities because the people did not repent even though he had done so many deeds of power there (Matt 11:20–24; Luke 10:13–16).

Bethsaida was east of Galilee, located in Herod Philip's territory, and the hometown of the disciples Philip, Simon Peter, and Andrew. (Peter apparently married a woman of Capernaum and moved there with Andrew; see John 1:44; Mark 1:30.) Jesus healed many here, including a blind man

JESUS'S MINISTRY IN GALILEE AND NEARBY TERRITORIES map 56

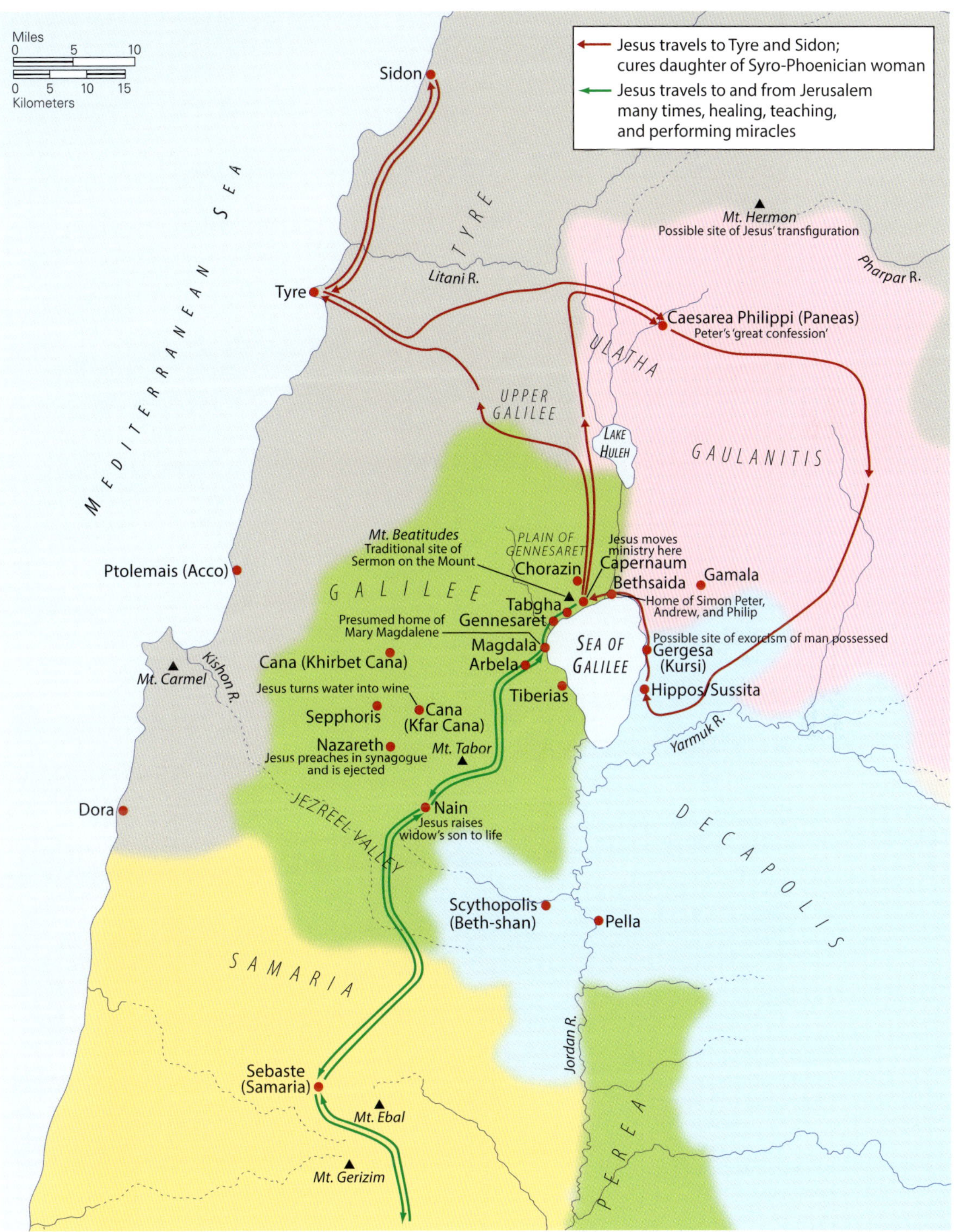

Aerial view of the excavations at Capernaum. The octagonal roof covers the structure identified as Simon and Andrew's house. The larger structure at the lower left is the 4–5th century CE synagogue built on the foundation of the probable 1st century CE synagogue.

(Mark 8:22–26). According to Luke 9:10–17, the feeding of the five thousand occurred near Bethsaida.

The Gospels recount Jesus's exorcising a man possessed by a legion of demons, casting them into swine that ran down a steep bank and drowned in the sea (see Matt 8:28–34; Mark 5:1–20; and Luke 8:26–39). Mark and Luke say this occurred in the country of the Gadarenes. Matthew says it was the Gerasenes—but the textual traditions are complicated with other names. A solution proposed in antiquity was **Gergesa**, modern Kursi, midway on the eastern shore.

Jesus made another trip outside of Galilee, north into the Gentile region of Tyre and Sidon (Matt 15:21–28; Mark 7:24–30), where he healed the daughter of the Syro-Phoenician (Canaanite) woman. Jesus made a trip to the northern portion of Herod Philip's territory, to the region around the capital city of **Caesarea Philippi** (Matt 16:13–20; Mark 8:27–30). This site had a long history as a pagan cult center, so it is perhaps significant that Peter confessed Jesus to be Messiah here.

It is also remarkable to note the prominent cities Jesus is never reported to have entered. **Sepphoris** was less than four miles north of Nazareth, and was Herod Antipas's initial capital. For a wood or stone craftsman, as Jesus was, it is likely that steady work was available there. In 20 CE, Herod Antipas founded **Tiberias** as his new capital, to replace Sepphoris. **Hippos** (**Sussita** in Aramaic) was one of the cities of the Decapolis, perched high above the Sea of Galilee on its eastern shore. Visible from almost every point around the sea, it was a city built on a hill that could not be hid (Matt 5:14). **Scythopolis**, known as Beth-shan in the Old Testament, was another large Decapolis city, about fifteen miles south of the Sea of Galilee, at the strategic juncture of the Jezreel Valley and Jordan River routes. Each of these cities had a pronounced Hellenistic and non-Jewish character, which perhaps accounts for why Jesus may have avoided them.

Jesus's Journeys to Jerusalem

"Yet today, tomorrow, and the next day I must be on my way, because it is impossible for a prophet to be killed outside of Jerusalem" (Luke 13:33).

Jerusalem was the center of both Jewish religion and economy in Jesus's day. Three times each year, Jewish men were expected to make a pilgrimage to Jerusalem to celebrate the ancient harvest festivals.

- Passover remembers the exodus; celebrated in March or April
- Shavuot, or Feast of Weeks, or Pentecost (which refers to its occurring fifty days after exodus) remembers the giving of the Torah
- Sukkoth, or Feast of Booths, commemorates the wilderness wanderings; celebrated in September or October

There was a tremendous influx of people and money into Jerusalem. Jesus, as an observant Jew, participated in the pilgrimages.

Depending on the terrain, a person could walk about 15 to 20 miles (24 to 32 km) per day. Depending on the starting point, a trip from Galilee to Jerusalem would take between three and six days. There were three possible north-south routes. The longest, and least likely, follows the Great Trunk Road through the pass at Leggio (ancient Meggido), south to Lydda, and from there east to Jerusalem. A more common route—and most direct—was to follow the Central Ridge Road directly south. The other route went down the Jordan River valley, and then up to Jerusalem from Jericho.

Luke's Gospel describes how twelve-year-old Jesus stayed behind after his family had traveled to Jerusalem to celebrate the yearly Passover (2:41–51). Once Jesus began his ministry, John's Gospel records Jesus making multiple journeys to Jerusalem. John 2:13 reports that Jesus went up to Jerusalem for Passover. During this visit, he had a conversation with Nicodemus (John 3). In John 4, Jesus leaves Jerusalem and returns north following the Central Ridge Road, which brought him to the encounter with the Samaritan woman at Sychar.

In John 5 Jesus again returns to Jerusalem for another festival during which time he heals the disabled man at the Beth-zatha (Bethesda) Pool. In chapter 6 Jesus is back in Galilee, but in chapter 7 he goes up to Jerusalem for Sukkoth. Apparently, Jesus stayed in Jerusalem for a few months, since in 10:22, he is present for the Feast of Dedication (Hanukkah). In chapter 11 he raises Lazarus in Bethany, just east of Jerusalem, and this motivates a plot to kill Jesus and causes him to retire "to a town called Ephraim in the region near the wilderness" northeast of Jerusalem (11:54). He stays there with his disciples until six days before Passover, when he returns to Bethany, where he is anointed by Mary.

In the Synoptics, Jesus's ministry is conducted in Galilee until he makes his final journey to Jerusalem. According to Luke 9:51–56, Jesus and his disciples initially headed south along the Central Ridge Road, but faced hostility when entering a Samaritan village. Luke then narrates a long travel section, apparently taking the Jordan Valley route, since in 18:35 Jesus is approaching Jericho. Matthew 19:1 and Mark 10:1 describe Jesus and his disciples going through the "region of Judea (and) beyond the Jordan," but they similarly arrive at Jericho. There Luke recounts Jesus's encounter with Zacchaeus (19:1–10), and all three report Jesus healing a blind man (Matt 9:27–31; Mark 10:46–52; Luke 18:35–43) before continuing up to Jerusalem.

JOURNEYING TO JERUSALEM

map 57

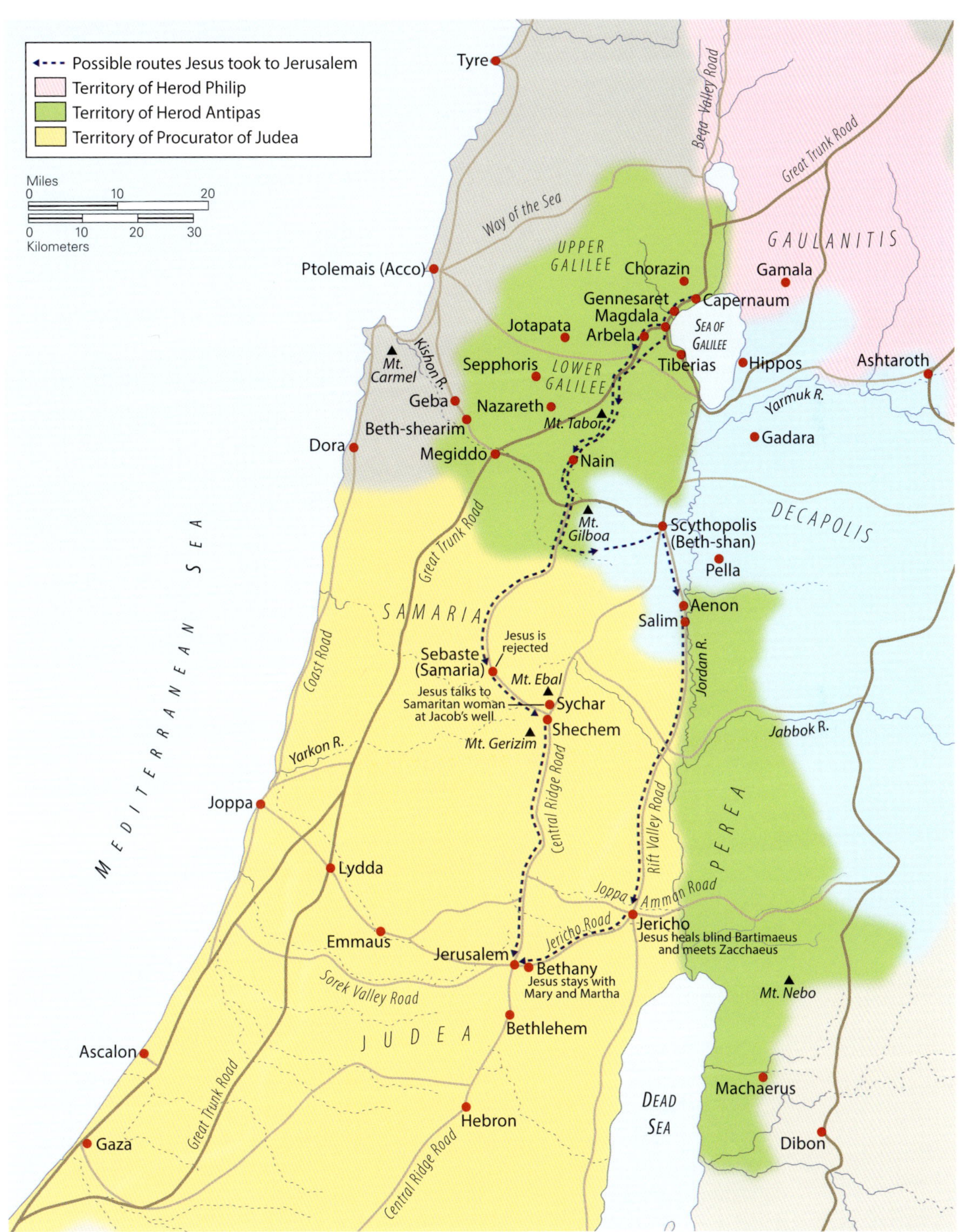

JESUS'S FINAL WEEK IN JERUSALEM

map 58

Jesus's Last Week in Jerusalem

Jesus's last week in Jerusalem can be reconstructed in broad outline, even though the Gospels provide differing details. On Sunday, coming from Bethany and nearby Bethphage, about 1.5 miles (2.4 km) east of Jerusalem, on the southeast slope of the Mount of Olives, Jesus approached Jerusalem riding on a donkey with the acclamation of the crowds.

Jesus visited the Temple Mount a number of times from Sunday to Wednesday, and at some point chased out the merchants and money-changers. He also taught publicly on the Temple Mount and privately to his disciples on the Mount of Olives. Mark and Matthew (and John?) indicate that he spent most nights in Bethany.

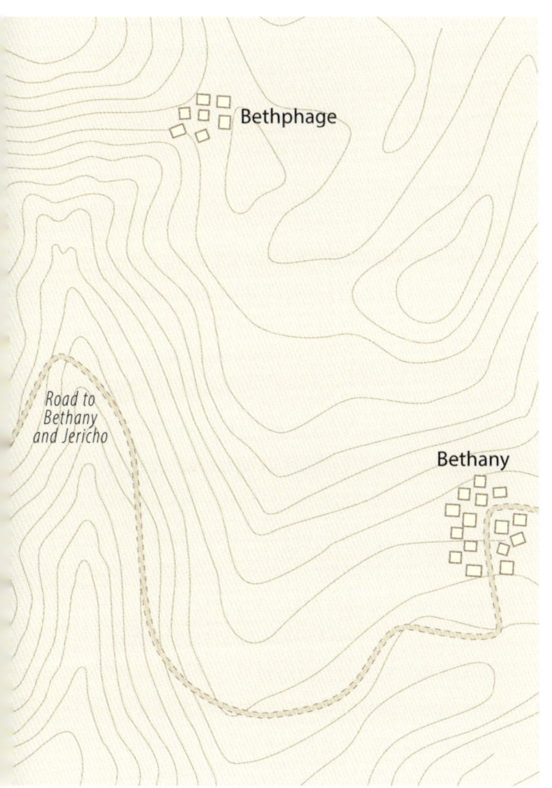

On Thursday evening Jesus ate a meal with his disciples. Tradition has located this on the western hill of the city, an area also known as Mount Zion. Afterward they went to a garden, Gethsemane, on the Mount of Olives, where Judas identified Jesus to the authorities, who arrested him. That same night, Jesus was subjected to trial before the high priest, and Peter denied Jesus three times. The location of this trial is uncertain, but tradition has located it at the Church of Saint Peter in Gallicantu, also on the western hill of the city.

Early on Friday morning Jesus was handed over to Pontius Pilate, the Roman prefect over the province of Judea, who was in Jerusalem to maintain order during the Passover festival. According to Luke 23:6–11, when Pilate discovered that Jesus was from Galilee, he tried to pass responsibility to Herod Antipas, tetrarch of Galilee, who also was in Jerusalem for Passover. Herod probably stayed at the old Hasmonean palace. When Jesus refused to cooperate, Herod sent him back to Pilate. According to John 19:13–16, Pilate presented Jesus to the crowds at the Stone Pavement (Gabbatha) just west of the city wall, at the former Herodian palace, where Jesus was rejected and handed over to be crucified.

Carrying his own crossbeam, Jesus was led outside the city walls to Golgotha, a Hebrew word meaning "Place of a Skull." This was a rocky outcrop that was part of an old quarry used in the construction of the buildings and walls of Jerusalem.

Jesus's Resurrection Appearances

Jesus died late on a Friday afternoon with just enough time before the Jewish Sabbath started that evening to allow for a quick burial. Each of the Gospel accounts record the boldness of Joseph of Arimathea in going to Pilate and requesting the body of Jesus. Crucified victims were often left on their crosses, but in this instance Pilate granted permission. Joseph wrapped Jesus's body in a linen cloth and laid it in his own unused, rock-hewn tomb. (According to John 19:39–40, Nicodemus also helped and provided the appropriate burial spices.) With this type of burial, the body would decompose, and a year later the bones would be gathered and placed in a box called an ossuary.

The traditional location of Jesus's tomb in the Church of the Holy Sepulcher has significant support for being the correct site. Golgotha was just outside the city wall at that time, in an old quarry, and there are other tombs nearby that were carved into the quarry walls (see map on p. 142). Evidence has also been found to confirm the claim made in John 19:41 that the quarry had been filled in and was being used as a garden.

It is difficult to harmonize the accounts of Jesus's resurrection appearances:

- In John 20:1–13, Mary Magdalene sees the stone rolled back from the tomb and reports it to Peter and another disciple, who run to the tomb and confirm that it is empty. After they leave, Mary looks in to the tomb and sees two angels. Turning around, she sees someone she supposes to be the gardener—until she recognizes him as Jesus when he calls her name. John 20:19–23 describes Jesus appearing to the disciples that same evening, but Thomas is absent and disbelieves their report. A week later, still in Jerusalem, Jesus appears again, and Thomas confesses Jesus to be his Lord and God. John 21 records another appearance, to seven of the disciples while they are fishing on the Sea of Galilee. Jesus prepares breakfast on the beach for them, and the Church of the Primacy of Peter, on the sea's northern shore near Tabgha, commemorates this event.
- 1 Corinthians 15:3–7 lists several appearances but does not specify where or when exactly they occurred.
- In Mark 16:1–8, the "young man" at the empty tomb tells the women to direct the disciples to Galilee, where they will see Jesus, but there is no account of that appearance.
- In Matthew 28:1–10, the angel at the tomb also tells the women to send the disciples to Galilee to see Jesus. As they leave the tomb, they encounter Jesus, who repeats the message they are to give to the disciples. In 28:16–20 the eleven disciples encounter Jesus in Galilee on "the mountain to which Jesus had directed them" where he gives them the Great Commission. It is unclear what mountain is intended.
- At the empty tomb in Luke 24:1–12, "two men in dazzling clothes" announce the resurrection of Jesus to three women who report to the disciples. Luke 24:13–35 records that "on that same day two of them were going to a village called Emmaus, about seven miles from Jerusalem" (map shows possible sites) when they encounter Jesus, who remains hidden from their perception, until he is revealed as he blesses and breaks bread that evening. When they return to share the news with the disciples in Jerusalem, they hear that Jesus has also appeared to Peter. As they are talking, Jesus appears in their midst and demonstrates his physical reality.

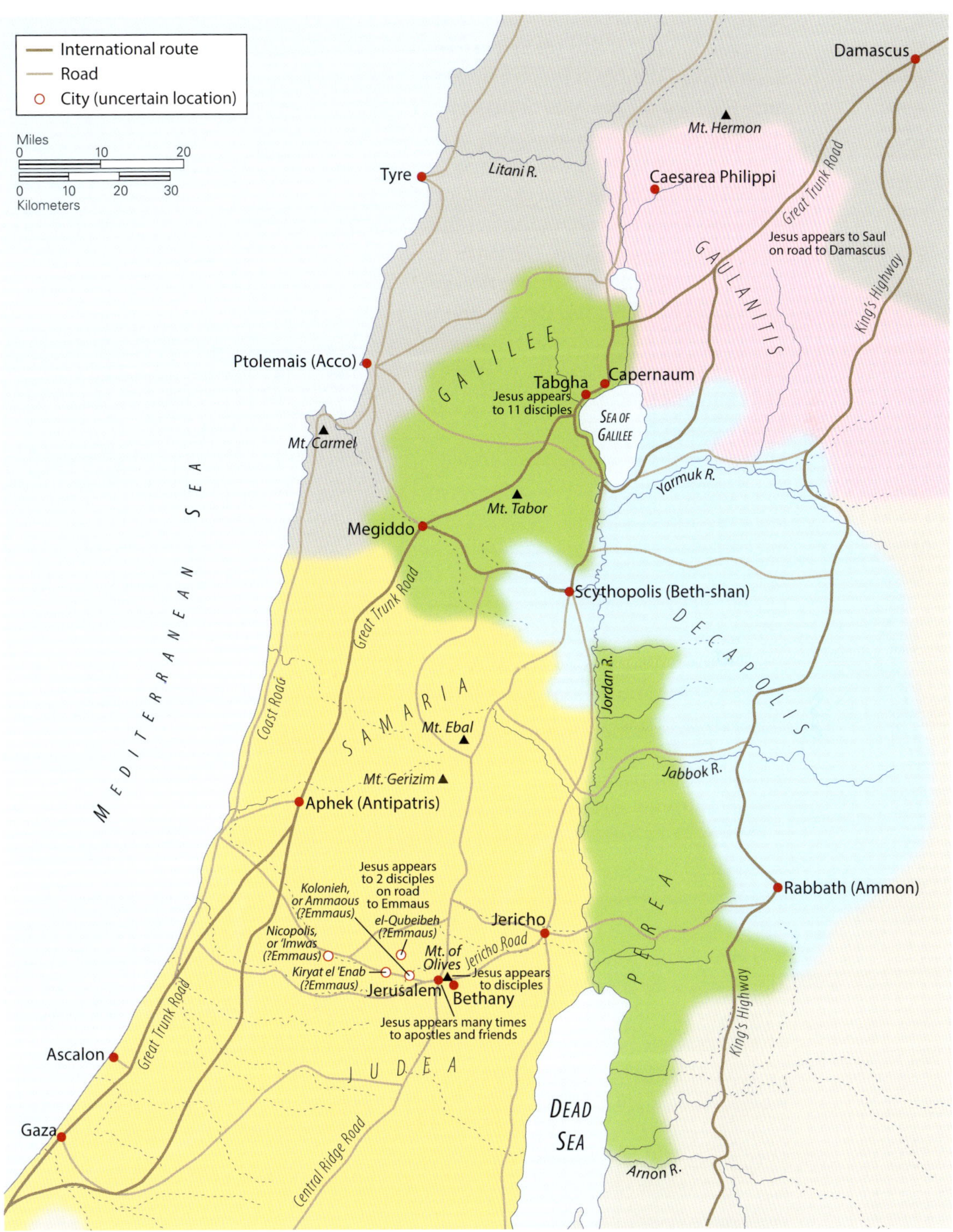

International route
Road
City (uncertain location)
Miles
0 10 20
0 10 20 30
Kilometers
Damascus
Mt. Hermon
Tyre
Litani R.
Caesarea Philippi
Great Trunk Road
Jesus appears to Saul on road to Damascus
GAULANITIS
King's Highway
GALILEE
Ptolemais (Acco)
Tabgha
Jesus appears to 11 disciples
Capernaum
SEA OF GALILEE
Mt. Carmel
MEDITERRANEAN SEA
Yarmuk R.
Mt. Tabor
Megiddo
Scythopolis (Beth-shan)
DECAPOLIS
Great Trunk Road
Coast Road
Jordan R.
SAMARIA
Mt. Ebal
Mt. Gerizim
Jabbok R.
Aphek (Antipatris)
Jesus appears to 2 disciples on road to Emmaus
Kolonieh, or Ammaous (?Emmaus)
el-Qubeibeh (?Emmaus)
Nicopolis, or 'Imwas (?Emmaus)
Kiryat el 'Enab (?Emmaus)
Jericho
Jericho Road
Mt. of Olives
Jesus appears to disciples
Jerusalem
Bethany
Jesus appears many times to apostles and friends
Rabbath (Ammon)
PEREA
King's Highway
Ascalon
Great Trunk Road
JUDEA
Gaza
Central Ridge Road
DEAD SEA
Arnon R.

The Birth of the Church

The Gospel accounts are vague about the timing of events between Jesus's resurrection and ascension. Luke 24:50–53 seems to suggest that the ascension happened on the day of his resurrection, after Jesus led the disciples to Bethany. In Acts 1:3, however, Luke reports that Jesus appeared to the group for forty days before ascending from the Mount of Olives. There are two traditional sites recounting the Ascension. The Pater Noster Church was an early pilgrimage location, but there is also the Chapel of the Ascension, which is now part of a mosque complex just to the west of that church (see map 58).

Most of the information about the earliest church comes from Acts. The disciples stayed in Jerusalem for the fifty days after Passover, until the pilgrimage Feast of Pentecost (Weeks), which attracted believers from throughout the Jewish diaspora (Acts 2:8–11). The disciples were "all together in one place" in a house when the Spirit filled them. If three thousand people were baptized that day (2:41), we should imagine this happening either at the Beth-zatha (Bethesda) Pool, northwest of the Temple Mount, or the Siloam Pool, at the southern tip of the city.

Acts 3 continues the story of the church in Jerusalem as it recounts Peter and John healing a crippled beggar at the "Beautiful Gate" of the temple. A crowd gathers in Solomon's Portico, which ran along the eastern side of the Temple Mount (Acts 3:11). Peter and John were arrested and the next day appeared before the Jewish Council (Sanhedrin) before being released with a warning. The apostles, however, continued to teach and heal in Solomon's Portico (5:12–16) and the Temple Courts itself (5:17–25). The ongoing conflict between the Christians and the Jewish authorities culminated with the stoning of Stephen (7:54–60). Tradition has located this event outside the city, at what is now known as Stephen's Gate located on the eastern wall of the Temple Mount, toward the northern end. There is a Greek Orthodox Church below the gate, at the foot of the Kidron Valley. An earlier tradition, however, locates Stephen's stoning near the Damascus Gate, beyond the northern wall.

THE DIASPORA JEWS AT PENTECOST

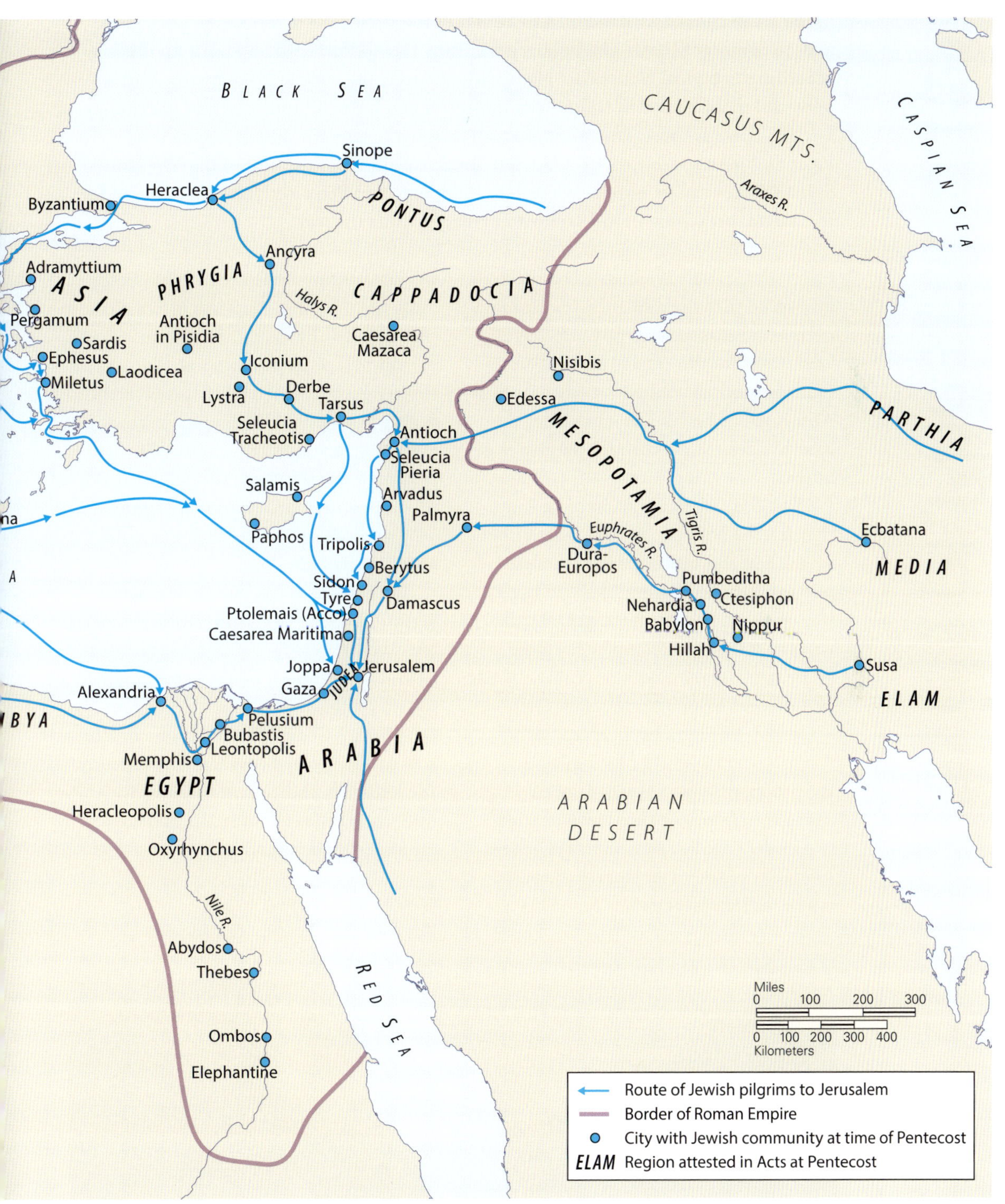

BLACK SEA
CAUCASUS MTS.
CASPIAN SEA
Araxes R.
Sinope
Heraclea
Byzantium
PONTUS
Ancyra
Adramyttium
ASIA
PHRYGIA
CAPPADOCIA
Halys R.
Pergamum
Antioch in Pisidia
Caesarea Mazaca
Sardis
Ephesus
Laodicea
Miletus
Iconium
Nisibis
Edessa
Lystra
Derbe
Tarsus
PARTHIA
Seleucia Tracheotis
Antioch
MESOPOTAMIA
Seleucia Pieria
Salamis
Arvadus
Palmyra
Paphos
Tripolis
Euphrates R.
Tigris R.
Ecbatana
Dura-Europos
MEDIA
Berytus
Sidon
Tyre
Damascus
Pumbeditha
Ctesiphon
Nehardia
Ptolemais (Acco)
Babylon
Nippur
Caesarea Maritima
Hillah
Joppa
Jerusalem
Susa
JUDEA
Alexandria
Gaza
ELAM
Pelusium
Bubastis
Leontopolis
ARABIA
Memphis
EGYPT
ARABIAN DESERT
Heracleopolis
Oxyrhynchus
Nile R.
Abydos
Thebes
RED SEA
Ombos
Elephantine
Miles
0 100 200 300
0 100 200 300 400
Kilometers
Route of Jewish pilgrims to Jerusalem
Border of Roman Empire
City with Jewish community at time of Pentecost
ELAM Region attested in Acts at Pentecost

The Early Travels of Philip and Peter

The martyrdom of Stephen (Acts 7) results in the scattering of all the Christians "except the apostles" throughout the areas of Judea and Samaria (Acts 8:1). Philip, one of the seven chosen with Stephen to attend to the Hellenists in Jerusalem (Acts 6:5), goes to Samaria Sebaste and begins preaching. Herod the Great had built up this city according to typical Hellenistic plans with an imposing temple to Augustus. Philip's powerful message and healings even impress a magician, Simon, who had previously awed the people there. Due to Philip's success, the Jerusalem church dispatches Peter and John to confirm his work and disabuse Simon of the notion that the Holy Spirit's power can be purchased. Acts 8:25 reports that Peter and John then return to Jerusalem, preaching in the Samaritan villages along the way.

Philip subsequently is motivated by an angelic message to go to the wilderness road leading from Jerusalem southwest to Gaza. There, he explains Scripture to and baptizes the Ethiopian eunuch. Philip is snatched away to Azotus and makes his way north along the coast to Caesarea, proclaiming the gospel as he goes.

Saul (Paul) enters the drama of the early church at this point (see the next chapter), but we also hear about Peter healing a paralyzed man in Lydda and reviving Tabitha in Joppa (Acts 9:32–43). This sets the stage for Luke's narrative of the expanding influence of the gospel, which now includes the gentiles. In Acts 10, Cornelius, a God-fearing Gentile centurion in Caesarea Maritima, has an angelic vision that causes him to send for Peter in Joppa. Peter, meanwhile, has a vision of unclean animals being declared clean and is directed to go with Cornelius's messengers to Caesarea. After Peter proclaims the gospel to them, they receive the Holy Spirit and are baptized. Peter will subsequently need to defend this Gentile mission to the Jewish Christians in Jerusalem (Acts 11:1–18). By 44 CE, the Christian movement is perceived as a threat, which causes Herod Agrippa I, whom Rome had established as king over Judea, to kill the disciple James. Herod also imprisons Peter in Jerusalem, but Peter miraculously is delivered (Acts 12:1–19). After Herod goes to Caesarea, Luke reports of his untimely and painful death due to his impiety (Acts 12:20–23).

Prior to this event, Luke notes that the persecution that began with Stephen had caused believers to travel as far as Phoenicia, Cyprus, and Antioch (see Map 62). Antioch was one of the important centers of early Christianity, where both Torah-observant Jews and Hellenized Jews were converted. The Jerusalem church sent Barnabas to Antioch to assess the situation, and he confirmed their faithfulness.

Theater at Caesarea Maritima.

THE EARLY TRAVELS OF PHILIP AND PETER

map 61

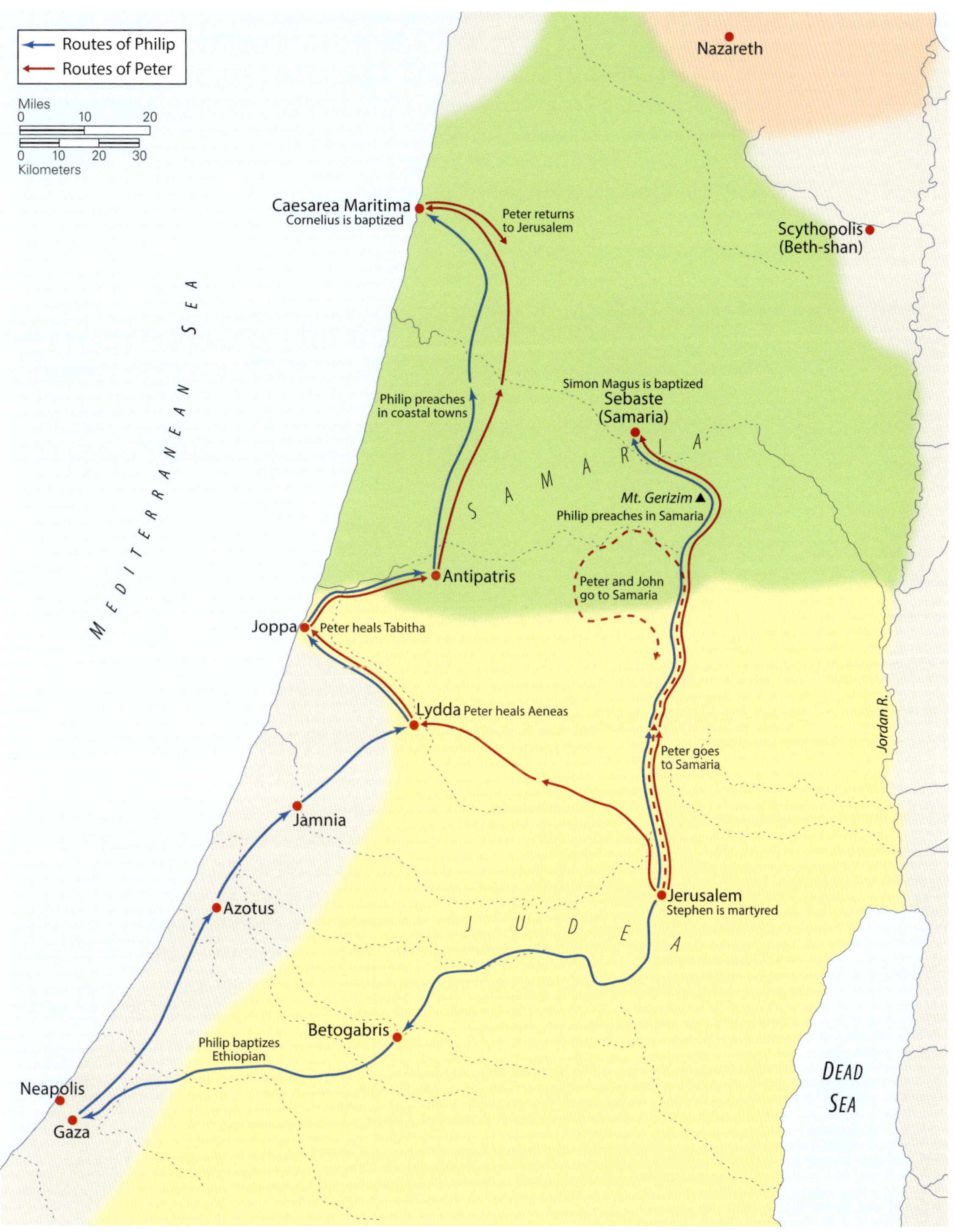

The Calling of Paul

Saul, who will be named Paul in Acts 13:9, was an observant Jew and Roman citizen from Tarsus in Asia Minor. He is first mentioned in Acts 7:58 as present at, and approving of, the stoning of Stephen. As Philip and Peter are active in Judea and Samaria (Acts 8:4–40; see p. 148), Saul begins persecuting the Christians in those areas. Saul is mentioned again in Acts 9 as he goes to Damascus to persecute the Christians. He is blinded as he encounters Jesus in a heavenly vision of light, an event occurring sometime around 35 CE. After recovering his sight at the hand of Ananias, Saul begins preaching that Jesus is the Messiah in Damascus and the surrounding area of Arabia until his life is threatened.

Saul escapes Damascus (Acts 9:23–25; 2 Cor 11:32–33) and goes to Jerusalem, but is not welcomed by the church there until Barnabas vouches for him. Non-Christian, Hellenized Jews in Jerusalem oppose Saul and once again threaten his life, so he goes to Caesarea Maritima and on to Tarsus, where he preaches in the regions of Cilicia and Syria for many years (Gal 1:21–2:1).

Chapters 10 and 11 of Acts describe the rise of Gentile Christianity (see previous chapter), and 11:19–26 notes the growth of the church in Antioch, which included a significant number of Hellenized Jews. Barnabas is sent from Jerusalem to confirm the ministry. To further the work there, Barnabas goes to Tarsus and brings Saul back to Antioch, where together they work for a year, sometime around the mid-40s CE. In response to a famine, Barnabas and Saul bring an offering to the believers in Judea (Acts 11:27–30) and later return from Jerusalem to Antioch, bringing John Mark along with them (Acts 12:25).

At this point in the early church's growth, Jerusalem is the center for a traditional Jewish Christianity, while Antioch has become the base for a more mixed group of Jews, Hellenized Jews, and gentiles worshiping and eating together. The ongoing conversion of gentiles in Antioch and in Asia Minor (see Barnabas and Paul's missionary journey, pp. 152–53) became a critical problem for some Jewish Christians, who insisted that gentiles must first convert to Judaism—in particular, the men must be circumcised—before they could be assured of salvation through the Jewish Messiah, Jesus.

Paul and Barnabas, along with Judas Barsabbas and Silas, are appointed by the Antioch church to go to Jerusalem to discuss the issue with the apostles and elders there. The issue is addressed directly at the council in Jerusalem, which occurs around 49 CE, and is described in Acts 15. Peter reports his experience with Gentile believers, and asserts that all are "saved through the grace of the Lord Jesus" (Acts 15:11), a claim that is confirmed by the report of Barnabas and Paul. The decision by James, the brother of Jesus, is that gentiles are saved as gentiles, but that they should abstain from fornication and observe food laws that would prohibit Jewish Christians from sharing table fellowship with them. The delegates return to Antioch with a letter confirming this decision, and continue to minister there.

THE CALLING OF PAUL AND HIS EARLY TRAVELS

map 62

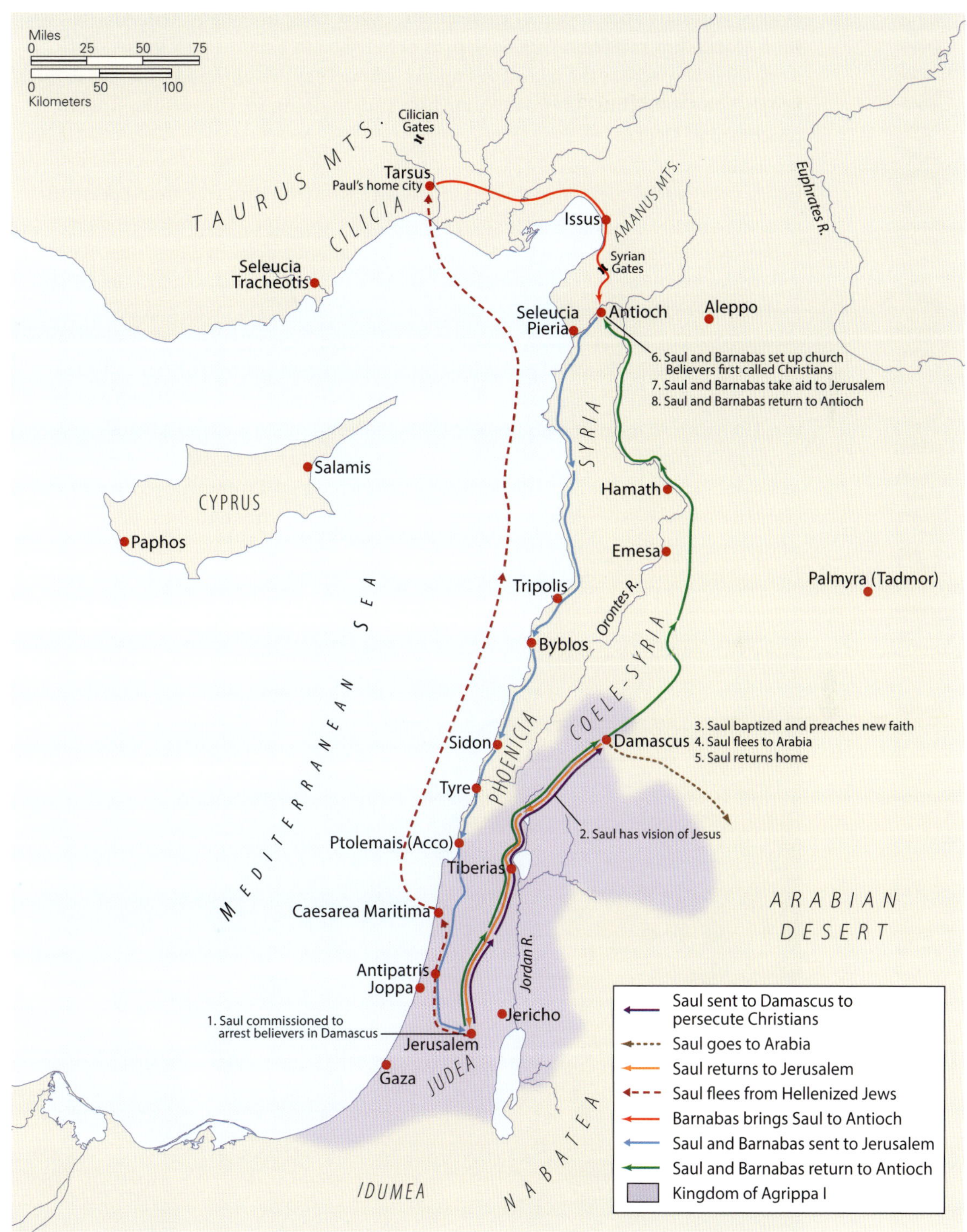

Paul's First Missionary Journey

The church in Antioch in Syria was an important center of early Christianity and commissioned evangelism efforts. In Acts 13:1–3, around 48 CE, as directed by the Holy Spirit, Barnabas and Saul (henceforth called Paul) are appointed. Assisted by John Mark, they sail from Antioch's port of Seleucia to Salamis on Cyprus. They work their way across the island to Paphos, where they are opposed by a Jewish false prophet and magician. They overcome him and, in doing so, convert the Roman proconsul of Cyprus.

Sailing from Paphos, they arrive at Perga in Pamphylia, on the southern coast of modern Turkey (Acts 13:13). John Mark leaves them and returns to Jerusalem, but Barnabas and Paul journey to Antioch in Pisidia. As will become a pattern, they attend a synagogue service on a Sabbath when Paul makes a persuasive presentation of the gospel of Jesus based in Jewish Scripture and history, and the message is well-received. Jews who are not persuaded, however, raise an alarm, but that causes the message to be extended to gentiles who receive it gladly. Facing persecution, Paul and Barnabas move eastward, following an ancient road that runs from Ephesus to Antioch in Syria, and arrive at Iconium. Here also, after staying a long time, they get a mixed reception, and to avoid being stoned, they flee to Lystra and Derbe, cities of Lycaonia (Acts 14:1–7).

Paul heals a paralyzed man in Lystra, but this causes the locals to hail Barnabas as Zeus and Paul as Hermes his messenger and to try to offer sacrifices to them. It gives them occasion for preaching to these gentiles. However, Jews from Antioch and Iconium

Part of the remains of the Graeco-Roman city of Perga.

THE FIRST MISSIONARY JOURNEY OF BARNABAS AND PAUL map 63

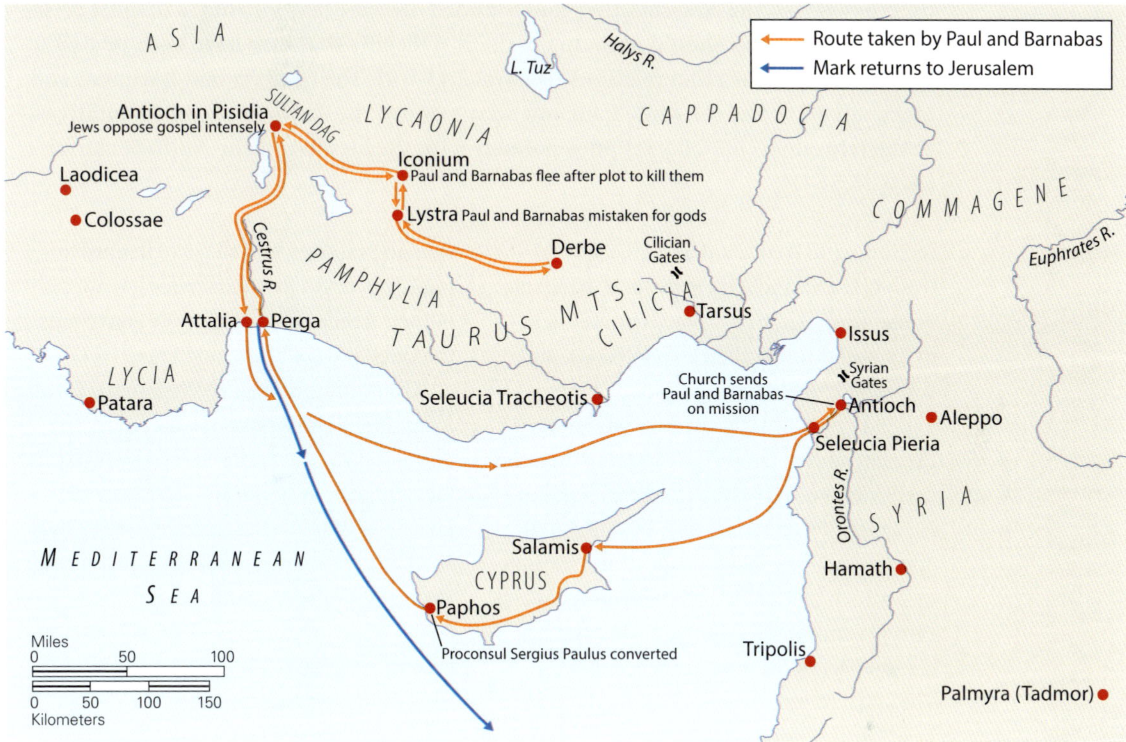

come to Lystra, incite the crowds to the point that Paul is stoned, dragged outside the city, and left for dead. When the believers gather around him, he gets up and goes on to Derbe with Barnabas (Acts 14:8–20).

Acts 14:21 reports that Paul and Barnabas made many disciples in Derbe, and that they then retraced their steps through Lystra, Iconium, and Antioch. They encouraged the believers along the way, and appointed elders in each church. Continuing on, they returned to Perga to preach, and then went to the nearby port town of Attalia. From there they sailed back to Antioch in Syria and reported to the church how God "had opened a door of faith for the Gentiles" (Acts 14:21–27).

Paul and Barnabas remain in Antioch "for some time" (Acts 14:28), but the success of the mission to the gentiles precipitates the need for the Jerusalem church to resolve how gentiles fit within a Jewish understanding of salvation based on faith in Jesus as the Messiah. The result, as described on p. 150, was a council in Jerusalem (Acts 15).

Paul's Second Missionary Journey

The settlement at the Jerusalem council (Acts 15) regarding the inclusion of Gentile believers as gentiles does not solve every problem. When Paul proposes to Barnabas that they revisit the churches they had founded on their first journey, a dispute arises whether John Mark should accompany them, a dispute that may have been related to Jewish-Gentile Christian relations (see Gal 2:11–14). The result is that Barnabas and Mark sail off to Cyprus while Paul and Silas—one of the Antiochene representatives to the Jerusalem council—set off separately with the blessing of the Antioch church (Acts 15:36–41).

According to Acts, Paul and Silas go through Syria and Cilicia by land, likely via a road from Antioch to Paul's hometown of Tarsus, through the Cilician Gates, and from there to Derbe and Lystra, cities that Paul had previously visited. While there, they encounter Timothy, who joins them on their mission (Acts 16:1–5). Paul's itinerary is vaguely described in Acts 16:6–8, but it appears that they head north from Iconium or Antioch in Pisidia into the regions of Phrygia and Galatia, not west into the central part of the area known as Asia. The spirit of Jesus does not allow them to head further north into Bithynia, so they apparently travel along the northern edge of Mysia until they arrive at Troas on the Aegean Sea coastline.

In Troas, Paul experiences the vision of a "man of Macedonia" pleading for him to come to Macedonia (Acts 16:9–10). Following typical coastal routes, they sail to Samothrace and on to Neapolis the next day. They then walk the Via Egnatia to Philippi, a leading city and Roman colony. Apparently, there were not enough Jews to have their own synagogue, so Paul and his companions go outside the city gate to a likely place of prayer near the river. There they meet Lydia, a "God-fearer" and dealer in purple cloth from Thyatira, who converts and with her household is baptized and supports Paul's work in Philippi. While there, Paul expels a spirit of divination from a slave-girl. Her owners charge Paul and Silas with anti-Roman practices, and they are flogged and imprisoned. An earthquake results not only in their freedom but also in the conversion of the jailer and his household (Acts 16:11–40).

Continuing along the Via Egnatia through Amphipolis and Apollonia, they arrive in Thessalonica, where there was a synagogue. Like the pattern in his first missionary journey, Paul preaches, converts some Jews and God-fearing Greeks, but then arouses a violent response from Jews, who attack Jason, owner of the house where Paul and Silas had been staying (Acts 17:1–9). Fleeing west to Beroea, they are welcomed in the synagogue there, until some Thessalonian Jews come and incite trouble. Silas and Timothy remain in Beroea, but Paul is escorted to the Aegean coast and sails to Athens (Acts 17:10–15).

In Athens, Paul testifies in the synagogue with Jews and God-fearers and in the marketplace (agora), which he finds filled with idols. His teaching leads to an opportunity to speak with the philosophers at the Areopagus, a prominent hill overlooking the marketplace and near the entrance to the Acropolis (Acts 17:16–34).

From Athens, Paul moves on to Corinth, where he stays with a Jewish couple, Aquila and Priscilla, and works with them as tentmakers. Paul preaches in the synagogue to Jews and God-fearers, but again he ends up being rejected by many of the Jews and begins to focus on the gentiles. Paul experiences significant success in Corinth, spending a year and a half there. The Jewish

PAUL'S SECOND MISSIONARY JOURNEY map 64

authorities bring Paul before the proconsul of Achaia, Gallio, and charge him with trying to persuade people to worship God contrary to the law. But Gallio dismisses the charge as a mere religious matter (Acts 18:1–17).

When Paul decides to leave, Priscilla and Aquila accompany him. Departing from Cenchreae, Corinth's port on the Aegean, they sail to Ephesus. Paul stays briefly and promises to return and then sails on to Caesarea. He continues to Jerusalem for a short visit, before returning to Antioch (Acts 18:18–22).

Paul's Third Missionary Journey

Paul's third missionary journey begins from Antioch, but he goes on his own and perhaps without the church's blessing (see Acts 18:23). He follows the initial land route of his second journey, again visiting the churches he had founded in Galatia and Phrygia. Paul's goal, however, is Ephesus. As he is on his way to Ephesus, Acts 18:24–28 reports that Priscilla and Aquila (the couple Paul had met in Corinth) are ministering in Ephesus along with the tutor Apollos, a native of Alexandria. Apollos will move on to Corinth and become a prominent figure in the church there (see 1 Cor 1:12; 3:4–6, 22; 16:12).

When Paul arrived in Ephesus, he started preaching in the synagogue until Jewish opposition grew, when he opened his ministry to both Jews and gentiles. Paul stayed more than two years in Ephesus, performed miracles, greatly expanded the Christian presence, and wrote some of his letters from here. As he began to make plans to visit his congregations in Macedonia and Achaia and return to Jerusalem, the success of the Christian movement alarmed the silversmiths and others involved in the worship of Artemis at the renowned temple in Ephesus. A near-riot erupted in the theater (Acts 19:23–41). Paul subsequently left and went through Macedonia (probably at least visiting Philippi, Thessalonica, and Beroea), apparently to Illyricum (according to Rom 15:19); perhaps following the Via Egnatia from Beroea and even sailing from Dyrrachium on the Adriatic Sea, and to Achaia (presumably Corinth) where he stayed for three months (Acts 20:1–3).

A plot was made against Paul's life as he was planning to return to Syria with the offering he had gathered for the Jerusalem church, so instead of sailing directly to Troas, he and his companions traveled north to Philippi and sailed from Neapolis to Troas. During the week's stay in Troas, a sleepy Eutychus fell out a window three stories to the ground, but was revived by Paul. From Troas, his companions sailed to Assos, while Paul walked the two-day journey there. From Assos they followed coastal sailing routes to Mitylene, past Chios, to Samos, and then to Miletus. Paul summoned the Ephesian elders to Miletus where he exhorted, encouraged, and bid farewell to them (Acts 20:17–38).

Sailing on, they went to Cos, Rhodes, Patara, past Cyprus, to Tyre for a short stay, and to Ptolemais, before arriving at Caesarea. After again being warned about the dangers ahead for him, Paul and his companions continued to Jerusalem.

It is not clear that the Jerusalem church accepted Paul's offering, since there were reports that his mission had taught Jewish Christians to abandon their Jewish piety. To assure them of his adherence to his Jewish identity, he agreed to sponsor a Jewish purification ritual for himself and four others (Acts 21:17–26). Non-Christian Jews from Asia who were in Jerusalem accused Paul of bringing gentiles into the temple and tried to kill him. Saved by the Roman cohort in the nearby Antonia Fortress, he made his defense to the crowd, who listened to his story until he reported of his commission to the gentiles. Because of his Roman citizenship, he avoided being flogged and was given a chance the next day to defend himself before the Jewish council (Sanhedrin). The Romans again had to rescue him. When it was discovered that there was a plot against his life, the Roman tribune sent him by night to Antipatris, and from there to Caesarea, where the governor Felix resided. Paul would remain in prison there for more than two years (Acts 24:27).

PAUL'S THIRD MISSIONARY JOURNEY

map 65

Paul's Voyage to Rome

During the years Paul was imprisoned at Caesarea, he had numerous opportunities to defend himself before religious and political leaders. Ultimately, because of his Roman citizenship, Paul appealed to the emperor's tribunal (Acts 25:6–12) in Rome. Acts 27:1–28:16 recounts Paul's long and dangerous journey to Rome under a centurion's guard.

Sailing north from the Caesarea harbor on a merchant ship, they stopped at Sidon before continuing along the southern coast of Asia, north of Cyprus, arriving in Myra in Lycia. Transferring to a grain ship from Alexandria bound for Italy, they sailed to Fair Havens on the island of Crete. Acts 27:9 reports that the Day of Atonement, a festival occurring in late September or October, had already passed. Mediterranean Sea travel was regarded as dangerous after mid-September, and Paul warned against going further. The ship's owner and pilot, however, wanted to make it to Phoenix, a safer winter harbor further west on Crete.

A break in the weather did not last, and a hurricane-force northeasterly wind drove them off-course and in jeopardy of running aground on the shallows off the North African coast. Paul's insistence that everyone stay onboard and encouragement that no lives would be lost proved accurate when the ship went aground on the island of Malta (Acts 28:1). After spending the winter there, they boarded another Alexandrian ship bound for Rome, making stops at Syracuse on Sicily, Rhegium, and then the Roman port of Puteoli. Luke reports that Christians from Rome came to accompany Paul at stops on the Appian Way. When he finally reached Rome, Paul was placed under house arrest (Acts 28:13–16).

As he had on previous mission stops, Paul preached to a Jewish audience with mixed results that ultimately confirmed the validity and viability of the Gentile mission. Acts 28:30 indicates that Paul spent two years in Rome openly preaching, but does not say anything further about Paul. According to some traditions, Paul was released and did accomplish his goal of going to the "ends of the earth," making it to Spain before being

The Forum, Rome.

PAUL'S VOYAGE TO ROME map 66

arrested and returned to Rome again (Rom 15:24, 28). There is better evidence to believe that Paul was executed by beheading under the Neronian persecution of Christians around 62 CE or within a few years thereafter and buried outside Rome on the Via Ostiensis. Peter is supposed to have been crucified in Rome around the same time and buried in St. Peter's Basilica in the Vatican.

Only reckoning the four journeys described in Acts, Paul travelled more than ten thousand miles. Travel was expensive and perilous. In addition to all his other hardships, Paul mentions danger from rivers and robbers in cities, in the wilderness, and at sea. The shipwreck that occurred during the journey to Rome was just one of three times this happened to him (2 Cor 11:21–29). Paul's enduring influence is not only because he founded Christian communities, but also because of the letters he wrote that provided encouragement and guidance, some of which were written from prison, either while he was in Ephesus on his third journey, in Caesarea after his arrest in Jerusalem, or in Rome just before his martyrdom.

The Jewish Revolt

Judaism during the time of the Herodian Temple was represented by various groups divided by religious, political, ethnic, regional, and economic differences. The emerging group that confessed Jesus as Messiah further complicated matters. For most Jews, except for the Herodians and some of the elites, a unifying factor was their opposition to Roman imperial power.

Jews were outraged that Emperor Caligula had attempted to set a statue of himself in the temple in 40 CE. The heavy burden of taxation and other indignities Jews suffered came to a head in 66 in Caesarea Maritima, when gentiles conducted a mock sacrifice in front of the synagogue. Many Jews revolted, and the Roman procurator, Gessius Florus, worsened the situation by ordering further persecution. The result was a full-scale rebellion in Jerusalem. The rebels eventually won, but this also marked the beginning of strife among competing rebel groups that would continue throughout the war.

By now there was open violence between Jews and gentiles throughout the region. The disturbance caused the Syrian governor, Cestius Gallus, who oversaw the whole region, to lead Roman forces south from Antioch. Cestius's forces proceeded to Jerusalem and were on the verge of overtaking the city before inexplicably retreating to their camp at Antipatris. As they retreated, they suffered a devastating defeat at the Beth-horon pass, which emboldened the rebels and panicked Rome.

Through the fall of 66 into the spring of 67, the Jewish rebels organized, fought, and gained control of much of the country. Emperor Nero responded by sending Vespasian, a seasoned general, along with his son, Titus, to quell the resistance. Vespasian's forces arrived in May and headquartered at Ptolemais. Working their way through Galilee, Sepphoris again surrendered. After a lengthy siege, Jotapata was crushed, and the rebel commander Josephus, who later wrote a history of the war, surrendered. The Jews at Gamala had initial success before being destroyed. By the end of the year, all of Galilee and northern Samaria was under Roman control.

In the spring of 68 CE, Vespasian, now based in Caesarea Maritima, decided to cut off Jerusalem from the east. All Perea except for Machaerus were quickly conquered in the Transjordan. The western plains of Judea and Samaria fell, and after that the western side of the Jordan Valley, including the Essene community at Qumran, ultimately resulting in the capitulation of Jericho.

In the spring of 69, Vespasian resumed the attack, and by the summer, the Jewish rebels held only Jerusalem and the fortresses at Herodium, Masada, and Machaerus. In July 69, Vespasian was proclaimed emperor, and he handed responsibility over to his son Titus. In the spring of 70, Roman legions approached Jerusalem from Emmaus on the west, from Samarian Gophna on the north, and from Jericho on the east. By May, they had broken through the two outer walls of northern Jerusalem. In August, the Temple Mount was breached, and the temple was burned down. The rest of the city was captured and destroyed soon after.

In 71, Herodium was conquered, and in 72, the Jews at Machaerus surrendered. Only Masada was left. In 73, after a prolonged siege, Josephus reports that the 960 zealots there committed suicide rather than be killed or enslaved by the Romans. The war was over, and Jerusalem was in ruins.

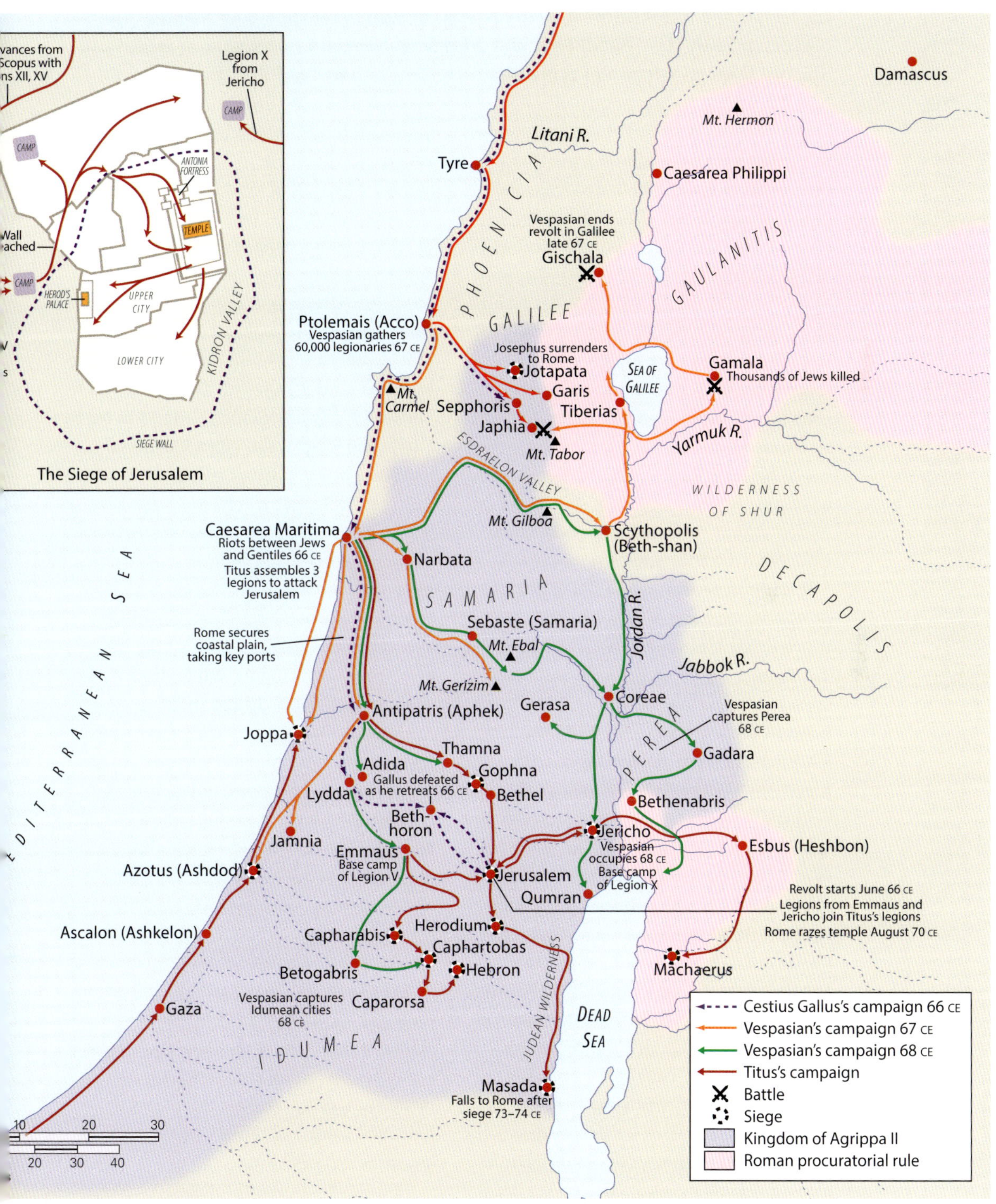
The Siege of Jerusalem
Legion X from Jericho
CAMP
ANTONIA FORTRESS
TEMPLE
HEROD'S PALACE
UPPER CITY
LOWER CITY
KIDRON VALLEY
SIEGE WALL
Damascus
Mt. Hermon
Litani R.
Tyre
PHOENICIA
Caesarea Philippi
Vespasian ends revolt in Galilee late 67 CE
Gischala
GAULANITIS
GALILEE
Ptolemais (Acco)
Vespasian gathers 60,000 legionaries 67 CE
Josephus surrenders to Rome
Jotapata
Garis
Sea of Galilee
Gamala
Thousands of Jews killed
Mt. Carmel
Sepphoris
Tiberias
Japhia
Mt. Tabor
Yarmuk R.
Esdraelon Valley
Wilderness of Shur
Mt. Gilboa
Scythopolis (Beth-shan)
Caesarea Maritima
Riots between Jews and Gentiles 66 CE
Titus assembles 3 legions to attack Jerusalem
Narbata
Samaria
Decapolis
Sebaste (Samaria)
Mt. Ebal
Jordan R.
Rome secures coastal plain, taking key ports
Jabbok R.
Mt. Gerizim
Coreae
Mediterranean Sea
Antipatris (Aphek)
Gerasa
Vespasian captures Perea 68 CE
Joppa
Perea
Thamna
Gadara
Adida
Gophna
Gallus defeated as he retreats 66 CE
Lydda
Bethel
Bethenabris
Beth-horon
Jericho
Jamnia
Vespasian occupies 68 CE
Esbus (Heshbon)
Emmaus
Base camp of Legion V
Azotus (Ashdod)
Jerusalem
Base camp of Legion X
Qumran
Revolt starts June 66 CE
Legions from Emmaus and Jericho join Titus's legions
Rome razes temple August 70 CE
Herodium
Ascalon (Ashkelon)
Capharabis
Caphartobas
Hebron
Machaerus
Betogabris
Judean Wilderness
Gaza
Vespasian captures Idumean cities 68 CE
Caparorsa
Dead Sea
Idumea
Masada
Falls to Rome after siege 73–74 CE
Cestius Gallus's campaign 66 CE
Vespasian's campaign 67 CE
Vespasian's campaign 68 CE
Titus's campaign
Battle
Siege
Kingdom of Agrippa II
Roman procuratorial rule
10 20 30
20 30 40

Judaism and Christianity after 70 CE

Over twenty thousand residents lived in Jerusalem before the war, but after 70 CE the city was in ruins, occupied by the Roman Tenth Legion. With the destruction of the temple and its sacrifices and rituals, Jews needed to redefine their identity. The Essenes, priestly class, Sadducees, and other Jerusalem elites were gone or irrelevant. The two main Jewish groups remaining were the Pharisees and the Christians.

During the early turmoil of the Jewish rebels in Jerusalem in 67, tradition reports that the Christian leadership fled to Pella, a city of the Decapolis east of the Jordan River. Jewish Christians acknowledged greater allegiance to Jesus than to the temple, so the temple's destruction was not devastating and even confirmed Christian beliefs. Christianity expanded rapidly in the Roman Empire beyond Jerusalem to new Christian centers in Antioch on the Orontes, Ephesus, Rome, and Alexandria.

As for Jews, Rabbi Yochanan ben Zakkai, a Pharisee, escaped Jerusalem shortly before its destruction, relocated at Jamnia (Yavne), established a school, and convened the Sanhedrin there. This marks the beginning of what would become rabbinic Judaism which defined Jewish identity in terms of Torah observance, piety, liturgy, and calendar apart from the temple. Tradition also locates here one of the turning-points in Jewish-Christian relations. The primary Jewish prayer, the eighteen benedictions, called "The Amidah," added a curse against apostates and specifically the Naziarim (i.e., the followers of Jesus the Nazarene). This curse made it impossible for Jewish Christians to remain in the synagogues, a situation envisioned in the Gospel of John. In addition to Jamnia and the longstanding community in Babylon, other cities that would become important in post-70 Judaism include Usha, Sepphoris, Beit-She'arim, and Tiberias.

Jews regarded Christianity as heretical, while Rome considered it a dangerous superstition that threatened the social order. Non-Christian Jews also continued to be oppressed in the Roman Empire, resulting in various Jewish uprisings in Egypt, Cyrenica, and at Lydda during the reigns of Trajan and Hadrian. Hadrian, as part of his program of Hellenization, banned castration, which apparently included circumcision. When he visited Jerusalem in 130, he announced plans to rebuild Jerusalem as a Roman city renamed Aelia Capitolina, with a new temple to Jupiter where the Jewish Temple had stood. The Jewish revolt began in 132 and was led by Simon ben Kosiba, also given the messianic name Bar Kokhba, meaning "son of the star," by Rabbi Akiva (see Num 24:17). The Jews had some remarkable initial successes that allowed them to claim control of the land for a time, and it took six Roman legions to finally overcome the rebellion. Bar Kokhba, later renamed "bar Kozeva" meaning "son of a lie," ended up being starved to death in the last stronghold at Beth-ther (Beitar).

Roman tolerance for Jews was exhausted. Jews were banned from Jerusalem except for Tisha B'Av, a day of fasting and mourning in July/August, which recalls the destruction of both the First and Second Temple. The Temple of Jupiter was built where the Jewish Temple had stood. Since Christians were regarded as a Jewish sect, they also were prohibited from Jerusalem, and a Temple of Venus was built on a site apparently venerated by Christians as the site of the crucifixion and tomb of Jesus. Today this is the site of the Church of the Holy Sepulcher. To further eradicate the Jewish memory, Hadrian removed the designations of Judea and Israel, and the land was henceforth known as Syria Palestina.

JUDAISM AND CHRISTIANITY AFTER 70 CE

map 68

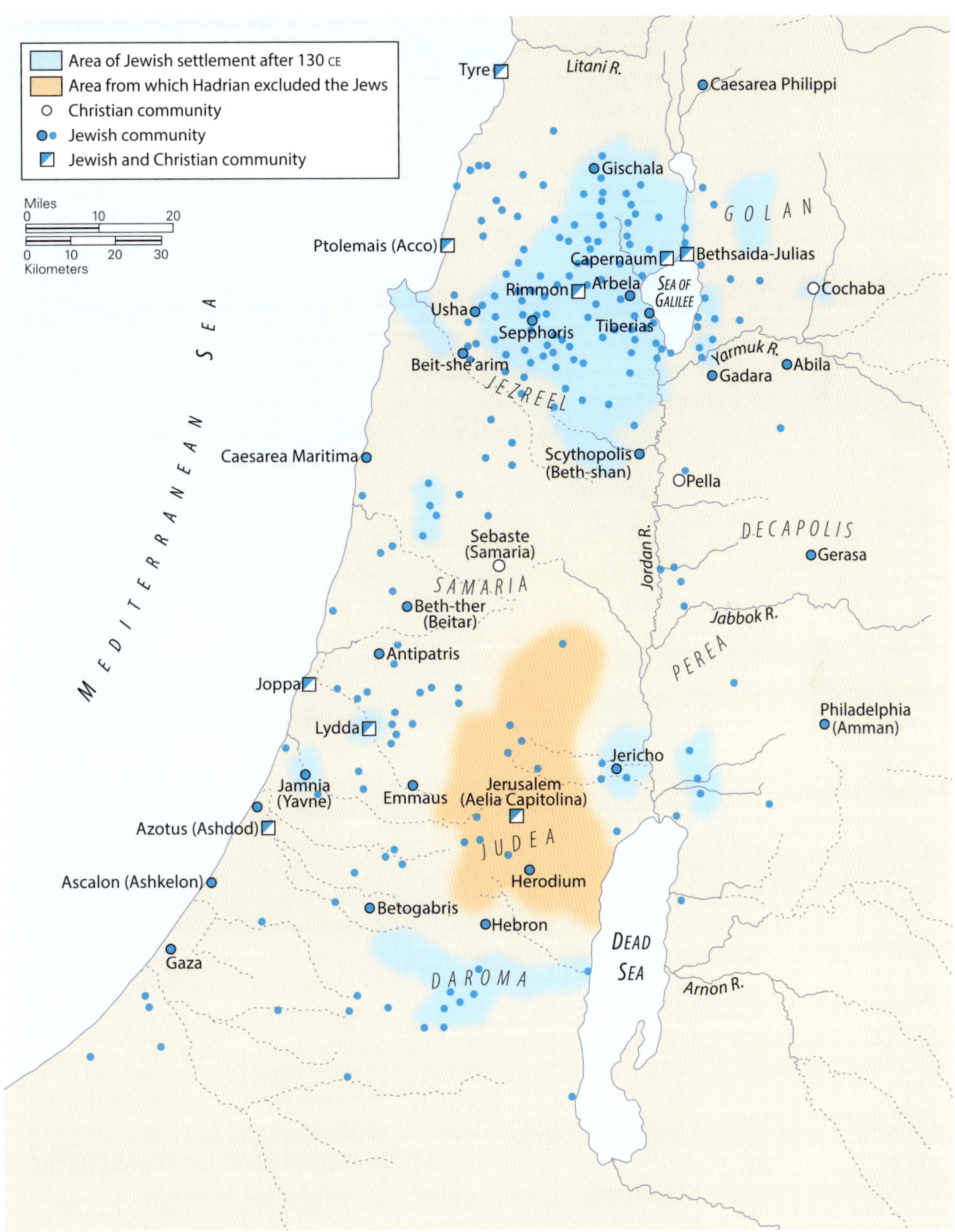

The Seven Churches of Revelation

The author of Revelation had been exiled to the barren island of Patmos, off the coast of Asia Minor (modern Turkey), due to his witness to Jesus. There he received a revelation (*apokalypsis*) of Jesus that he was to share with fellow Christians, and specifically to seven churches in Asia Minor. The most likely context is around 95 CE, during the reign of Emperor Domitian, when Christians were pressured to show loyalty to the Roman Empire by participating in the imperial cult and to accommodate to the pagan culture.

The seven churches were linked by established roads and are addressed in a clockwise manner beginning with Ephesus. Each was an important center of civic administration in its day.

1. **Ephesus** (Rev 2:1–7) was significant for both Pauline and Johannine Christianity. It was the fourth largest city in the empire, with about 250,000 people, and an important seaport. It was famous for its Temple of Artemis (see Acts 19:23–41). The Ephesian church is commended for its endurance, but also admonished to revive their initial fervor.
2. **Smyrna** (Rev 2:8–11) was a port city that claimed to be "first of Asia" due to its prominence as a center of imperial worship. The church receives strong commendation for its perseverance considering its tribulation and poverty, and for enduring suffering at the hands of anti-Christian Jews. Of the seven churches, only in Smyrna has a church survived from ancient to modern times.
3. **Pergamum** (Rev 2:12–17) was a magnificent city in the first century CE. "Satan's throne" (2:13) could refer to Pergamum's status as guardian of the imperial temple, since in 29 BCE Augustus had granted the city that coveted right. Another possible referent for Satan's throne is the Altar of Zeus on the acropolis whose raised platform and U-shape looked like a throne. The church in Pergamum is warned against the kinds of idolatry encouraged by the prominent civic structures in the city.
4. **Thyatira** (Rev 2:18–29) was an important commercial center on trade routes linking it to Pergamum, Smyrna, and Sardis, and known for its wool trade. It was the home of Lydia who dealt in purple cloth (Acts 16:14). The church is commended for its faithful endurance, but chastised for tolerating a false prophetess who promotes immorality and eating food sacrificed to idols.
5. **Sardis** (Rev 3:1–6) served as an administrative center of the Persians Cyrus and Darius (sixth century BCE) who built the Royal Road from Sardis to Susa, nearly 1,700 miles (2,700 km) away in Mesopotamia. It was still a prominent city in Roman times, notable for the immense Temple of Artemis there. The church is described as "dead" in Revelation 3:1, with only a few left who are faithful, but Sardis was home to Melito, a well-known bishop of the second century, and there is a fourth-century chapel attached to the Temple of Artemis that is one of the earliest surviving Christian structures.
6. **Philadelphia** (Rev 3:7–13) had strong imperial connections that honored the emperor by renaming itself Flavia for a time, in honor of the Flavian family of Vespasian, Titus, and Domitian. Earthquakes demolished the city in 17 and 23 CE. Like the Smyrna church, Philadelphia receives commendation only for their perseverance, despite their weakness and the harassment from the "synagogue of Satan."

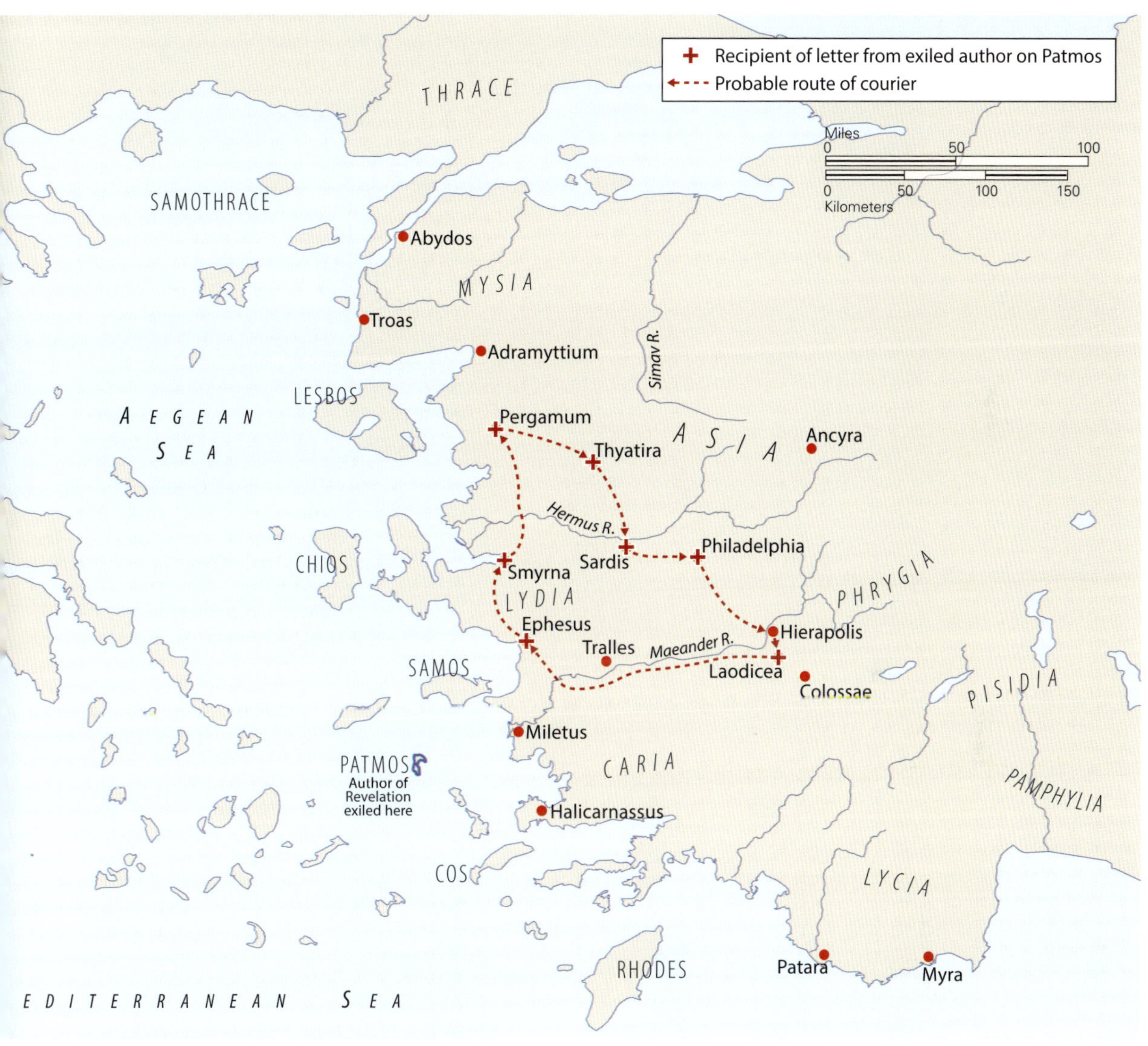

7. **Laodicea** (Rev 3:14–22) was founded in the third century BCE, but by Roman times it was a wealthy trading center on a major crossroads, noted for the luxurious black wool it produced and the nearby medical center. When a major earthquake in 60 CE devastated the city, it refused imperial assistance and rebuilt on its own. Revelation only has condemnation for the church. It accuses them of being lukewarm, perhaps an allusion to the hot springs at Hierapolis to the north, and the cool water brought to the city from the hills five miles to the south via an aqueduct. Though they think they are rich, they are unaware of how poor they are.

Gazetteer

This is an index of the labels on the maps - names of countries, settlements, geographic features, peoples etc. (A few names represent features included (mainly at map edges) to set the context and are not indexed here.) Numbers are page numbers, not map numbers.

Index